Praise for *On Microfasc*

T0160814

"*On Microfascism* stands out as a uniquely impo.... n which Bratich goes further and deeper than almost every text dedicated to naming and understanding the fascism(s) of today. In this rigorous and righteous book, Bratich rightly insists on the insufficiency of seeing fascism only when it arises in state regime form. Through which subjectivities, practices, hierarchies, and cultural forms do fascistic constellations permeate and grow? Bratich's razor-sharp analysis provides invaluable answers, and in so doing, offers a crucial tool for antifascist praxis.

—**Natasha Lennard**, author of *Being Numerous: Essays on Non-Fascist Life*

"*On Microfascism* is a profoundly original and compelling analysis of fascism's deep roots in Western traditions of patriarchy. By pinpointing the foundational role of the concept of autogenetic sovereignty and charting its many implications for how we live and die, Bratich equips readers with the intellectual framework necessary to wage not only an antifascist struggle, but an anti-*micro*fascist struggle."

—**Mark Bray**, author of *Antifa: The Anti-Fascist Handbook*

"It was hard to miss the wake-up call: fascism is back, no doubt about it, but in the novel formations of a microfascist culture that is directing the contemporary production of subjectivity. Jack Bratich not only undertakes a probing analysis of the mechanisms of the misogynistic, racist death-style of the self-affirming sovereign microfascist subject, but he most importantly proposes a number of welcome responses for living, to paraphrase Foucault, a micro-antifascist life. This book puts its readers on the path to such an art of living."

—**Gary Genosko**, Professor of Communication and Digital Media Studies at Ontario Tech University, Oshawa, Canada

On Microfascism

On Microfascism

Gender, War, and Death

Jack Z. Bratich

Brooklyn, NY
commonnotions.org

Contents

Acknowledgements

Writing a book on fascism requires an initial nod to the long history of antifascist multitudes. Along these lines, this book's direction would not exist without my parents, Milovan and Vasilija Bratic, whose tales of Yugoslav Partisans formed some of my early dispositions.

My fourteen years of living in New York City's anti-authoritarian and anarchist milieu were indispensable to forming the thoughts herein. An archipelago of radical spaces (16 Beaver, Not an Alternative, Bluestockings, Woodbine, The Base) provided shelters and incubators for thinking and practicing antifascism. Elements and moments of Occupy Wall Street, BlackLivesMatter, and the less visible antifascist resistance in NYC also demonstrated ways to ward off fascism's varying forms. As a zine library staffer and an advisory board member at ABC No Rio, I have seen the successful efforts, both collective and individual (shout out to Steven Englander!), to maintain an organization run on anti-authoritarian, inclusive, and community-oriented principles. Since moving to Philadelphia I have connected with these operationalized values at Making Worlds Bookstore and Social Center.

This book's initial ideas came together thanks to *Fifth Estate*'s editor-in-chief Peter Werbe, who asked me to write for a special issue of that venerable anarchist magazine. Thank you to Carrie Rentschler for the chance to guest lecture in her McGill graduate seminar "Cultural Studies of Political Affects," where students read and generated a fruitful conversation around that essay. A pivotal moment came when Andrew Culp at California Institute of the Arts invited me to participate in their West Hollywood Aesthetics and Politics speaker series. Not only did I get to present my thoughts on necropopulism and aesthetics for an hour (a luxury in academic time), I also had a stimulating and lively conversation with the Masters students there, especially my interlocutor Claudia Grigg Edo. Grant Kien graciously offered me a plenary platform at the 2019 Union for Democratic Communication conference, resulting in audience feedback that was challenging and even moving. An important thread of the book was presented at the Media, Gender and Feminism Symposium at the London School of Economics, where astute insights from feminist scholars elevated and sharpened the project's intellectual contribution.

Institutional support is always crucial for these projects, so I thank Rutgers University's sabbatical program (due in part to the hard-won efforts by the faculty union) and the School of Communication and Information's approval for a well-timed Fall 2020 leave. The book was almost exclusively written during pandemic-induced home time, which was split between Philadelphia and London. As fate would have it, Sindhu Zagoren and David Raskin had a house-sitting opportunity that gave me a much needed six-week writing retreat in Germantown/Mt. Airy, North Philadelphia. A special thanks goes to Neve Gordon and Catherine Rottenberg, whose conviviality, hospitality, and intellectual probing kept me nourished and on track while in the UK's capital.

Conversations with Marco DeSeriis, James Hay, and Spencer Sunshine all helped sharpen the ideas around populism and antifascism. A trip with Stevphen Shukaitis and his son Gustav to see Clapton CFC play a match in East London was an adventure in antifascist fandom and popular culture. Thanks especially to Miriam Tola who introduced me to the *Non Una di Meno* movement as we walked to a related demonstration in Rome in 2017.

While writing the book, I had fruitful discussions with friends who were doing the same. Lindsay Caplan, Paloma Checa-Gismero, Jayson Harsin, Chenjerai Kumanyika, and Daniel Tucker all got me thinking about what a book can do. Check out their books when they come out! Thanks goes to a number of Rutgers doctoral students who assisted this project whether via engaged feedback or meticulous bibliographic work: Alptug Okten, Dane Spudic, Holly Avella, and Bryan Sacks.

Working in cahoots with the astounding Common Notions publishing collective has been a real treat. Andy Battle got me out of the rabbit holes of my mind, nudging my writing to become more inviting to a range of readers. From concepts to commas, Erika Biddle has solidified her reputation as copyeditor extraordinaire. Together they turned the manuscript into something that can sing, even if the songs are occasionally dirges. Thanks to Nicki Kattoura for the thorough indexing, to both Nicki and Alexander Dwinell for their promotional work, and to Morgan Buck for the zinging final layout. I'm honored to have my words linked to any of Josh MacPhee's images, and especially here with the cover design. Finally, friend, comrade, and co-thinker Malav Kanuga's exceptional editorship was vital in jump-starting this as a book and situating it in salient reader-communities. He provides the sustenance and solidarity that allows an author to be both singular and common. With the immense care and trust put into this process, Common Notions provides a model for how commoning can happen in book production.

Finally, most of all, I give copious gratitude to Sarah Banet-Weiser, whose thoughtful and perceptive feedback was crucial in developing drafts of the manuscript. Her advice, patience, and support were essential whether across an ocean or in the next room. Her influence can be found explicitly in the project's centering of gender. More subtly, its traces are evident in the ways I've been able to displace my own autogenetic sovereign tendencies in favor of an entwinement of hearts and minds. The book is launched into the stream of this kind of love, one that also fuels the anonymous, pseudonymous, ancestral, and future antifascists who continue the fight inside and out.

Introduction

Why the Micro Matters for Fascist Culture

W<small>HAT COMES TO MIND WHEN WE THINK OF</small> J<small>AMES</small> A<small>LEX</small> F<small>IELDS</small>, J<small>R</small>., the 2017 Charlottesville killer? Images of his khaki pants, white polo shirt, and freshly buzzed undercut hairstyle likely appear. The alt-right, white nationalist uniform itself might be sufficient to identify him as fascist. His high school teacher noted that Fields was obsessed with Adolf Hitler. A good case could be made for fascist leanings there. Some might recall the telling detail conveyed by a classmate about a school trip to a former concentration camp in Germany, where Fields quipped, "This is where the magic happened."[1] We *can* imagine this, too, would quickly associate him with fascism.

But in the retelling of Fields' vehicular homicide of antifascist counterprotester Heather Heyer during the 2017 "Unite the Right" rally in Charlottesville, Virginia, how many remember the fact that Fields' wheelchair-bound mother called the police three times over the prior years due to his violent behavior against her? On one occasion, he struck her in the head and forced his hands over her mouth when she tried to impose limits on his video game play time. In another incident, he threatened her with a foot-long knife. He also spat on her. Before Fields was born, his grandfather killed his grandmother and then committed suicide. While this personal and familial misogynistic history has been noted in passing, it subsided in the narrativization of the Fields. So, what about this history's relation to fascism?

One might debate about whether *any* of these elements in the Charlottesville case are in themselves sufficient to call it fascism, much like commentators mused over whether to consider Donald Trump a fascist. This book is not designed to persuade you one way or the other. But if your starting point is antifascist, and you do consider Charlottesville an event steeped in or tied to fascism, then this book asks you to consider what role Fields' misogyny and domestic violence against his mother had to do with it. To do so, we need to expand our notion of fascism.

Fascism is an elusive and contested term. Andreas Huyssen modifies Theodor Adorno's statement on nationalism when he suggests that the word "fascism is both obsolete and up-to-date."[2] The literature on fascism is sprawling, complex, and multidisciplinary.

When fascism (new or old) is studied, the focus tends to be on a leader or styles of leadership, named organizations, particular national contexts, or economic conditions. Such analyses foreground fascist politics as institutionalized and systematized. There are stubborn attachments, as some writers and readers will never let go of the idea that fascism is *extraordinary* rather than ordinary. Others see fascism as a *recent* phenomenon (either as European interwar event or, at its most expansive, a reaction to modernity). Still others will only consider it a *state* affair. Finally, there are those who deploy the term only when ethnonationalism is primary.

Rather than hold up historical expressions of fascism as paradigms, I orient toward Alberto Toscano's position that the usual set of "checklists, analogies, or ideal-types cannot do justice to the concrete history of fascism."[3] Debates over fascism's definition and features are sometimes pedantic affairs, but as praxis they matter because they set the stage for what it means to be antifascist.

When fascism arrives, it does not always announce itself with sleek uniforms, amassed crowds, and spectacular stage presentations. Nor does it appear only or primarily as a state affair. As French philosopher of antiracism Pierre-André Taguieff reminds us, fascism will not "do us the favor of returning in such a way that we can recognize easily. If vigilance was only a game of recognizing something already well-known, then it would only be a question of remembering. Vigilance would be reduced to a social game . . . a consoling illusion."[4] In other words, if we fixate on expected characteristics that match other eras, we miss out on perceiving the particularities of the current one.

Alt-right, neofascist, and reactionary populist forces have swelled in the US during the second decade of the twenty-first century, becoming the object of significant journalistic coverage, academic analyses, and activist chronicling. Books on the subject fall into several categories. Given the period of this publication surge (2017–2020), many works focus on the rise of the alt-right, often with overlapping accounts of personalities (e.g., Richard Spencer, Andrew Weev, Steve Bannon), groups, and actions. A number of these are journalistic accounts that perceive the rise of the alt-right as a sign of expanding white supremacy or as an explanation for the 2016 Trump election victory—or both. In the United States, considerable focus is placed on the followers of Donald Trump, especially to make sense of Trump's ascendancy. They thus limit their analysis to the conditions leading to his victory and continued influence, including the militancy in the January 6, 2021 storming of the US Capitol.

At the same time, multidisciplinary accounts of fascism as a concept and historical formation have proliferated. While some are situated as defenders of liberal democracy, others are movement-based works that assess the contemporary resurgence of fascism. More explicitly antifascist analyses chronicle a series of recent and longer historical examples of white supremacist, neo-Nazi, ethnonationalist, and alt-right groups that often emphasize leaders and personalities.[5]

Much of the research on this reactionary milieu is oriented to political ideologies and explicit political phenomena, often using historical or sociological approaches. Whether named as the alt-right, radical right, or right-wing populism, they employ standard categories and frameworks about social movements. Phenomena are mostly linked to more institutionalized party politics. When movements are the focus, they tend to be ones with a proper name, studied for their formal components: decision-making protocols, functions and roles, planning efforts, strategic meetings, street actions, and principal individuals or groups. In sum, the research is oriented toward the organizational dimension of public actions. Moreover, when that movement is determined to be fascist, it is studied for its passage from the margins to the mainstream as a strategy of implanting itself as a fascist state.

These works form a vital and timely syllabus for contemporary fascism studies. Examining belief systems, organizations, and movements, studies of fascism give us grounding in historical patterns as well as their effects on contemporary elections, policies, and communities. As a collective body of work, these recent sources provide much insight into the old and new fascist aspects of our current context. Only some highlight the realm I consider crucial to microfascism: the cultural dimensions of fascism.

Antifascists have understood that social and cultural realms produce the values and ideas a fascist state draws upon. Neiwert, Ross, and Burley, for instance, build on Robert O. Paxton's "Five Stages of Fascism" model in which culture plays an early role in developing a populace ready for the state.[6] Stages allow clearer thinking about *proto*-fascism or *pre*-fascism. While such a model pinpoints different expressions well, the clarity that comes with steps also reduces certain realms to being steppingstones.

Recent authors have given significant attention to the cultural dimensions of the alt-right, mostly by focusing on Internet-based subcultures[7] or digital technologies.[8] Often these works classify media as news and information systems, with occasional mentions of idiosyncratic cultural expressions (such as neo-folk and Nazi punk). Most note the importance of the online worlds that have generated (mis)information, ideas, and sensibilities that have contributed to ethnonationalism and the alt-right.

When culture is foregrounded, it is positioned within the right's own terminology of "meta-politics." Shane Burley defines meta-politics as the "ideas, culture, and inclinations that motivate politics down the line. Meta-politics, in the neo-fascist sense, are the cultural projects that attempt to influence ideological positions without engaging strictly in political practice . . . [which] includes art, music, and philosophy."[9]

Culture is thus explicitly part of twenty-first century right-wing organizational strategy, encapsulated in the well-worn phrase "politics is downstream from culture." As meta-politics, culture tends to be equated with ideas and beliefs (encoded in art and pop culture artifacts) that are *strategically shaped* by organized actors. Those actors develop a fascist movement in order to establish a fascist state, moving from fringe Internet culture to alt-right to Trumpism.

In this formulation, culture matters only when it is instrumentalized for a body formed outside of itself, such as when actors recruit followers through it. For example, some commentators classify popular culture as "apolitical" until specific individuals and groups "hijack" or infiltrate it to guide it to their own ends. Culture can certainly operate as this kind of "strategic messaging," but reducing it to a weapon and a channel becomes too intentionalist and even conspiratorial. Moreover, such a focus on strategic hijacking only works in retrospect. The analysis is *already-too-late*; the moment to understand culture is over, since it only mattered in the moment it was instrumentalized and not when it was "apolitical." Such analysis hampers our ability to defeat fascism's future manifestations.

This book, while recognizing culture as *meta*-politics, centers culture and stays with it longer, since culture is the sphere where *micro*-politics take place. Such an approach is rooted in cultural studies, where culture is not apolitical, waiting for external actors to politicize it. Instead, culture is *always political*: not just in the sense of expressing political dynamics formed in other spheres, but as the realm where values, power relations, subjective encounters, and capacities for connection and freedom develop. Specifically, this book examines the realm of *microfascist cultural politics*, which is composed before being organized, directed, even named.

Fascism and/as culture

This project studies fascism as a fundamentally *cultural* phenomenon.[10] The vast intellectual output on interwar fascism includes key works on culture—whether as aesthetics[11] or as industry,[12] as religiosity and sacralization,[13] as embodiment,[14] as media spectacles, as the production of imaginaries and values.[15]

Zeev Sternhell, Mario Sznajder, and Maia Ashéri define fascist culture as a spirit of rebellion involving "the cult of *energy, of dynamism and power*, of the machine and speed, of instinct and intuition, of movement, will power, and youth."[16] Lutz Koepnick sees culture as profoundly central to fascist renewal and restoration, as it involves "breaking older bonds of solidarity while simultaneously rendering modern consumerism . . . a privileged ticket to national rebirth."[17] Christoffer Kølvraa and Bernhard Forchtner draw on early fascism scholar George Mosse's position on the importance of culture "to better understand the *existential imaginary* which drew people to fascism by looking beyond the latter's organizational forms, institutional structures, or concrete aims and policies."[18] Only after comprehending fascism's subjective structure formed through vision, ideas, and comportment can we get a proper sense of fascist self-understanding and therefore its appeal. And, in a nod to fascist philosopher Julius Evola, whose theories of subjectivity, war, and gender figure prominently in this book, Alexander Reid Ross notes, "Greater than mass-based civilization . . . was culture, which as he understood it could be carefully curated by elites to channel the energy of the masses toward destruction while leaving the higher echelon of spiritual warriors to play in the ashes."[19]

The most developed attention to culture for the purpose of the current project has been proposed by Roger Griffin.[20] Even within analyses that foreground culture he finds that the genre of fascist studies neglects "the attempts by Fascism and Nazism to engineer a *subjective revolution . . .* as an integral part of their project to regenerate the nation."[21] For Griffin, this means fascism is not best identified as a state-form, a conventional political party, or even a movement. Indeed fascism's "creation of a new type of state was the materialisation and externalisation of a subjective revolution in values and national character."[22] Griffin argues for an understanding of fascist culture as "a wholesale transformation of the world, of time/space coordinates as well as the direction of human development."[23] His focus on culture will be key for our close attention to microfascism, as will his emphasis on the transformation of subjectivity (the new/reborn man), and on the types of composition that he calls groupuscules (fluid and amorphous clusters that are not attached to formal parties or structures).

Fascism's two core features: restoration/renewal and eliminationism

Roger Griffin provides the first of two main features of fascism that will inform our concept of microfascism, *restoration/renewal* and *eliminationism*. In addition to centering culture in his analysis of fascism, Roger Griffin's methodological approach invites analysts to pay careful attention to what is essential and what is epiphenomenal in fascism. He asks us "to separate out those 'ineliminable,' definitional components from time- or place-specific, peripheral ones."[24] He finds that too often, a historically situated expression comes to stand in as the template, model, or even sole example of the set. Griffin distills fascism's definitional essence: "*Fascism is a political ideology whose mythic core in its various permutations is a palingenetic form of populist ultra-nationalism*."[25] Palingenetic refers to a temporal quality that seeks restoration, renewal, and rebirth. It's the continuous revival and return of the "original."

This project on microfascism takes up Griffin's notion of the palingenetic but with qualifications. Like many analysts, Griffin situates fascism as something opposed to modernity, especially liberal democracy. While certain expressions of microfascism (e.g., neo-reactionary subcultures, traditionalist groups, outright neo-Nazis) explicitly rail against liberal democracy, microfascism both precedes modernity and incorporates aspects of it. I will argue in this book that we should look for it in the constitution of states themselves. Fascism includes the modern production of *sovereign subjectivity*, defined here as the capacity of a subject to make its will reality (including its own reality as subject). Fascism is an extension of systems of power and oppression in what Walter Benjamin calls mythical violence: the mystical capacity of a state to simultaneously establish its foundation as monopoly on violence and justify it as reality itself.

Fascism is only conjuncturally—as an historically specific mode of becoming—a reaction to liberal democracy. For instance, the neo-reactionary component of the right wing, which at first blush appears as a *response* to liberal democracy, traces its roots to positions *prior* to modernity's rise. The contemporary reactionary position is a renewal of the positions *taken at the time* by royal sovereigns who saw liberal democracy as degenerate and sought to preserve their power. It is reactive in advance, posed against insurrections of the time, seeking to preserve and continue a type of sovereignty against revolt.[26] It was the failure of sovereigns to suppress the revolts that animates today's "response." Fascism is the imagined and enacted renewal of *sovereignty*, which now happens to be expressed as antimodern and antidemocratic.

Moreover, these forms of sovereignty never fully disappeared as a concession to the triumph of liberal democracy. As the Black Radical Tradition demonstrates, liberal democracy was always underpinned and organized by racial capitalism. The founding and perpetuation of that political project was tied to wage slavery, enslavement, settler colonialism, and the carceral complex. We thus need to push Griffin beyond the confines of a particular time/space framework into a more expansive one that includes *colonization* and *patriarchy*.

Griffin has given us the tools to overcome his own restrictions. He has asked us to not limit fascism to its historical expression/epiphenomenon. His version of the transhistorical (or the ineliminable) is still tied to a narrow frame of Western history—from twentieth-century interwar Europe to now. We need to expand the timeline to include understandings of racial capitalism and colonialism. But even anticolonial accounts are still focused on a Western moment, now coterminous with something called the "birth of modernity." We must stretch our analysis beyond the modern West to the state foundations, especially in its gendered and war contexts.[27]

Importantly, palingenesis occurs within a process of subjectivation that *preexists nationhood.* Nationalism is certainly in play as a mythic image for contemporary fascist restoration operations. But "nationalism" is only one set of values and identities being restored. By focusing on sovereignty, I highlight the *process* of restoration. What is restored is not a mythic past but the performance of founding itself—the capacity to make reality and the authority to establish order. The nation is a result of sovereign acts, mythic and otherwise, and not a fixed object for renewal. This subjective sovereignty preexists "nation" or "community" by originating in, and inaugurating, the authority of ordering as such. Such an ordering principle is found in the state, in patriarchal social order, and in war. What is palingenetic is the creation process itself, the founding and self-authorizing acts that seek to shape reality.

This book makes the controversial claim that microfascism is a resource that is not primarily antimodern. It is premodern and even helps form the modern through its primary subject, the sovereign. In the comforting story it tells itself, the modern heroically triumphs over tradition through the values of democracy and progress. Fascism is seen as the negation of this fragile displacement in favor of restoring a mythical past grounded in actual power relations. This book argues that we need to recast the modern, especially as it was forged in patriarchal pacts and an authoritative order based on transcendent (religious) values and war. Modernity's values depended on a subject and state-form that underpinned the system's authority. What Umberto Eco called *Ur-Fascism*—the deep structure of fascist tendencies in human history—was not displaced by the modern, it was just reconfigured as state-form.

Fascist philosopher Julius Evola would not fit into Griffin's notion of "palingenetic ultranationalism," as Evola's fulcrum for understanding authority and tradition is the state and not the nation. For fascist thinkers like Evola, nationalism is already a decadent swerve from the primary authority-making mechanism: the state and its autotelic sovereign.[28] He even goes so far as to oppose nationalism, as he sees it embodying a feminized political sensibility. Evola's traditionalism, as we'll explore later, leads him to invoke war, specifically the formation of masculine war societies called *Männerbunde,* as the origin of a sovereign subject. In other words, what is renewed in any palingenesis is much older than the nation and it's something much more gendered. This binding, this patriarchal pact, is what needs renewal and restoration: a palingenetic *ultra-statism* or *ultra-sovereignty*.

Eliminationism as violence

The second feature of fascism that anchors my project is what David Neiwert calls the violence of *eliminationism*. Eliminationism refers to a "politics and a culture that shuns dialogue and the democratic exchange of ideas in favor of the pursuit of outright elimination of the opposing side, either through suppression, exile, and ejection, or extermination."[29] Fascist power defines its opposition as "the embodiment of evil itself, unfit for participation in their vision of society, and thus worthy of elimination."[30] Eliminationism constitutes its enemy as whole blocs of the populace that need to be excised or exterminated by peaceful or violent means. The subjective orientation of eliminationism infuses culture—appearing as offhand comments, crude jokes, and microaggressions. Culture creates the conditions for eliminationist actions by providing the dehumanizing imagination and the normalizing permission to speak and act in vilifying ways.

Neiwert draws from Daniel Jonah Goldhagen, who coined the term "eliminationist antisemitism" in *Hitler's Willing Executioners: Ordinary Germans and the Holocaust*.[31] The most obvious versions of elimination associated with fascism involve state-sponsored murders and genocide. Settler colonial projects are quite visible expressions of eliminationism, resulting in genocide and social death in addition to establishing a race-based carceral apparatus, once again anchoring the claim that fascism as palingenetic eliminationism predates twentieth-century fascism.

I would add the following to Neiwert's contribution: before eliminationism becomes concretized, the violence of action is akin to what Walter Benjamin called *mythic violence*. James Martel summarizes Benjamin's development of the concept:

> Mythic violence is Benjamin's term for the way that illicit economic and political power has asserted itself over all human life, projecting a form of authority out into the world that then becomes accepted as reality itself. It is mythic because there is no true or ontological basis for the powers of liberalism and capitalism; its right to rule is self-proclaimed and then naturalized so that it becomes seen as fated

and inevitable. It is violent because, without a genuine basis for its authority, mythic violence must endlessly strike out, killing and hurting over and over again to establish its power and even its reality.[32]

Mythic violence is the shaping of reality in accordance with an abstraction that founds the state, based on a sovereign capacity that I'll argue derives from archaic masculine subjectivity. Mythic and foundational violence is not done in one strike nor does it recur as a single type. Its palingenesis is more pervasive, based on an *eliminationism spectrum*, or what I will be identifying as *reductionism* as it pertains to gender.

Gender changes the typical understanding of eliminationism, for instance, when it comes to its temporality. What is the measurement of speed and time for reduction, annihilation, extermination? Elimination can take the form of what Lauren Berlant calls *slow death*: "a condition of being worn out by the activity of reproducing life."[33] In this state of the long elimination, "dying and the ordinary reproduction of life are coextensive."[34] And, as she puts it, only some populations are "marked out for wearing out."[35]

Elimination is thus not the result but the *process* of "taking to the limit," reducing, de-animating, de-vivifying, and annulling. Elimination decapacitates but does not always kill. It is closer to what Jasbir Puar calls "'the right to maim': a right expressive of sovereign power that is linked to, but not the same as, 'the right to kill.'"[36] Elimination reduces capacity, it is "debilitation and the production of disability" that is ultimately an *inclusive* annulment. When it comes to gender, women are necessarily included but as reduced. Elimination is an ongoing management of this inclusive annulment, the continuous "taking to" (and past) the limit.

Eliminationism is a political and cultural tendency that only partially finds expression in the state. With US plantation-based enslavement systems, for instance, what was remarkable was precisely the ability for ordinary enslavers and their postbellum successors to reduce others with *impunity*.[37] In colonial relations, white settlers had a birthright to act with sovereign violence, an ongoing and pervasive eliminationism. Achille Mbembe's origin of necropolitics begins with war in the colonies waged for "civilization." Invaders imagine enemies to be nonhuman, allowing the culture of settler colonialism, apartheid, and the plantation world to deploy "social death" and generate "death-worlds."[38]

This project will focus on another systemic spectrum of elimination, patriarchy, whose fundamental features include the instrumentalization, objectification, and reduction of women. For what I'll be describing as microfascism, patriarchy takes the form of everyday sexism and misogyny as a slow elimination and includes policing limits of women's actions through threats, chasing women from public places (whether streets or the Internet), and reducing their capacities through ongoing attrition. Gendered eliminationism is a reductionism *towards* the limit, a nullification that deposits women into a sphere or a role in the patriarchal order.

Gendered eliminationism is the ongoing process of diminishment into a thing that teeters on becoming no-thing. Elimination as physical death systematically occurs in patriarchy, but it is not the only kind of reduction. Social death, slow death, the longue durée of feminicide, the spectrum of violence, the erosion of life—all of these are forms of what I am examining here as the gendered dimension of microfascism.

Palingenesis, I argue, renews not just a past or a foundation, but the exclusions and violence that allow it to "take place." Any particular fascist war of restoration (like a mythic lost nation) is also a restoration of the founding violence that instituted the order and of the *subjectivity* that subtends it. Combining these two key features (palingenesis and eliminationism) into a process opens a path to understanding microfascism.

Microfascism

Microfascism is a concept drawn from Deleuze and Guattari, primarily the latter. Developed across essays and in books, the concept was an effort to rethink the forms and scales of fascism. Microfascism delves into the subjective realm with three main characteristics that are also qualifications: 1) it takes place "before" but really *in excess of* the state; 2) it exists in minds but moreover in desires, bodies and practices; and 3) it is composed in culture to create individual and collective actions with their own specific fascist results.

The first feature of microfascism is defined by Guattari in this way: "Fascism is inseparable from a proliferation of molecular focuses in interaction, which skip from point to point, before beginning to resonate together in the National Socialist State."[39] Microfascism takes a "step" or a stage and expands it outwards, nonlinearly. There is a continuity to the micro beyond its temporal placement "before" the state, since we may not ever see a state formation that crystallizes. A focus on microfascism can identify processes that have effects even if they don't "creep" to another stage.[40]

For Deleuze and Guattari, microfascism exists prior to a capture by molar state apparatuses as well as before the formation of organizations. Microfascism sets conditions for fascism even before it becomes a *movement*. The *micro* does not refer to a small scale but something multiple and molecular rather than coherent and uniform—a proliferation of resonances, practices, and relations that can cohere into operative bodies and collective agencies with their own short- and long-term effects. This is the realm we'll be exploring as culture—as ordinary, as cultivation of subjectivity, as pervasive.[41]

Second, microfascism encompasses the relation between *desire* and fascism. In "Everybody Wants to Be a Fascist," Guattari posits that fascism "seems to come from the outside, but it finds its energy right at the heart of everyone's desire."[42] In his preface to *Anti-Oedipus*, Michel Foucault refers to it as the fascism "in our heads and in our everyday behavior." The fascism in our subjectivity is more than a psychological category—it's "in our heads" but also in our bodies. Better yet, it's in the embodiments and affective armor produced within our relationships. Foucault describes Deleuze and Guattari's project as excavating and warding off the "fascism in us all."[43] While we might temper this universalism, he prompts us to reflect on the tendencies in our relationships (familial, erotic, institutional)—as a microfascism appearing at various scales.

Gary Genosko has worked methodically through the concept. As he puts it, "fascism is immanent to desiring-production . . . [it] is everywhere and to desire is to activate it in some measure at different scales within a microphysics of power relations."[44] While some, like Wilhelm Reich, focused on desire as the impulse to be dominated (seeking a master and the comfort of conformity), for Deleuze and Guattari desire is much more expansive. It includes becoming master without a leader figure. This book examines the microfascist as a social investment in masculine forms of sovereignty, specifically the desire to give to oneself the powers of creation through a fear of realms and practices coded as "feminine." Why would it be necessary to examine these micropolitics when fascism disappears as state-form? Following Guattari as well as Umberto Eco, Genosko astutely answers that it's because fascism "has survived its historical mutations and adapted itself to contemporary institutions, knowingly or unknowingly clinging to subcultural and political expression."[45] For Guattari, fascism "passes through the tightest mesh; it is in constant evolution."[46]

Following their lead, combating fascism involves a change in perception: microfascism appears not only when white nationalists carry tiki torches to defend Confederate statues but also when the ghosts of fallen soldiers are invoked to generate the statues in the first place. We don't just see microfascism when the alt-right promotes its "TradWives," who invest desire in submissive social roles but also when the "manosphere" begins coordinating its masculine instrumentalization of women. We need to perceive how the *Freikorps* campaigns of Great War veterans, with their feminicidal impulses, have now mutated into veterans of the *World of Warcraft*. Most importantly, microfascism inhabits desires that don't always crystallize into nameable groups and it can erupt even in leftist movements. Microfascism is thus pervasive and latent, embedding itself in our relationships and our subjectivities. Any antifascism needs to also be *anti-microfascist*.

The third feature of microfascism is related to subjective action—now defined less as individual desire and more as coordinated operations, or what describe as the *compositional realm*. Microfascism has a connective dimension where fascism forms a social body. For Deleuze and Guattari, "what makes fascism dangerous is its molecular or micropolitical power, for it is a mass movement: a cancerous body rather than a totalitarian organism."[47] This mass is neither uniform nor dependent on conforming subjects. It is something more elusive as a coordinating and gathering force—it "occupies micro-black holes and resonates among them acting on the masses through millions of catastrophes."[48] It's not that individuals are formed "first" and then find each other in some sociological manner—although this is what social movement studies often presumes. As Guattari remarks, "These black holes swarm and proliferate across the social field" which draw in and transform subjectivities.[49] Desire is again central here, as the attraction to these networked black holes is already socially produced.

Fascism is connective and networked, best understood through "the language of mutation, proliferation, and molecularity."[50] The movement here is not nameable as an organized coordination (even one as loose as the alt-right) but is a roving, mutating throng of self-affirming subjects. In other words, fascist individuals, even in their rigid "black hole" interiors, do not simply end up that way through their personal encounters with fascist ideas and beliefs. They become fascists through mimicking and inspiring others, based on an already-existing desire. They may even be initiated, whether by an explicit act (e.g., redpilling) or echoes of archaic rites of masculine passage and differentiation from women. Much of this happens below the usual threshold of political perception.

Thinking of microfascism as a network of disconnected holes is puzzling, even paradoxical upon first blush. It warrants an analysis that attends to both the hyperindividualism (self-sealed subjects, black holes) and the ways those units compose in collective action. Atomization is part of a composition of a more interactive body that holds the holes in place but also increases their capacity for action, thus posing a profound danger in the world.

Microfascism, ultimately, is the growth of a fascist formation beyond organized efforts: "Fascism, like desire, is scattered everywhere, in separate bits and pieces, within the whole social realm; it crystallizes in one place or another, depending on the relationships of force."[51] A laugh, a red pill-induced epiphany, an inspirational act—these can produce a fascist leap or jolt of subjectivation. Microfascism is punctuated by such resonant flashes. While most accounts continue to work with concepts of mass, movement, leader, and nation, analyzing microfascism's new conditions means looking at production and circulation processes well before and beyond any state capture, organizational form, or charismatic leader.

Microfascism, we could say, occupies a place in our analysis that is analogous to fascist culture as discussed above: not just pre-state formation or passage to more organized forms, but a necessary realm of the production of subjectivity and composition of collective action, akin to what Eco calls *Ur-Fascism* or "Eternal Fascism." Microfascism is a *form of life* that finds expression in politics as well as cultural practices and subjective orientations. Microfascism is a structuring of everyday life that resonates with macro-structures without being reducible to or absorbed by them.

Microfascism and culture

When referring to culture as the principal domain for microfascism, a few caveats are necessary. Culture can include representations (the best contemporary example of microfascism would be the visual and sonic genre of "fashwave") but is not primarily about images, ideas, or information. Culture is not just a series of artifacts expressing identity or subculture, nor is it bounded by ethnic enclosures or the commonalities of nation-state.

Culture consists of the production of subjectivity and the making of reality. It is less knowledge-based (truth, beliefs) and more action-oriented (making/production), a psychosocial dimension of power and ideology "operating in the affective realm as much as the realm of ideas."[52] Culture is the sphere where capacities develop and forms of life proliferate, before organizational, even nameable, entities can be identified (e.g., the "alternative right" or alt-right).

The constellation of culture, gender, and fascism comes out most thoroughly and concretely in the work of Klaus Theweleit. His two-volume opus *Male Fantasies* examined the letters, diaries, and images from the nomadic veterans and new irregular recruits that took up vicious campaigns and settlements throughout post-WWI Germany as the *Freikorps*. These bloodthirsty independent volunteer units translated their war training into murderous domestic operations, now fueled by misogyny and anticommunism. These ad-hoc squads carried out massacres and became prototypes for Nazi troops.

Theweleit examines artifacts including personal letters, poetry, propaganda posters, ads, comic strips, and diaries. Through this treasure trove of an archive, Theweleit pieces together a profound gender analysis of the collective and individual bodies (actual and metaphorical) that set the stage for Nazi Germany's masculine warrior subject. Methodologically speaking, William Connolly notes that Theweleit "loosens readings of structural determinations as he probes volatile intersections between bodies, movements, and politics."[53]

"Bodies, movements, and politics": culture is where these intersect to produce subjectivity. As Michael Hardt and Antonio Negri put it, what needs studying even in "'leaderless' movements [is the] *production of subjectivity* necessary to create lasting social relations."[54] These processes of subjectivation involve the encounters, relationships, and convergences that have come to be called *composition*.[55]

Composition refers to how bodies enter into relations with one another— a coming-together which cannot be predicted from component parts or interactions. Composition thus refers to an entity's *emergent qualities*, the not-yet-formed in the passage to action.

I have argued elsewhere that the genealogy of crafting is a paradigmatic case for understanding composition (especially its gendered dimensions).[56] Crafting existed before, during, and after capitalism's arrival and crisis. Compositional analysis, therefore, would have to begin earlier and in another place than those imagined with the capital/labor relation.

What would it mean to examine fascism compositionally? *Compositionism* begins not with sovereignty as a juridical matter, or fascism as a state affair, but with social relations and the powers of ordering being in the world. Before a fascist social movement, a fascist body that *can* move or be moved develops. This book's compositionist approach to microfascist culture means examining a process tied to an underlying and ongoing social body infused with capacities.

Microfascist culture is the realm where this collective body forms its capacities. This means downplaying representations of reality (epistemology) in favor making reality through metamorphosis (ontology). A compositionist approach to microfascism helps understand not the mentality/psychological profile of movement members (in their heads), nor their explicitly sociological roots (proximate causes), but the emergent capacities that seek to order reality through the production of sovereign subjectivity.

Compositional culture is not apolitical, waiting for external actors to politicize it—it is *the space for cultural politics*, an immanent sphere where meanings, values, and pleasures are circulated to form social identities and social relationships.[57] Culture is the realm where life (and death) is given a form and a style. It involves sensibilities and connective action—the circulation of embodiments and disembodiments we will examine as *mimesis*. Culture is the milieu of subjectivation where we collectively work out the making of reality through the social production of desire.

Analyzing compositionist culture resonates with works that study fascist-embodied aesthetics, such as Simonetta Falasca-Zamponi's analysis of the style, enthusiasm, and assemblages of Mussolini's Italy, or the "politics of the piazza."[58] Composition is also highly mediated. Culture can include the mediated forms of affective mobilization, including radio and cinema in Italy and Germany. Media here do more than spread beliefs or recruit adherents. Susan Sontag located Nazi Germany's "transformation of reality" in the power of its media forms. She notes that with Leni Riefenstahl's *Triumph of the Will* "the document (the image) is no longer simply the record of reality; 'reality' has been constructed to serve the image."[59]

More than representation, mediation reshapes reality and the subjects within it. Media cultural studies have analyzed professional wrestling, reality television, meme magic, cosplay and deepfakes, among others, to define media less as representing reality than a series of techniques *intervening* in it. Media forms are technical systems that set some conditions for assembling capacities and associations with an orientation towards action. My analysis in *On Microfascism* follows in this tradition of media composition, specifically by homing in on the mediated production of a fascist collective body.

The mediated form of collective action, I argue, has moved from mass spectator to networked participant. The results are an increase in circulation, mimicry, and transmission—the digital media formatting of imagination and inspiration. Mediated culture now refers to Internet technologies producing aesthetics that generate renewal and elimination, affects like irony and fun, modes of initiation like redpilling, and forms of coordination like raiding squads and gaming swarms. The ensuing body is networked and operational, drawn heavily from chan boards and gaming platforms, and organized via logistics and squad-based campaigns. The result is a distributed—what Griffin calls *groupuscular*—composition of operations, maneuvers, and logistics channeling action into war with homi-suicidal results.

Like culture, this means not reducing the Internet to an instrument for organizing and recruiting as this would relegate microfascism to "bad actors" and their "tools." The compositional substratum that shapes not only subjective resources but the subjects themselves should no longer be marginalized in favor of organized and readily apparent forms. In summary, composition is the dimension where the desiring machines of microfascism proliferate and crystallize. The main elements of this archaic culture are: 1) the *gendered* dimension; 2) a *necropolitical* dynamic; and 3) the *war* context.

A key feature of microfascist culture is that it's where we see patriarchal differentiation from nature/women instrumentalized to establish man as transcendent and sovereign. This makes worlds and orders reality through palingenetic elimination. Microfascist culture is the realm where fascism as a collective body is composed (before being organized, directed, even named). It generates desensitization and armored relationships, producing abstractions and reducing some groups' capacities while augmenting others. This is the place of initiation rites and death-rituals, cultivating a masculine renewal of spiritual subjectivity while eliminating materiality (the feminine).

Fascism, after all, is a *binding*, emblemized by the bundle of rods with an axe projecting from it [*fasces*] used by Mussolini's followers. It is *collective-making*. What is new is that historical forms of binding are now networked. Microfascism is thus both archaic and hypercontemporary. The rise of connective technologies and digital culture become key for the contemporary expression of this long-standing subjective realm. Microfascism features millions of tiny command centers, each self-enclosed yet bonded in action-at-a-distance. Each black hole is sealed while also networked, resonating via imitation, inspiration, and transmission. This paradox (the cohesion of the disconnected) results in action, not a standstill. Social clusters emit from this assemblage as a transient collective assembling. Such clusters, this project argues, appear at the origin of fascism—the war bands, the squads, the patriarchal pacts.

Recently, scholars have been giving this non-state, non-organized cultural dimension more attention. Thinking through a post-organizational framework, Maik Fielitz and Holger Marcks speak of *digital fascism*, which they define as "a more fluid and ambivalent movement, which cannot be fully grasped with actor- or ideology-centered approaches."[60] Instead, they argue, contemporary fascism is most pervasive and installed "as a social phenomenon of cultural practices."[61] Rather than calling it *pre-fascist* or *proto-fascist* culture (which still favors the state-form of fascism) microfascism is closer to what Mark Bray calls *everyday fascism*. It is ordinary, pervasive, even latent. Temporally speaking, it lurks as an Ur-Fascism of the archaic in the mundane.

Natasha Lennard proposes ways of living the antifascist life by first pointing out "'fascistic habit'—formed of fascistic desire to dominate, oppress, and obliterate the nameable 'other.'"[62] Habit, for Lennard, is not the trivialized, normalized phenomenon that appears in commonsensical language but refers to "no less than the modes by which we live."[63] Lennard situates microfascism as "a perversion of desire produced through forms of life under capitalism and modernity: practices of authoritarianism and domination and exploitation that form us."[64] She lists some central black holes: "The individualized and detached Self, the over-codings of family-unit normativity, the authoritarian tendency of careerism—all of them paranoiac sites of micro-fascism in need of anti-fascist care."[65]

Lennard's last phrase is key. Ultimately, a focus on microfascism enriches an antifascist analysis and praxis. As Guattari puts it, examining a "micropolitics of desire means that henceforth we will refuse to allow any fascist formula to slip by, on whatever scale it may manifest itself, including within the scale of the family or even within our own personal economy."[66] Identifying the features of microfascism conceptually can assist in recognizing its emergent tendencies in our own lives.

Microfascism and transhistorical materialism

Some readers might ask straightaway, "Isn't a cultural approach too idealist? What about the material conditions?" There are plenty of works that address what we could call the material conditions or systemic determinations of the rise of fascism: the economic contexts, organizing efforts, party-building, and interwar state formations. We could call this kind of materialist analysis a structural one.

Brad Evans and Julian Reid, elaborating Deleuze and Guattari's broad analysis, assert that fascism cannot "be represented or understood as that of an historically constituted regime, particular system of power relations, or incipient ideology. Fascism, we believe, is as diffuse as the phenomenon of power itself."[67] Approaches to fascism that take up the European interwar version as its model can limit our understanding of the temporality of microfascism and could even produce an analytic attachment that allows microfascism (and fascism) to reappear and renew itself, especially when it doesn't do so in familiar ways.

For the purposes of this project, and to preserve Griffin's prompt that we distinguish historical expressions from ineliminable elements of fascism, I work with the notion that some systems appear through various conjunctures which end up being modes or conditional expressions of more enduring, ineliminable or *ur-qualities*. Fascism lurks deep in society, as "ephemeral and indistinct" features that can combine into a force that then takes perceptible contours.[68] Eco listed fourteen characteristics of Ur-Fascism that were latent but always proximate in modern societies, even archetypal. [69] These are fascism's enduring qualities. Andrew Johnson summarizes Eco when he says Ur-Fascism does not merely refer to the most obvious models, "but to future cases and the process of metamorphosis."[70] The aim is to identify and diagnose emergent forms based on previous expressions, as we are always walking with "eternal fascism."[71]

At times, my approach will take up the techniques of mining the past that traditionalists do. There is a fascist mode of doing so, involving the projection of contemporary ideological values into an ancient past in order to create a continuity that universalizes and therefore justifies fascist thought and action. But there is also an antifascist mode for finding the continuity of fascism in other times and places or an antifascist transhistorical method.

Guattari gives us another angle on the study of "the genealogy and the permanence of certain fascist machineries."[72] One example he gives is the

Inquisition, which "had already put together a type of fascist machinery which kept developing and perfecting itself up to our own time."[73] For Guattari, the continuity of these forces—the "fascist machineries"—beg our attention, as they reappear "in the family, in school, or in a trade union. . . . A struggle against the modern forms of totalitarianism can be organized only if we are prepared to recognize the continuity of this machine."[74]

Such continuity will be most explicit when we discuss patriarchy in Chapter 2, as I'll trace the resonances between archaic ur-qualities, as well as more delimited conjunctural systemic forms. How do we speak of patriarchy's reverberations through time, systems, and subjects? One obviously does not need to valorize it to analyze it as archaic and continuous. Microfascism, like misogyny, is not an unbroken or universal story. Aligned with Eco's Ur-Fascism and Guattari's "continuity" of fascist machineries, I am arguing that microfascism appears earlier than modernity (with its liberal democracy, nationhood, and Western systems). By tracing contemporary microfascism's resonances with archaic ones, we address Guattari's antifascist question: "What is this bizarre totalitarian machine that traverses time and space?"[75]

The microfascist machineries return in conjunctures that are unstable. There is a crisis in the effectiveness of the mythic foundation of the state and, for our purposes, the sovereign subject that underpins it: "the 'phantasmagoria' is unraveling and is no longer doing the job of producing political and economic quiescence," says Martel, applying Benjamin to our times.[76] Ideological cohesion is crumbling, and stark expressions of violence increasingly work to police and secure a declining order. In Michel Foucault's terms, a political order built on a "rationality of calculations, strategies, ruses, [and] . . . technical procedures" erodes, reverting to its origins in war.[77]

For this project, that means an acute revival of what Silvia Federici calls "the war on women." A conjuncture or system in decline asks for an analysis that maps its volatile elements rather than its relatively stable terms. The primary *ur-microfascisms* this book takes up are gender and patriarchy. Before exploring those in detail, some necessary gestures must be made to two other systems central to microfascism: colonialism and capitalism.

Colonialism and race

Social theorist Alberto Toscano poses a challenge to recent analyses of fascism, asking what would happen if the discussion "of fascism were not dominated by the question of analogy?"[78] He is referring to the way interwar Europe tends to stand in for all forms of fascism. Toscano turns to thinkers who situate fascism in other lineages, namely race and colonialism. Aimé Césaire famously talked of Nazi Germany as the boomerang of European imperialist violence. George Padmore wrote "Fascism in the Colonies" in 1938, seeing in South Africa "the world's classic Fascist state." Cedric Robinson, Amiri Baraka, and Langston Hughes all noted that being Black means being intimately familiar with fascism in the form of white supremacy. George Jackson and Angela Davis used the term "fascism" to make sense of the US prison-industrial complex as "the ongoing fact of racialized state terror."[79]

Moving to the cultural sphere, we could say microfascism is marked by the ruinous project of whiteness on an everyday level. Whiteness is not just a demographic or a "working class left behind" that then turns into a racist bloc. Whiteness is a mythic abstraction that galvanizes expansion and control as a matter of habit and practice. The modern Western state does not exist without the colonial and settler violence at the root of the state's mythic violence.

The mission of whiteness at the basis of the American project is composed of coordinated action through renewal and elimination. As capitalism abandons its laborers and resources, we see what David Roediger calls a decline in "the wages of whiteness."[80] Such a feeling of dispossession and despair are part of what I call a *downsurgency* organized by right-wing activist groups.

A reorientation of fascism away from interwar Europe and towards scenes of colonial and racial sovereignty is indispensable to understanding fascism. In a moment when race is front and center for insurrections both fascist and antifascist, the displacement of the European expression is historically urgent.

When we discuss necropolitical sovereignty in Chapter 4, we'll find one of its early laboratories in the colonial encounter, which extends to the carceral system. The twenty-first century legacy includes massacres and lone-wolf killings in the Global North, often based on the reactionary idea of the "Great Replacement" in which refugees and immigrants are targeted. White supremacy—whether it be anti-Blackness, Islamophobia, anti-Semitism, Indigenous genocide, or hostility to Asian and Pacific Islanders—has been a growing multinational movement with lethal results. Antifascist work must necessarily chronicle and combat this global resurgence.

This long-standing global supremacist project of whiteness has become accelerated via networked communication technologies to form what Jesse Daniels calls "a translocal whiteness—that is, a form of white identity not tied to a specific region or nation but reimagined as an identity that transcends geography and is linked via a global network."[81] Daniels grasps the power of digital culture beyond the means "of recruitment or political mobilization" to "*the real epistemological challenge* it poses to undermining the very basis of racial equality."[82] Whiteness seeks to ground itself and its values as nationalist common sense and as sovereign truths (in fascist lingo, to be "based"). I would add that this epistemology is tied to an *ontology*, the production of subjectivity to shape a world in which these claims make sense. Moreover, such a subject gives itself the authority to make an action stick. Race and microfascism are inextricably linked as the ongoing sphere of the production of subjectivity, shaping reality, and establishing sovereignty under the sign of whiteness.

The racial project of whiteness and colonialism complicate palingenetic ultranationalism since whiteness preexists the nation-state. Nationalism remains a modern project, while fascism has older roots in forms of authority, command, and state formation—the settler colonialism of the state.

Capitalism

When it comes to capitalism, we need to acknowledge both its recent form as well as its longer-standing structure. First, as a persistent system of extraction and destruction, capitalism is closely tied to death-making. As we'll explore in Chapter 4, capitalism subsumes, systematizes, and expands death into a planetary machine, which Justin McBrien calls the "Necrocene" or "Capitalocene." The Capitalocene's conditions systematize a homicidal and suicidal sovereignty writ large in the so-called Anthropocene.

In addition, Silvia Federici expertly traces the intersection of patriarchy and capitalism through a necessary figure for capitalism's origins in primitive accumulation: the witch. The destruction of women's knowledges and practices under the sign of the witch inaugurates the role for women within capitalism, which in sum involves social reproduction without inclusion into wage relations.[83]

On a more conjunctural plane, capitalism's specifically neoliberal expression sets the stage for contemporary fascism by being always-already in *crisis*. Verónica Gago, Marta Malo, and Liz Mason-Deese posit that the crisis of neoliberalism will lead to "the advance of social fascism on the micropolitical plane."[84] This plane includes religious fundamentalism and other feminicidal subjectivities that "reinforce the divisions between the human and what is categorized as less-than-human (the feminized, racialized, and naturalized) that sustain necropolitics."[85] The current context is thus "a particular conjunction between a neoliberalism that refuses to die and fascist forms that come to save it."[86] Neoliberalism in decline thus unleashes and activates microfascism that is the nexus of gender, war, and death on women.[87]

Keeping in mind both the cyclical persistence and crisis-laden ruptures described by Gago and her collaborators, this book takes capitalism into account not as the totalizing machine that determines forms of gender violence, but as itself an event in history within a broader patriarchal ordering and gender-based microfascism. Patriarchal capitalism, sure, but also *capitalist patriarchy*, the latter referring to a mode of patriarchy that reigned for some time and is now in crisis.[88]

This book's project displaces nation from the center of analysis to locate fascism in another material dynamic of sovereignty and subjectivity—the premodern, pre-liberal democracy lineage that operates primarily in the mode of gender.[89] This project thus examines microfascism as marked by archaic and ongoing production of sovereign subjectivity. To that end, my project centers on the cultural domain as its own specific sphere of producing subjective formations, relational dynamics, and affective appeals.

Discerning morbid phenomena as antifascist praxis

This book's understanding of antifascism is rooted in a Deleuzo-Guattarian anarcho-feminist approach, one that finds fascism in microspheres of everyday life as well as the usual social and political venues. The project is a study in perception that encourages readers to become more attuned to that which does not always reveal itself in familiar ways. It aims to understand fascism's *emergent dimensions*—the subtle dynamics in play before historical expressions manifest. Such perceptions allow us to identify fascism before it turns into a movement or settles into state-forms, and it comes with an expansive notion of *antifascist praxis* as a preemptive strike, as ongoing *anti-microfascisms*. Until we understand the subjective and cultural dimensions of microfascism, we will continue to feel morally superior in our analysis ("racists are racists!") while ignoring the terrain we're on *and that lurks in us* as microfascism.

This book is written in a conjuncture marked by decline and crisis—this is not news to many. A waning of liberal centrist integrative capacities is generating a crisis so severe it is becoming what Antonio Gramsci calls an *interregnum*: the passage between conjunctures. He announces that in these moments "the old is dying and the new cannot yet be born . . . morbid phenomena of the most varied kind come to pass."[90] Tracing some of the interregnum's morbid phenomena as they fundamentally reshape reality, this book foregrounds culture as the realm where pervasive "latent" tendencies rest and move.

We are in an interregnum where foundational violences return as morbid phenomena, drawing from simultaneously archaic and hypercontemporary processes. We are not just seeing crises in particular systems (e.g., racial patriarchal capitalism) but in their foundational ability to authorize themselves, which I will argue rests on the ontological structure of Western masculine subjectivity. A war of restoration has been unleashed in which sovereign subjects seek renewal by reverting to their primordial operations. They seek to restore not just a prelapsarian world but the founding act of sovereignty that can make that world. Any such renewal is accompanied by eliminationist power.

Ultimately, microfascist culture is a *deathstyle*. It replaces life with abstractions, it flees life to reproduce it without women. These palingenetic and eliminationist processes make death-worlds and a life-destroying reality. The project of this book is to trace this deathstyle through gender, war, and sovereignty as well as point to some core elements of an anti-microfascism.

1

Autogenetic Sovereignty

Subjectivity and the Violence of Authority

Daryush "Roosh V" Valizadeh is an award-winning misogynist. It was perhaps too early in a year that saw the rise of Gamergate and Milo Yiannapolis to dub him, in February 2014, as the "Web's most infamous misogynist," but he didn't let his competitors take the spotlight so easily.

Roosh V is a self-made man. Not that he has cultivated an independent livelihood nor even lived the good neoliberal life by taking responsibility for his entrepreneurial self. Instead, and perhaps counter to the commonsensical notion of the self-made man, Roosh V's life trajectory in the 2010s encapsulates a microfascist masculinity, or what I am calling *autogenetic sovereignty*.

Roosh V rose to prominence as a pick-up artist (PUA) with a global orientation and a series of sex tourism books on how to get laid in different nations.[1] This could be seen as microfascist performance art, since it was unlike any modern, plebian variation of dating con-artistry. Instead, as his website *Return of Kings* heralded, his was a self-ordained royal lineage. The newness of what he dubbed "neomasculinity" resulted from rummaging through the past (reactionary Christianity, ideological evolutionary biology, and Stoic philosophy) to find "old ways of helping men" restore a lost patriarchal order. His mission: to renew and spread a *monarchical masculinity*.

Like any good traditional hero, Roosh V has faced some existential ordeals, which in his case could all be conveyed in one word: women. His entire PUA project is founded on the notion that female consent is a "barrier to be surpassed or sidestepped."[2] Roosh V *needed* women as an impediment to overcome and renew the sovereignty he always innately had anyway. Feminists were especially an obstacle, as they were the "reason that the 'masculine man' has apparently disappeared from the world."[3] His response to this crisis, a (since-deleted) blog post titled "How to Turn a Feminist Into your Sex Slave," was to remind everyone of his sovereign power by reasserting mastery over them.

Despite being a self-made man, Valizadeh relied on women as objects to blame and instruments to renew his status. Valizadeh's rallying cry was that "women forced him to act in a certain manner."[4] Men were sovereigns but under constant threat. Feminists in particular were so perniciously clever that he even blamed them for misogynistic killings, calling Elliot Rodger "the First Feminist Mass Murderer." Classicist Donna Zuckerberg has pointed out that, for all Valizadeh's claimed affiliation with Stoicism, "it is difficult to imagine a less Stoic pastime than ridiculing and attacking feminist writers for their ideas and physical appearances."[5] The self-made man, always on the brink of losing his subjective kingdom, must remake himself. This is done again and again through the reduction of women.

Valizadeh's sovereign acts include edicts: to repeal women's suffrage and for men to pass pro-men laws; to redefine rape according to his own standards ("All Public Rape Allegations Are False"); and to revive more traditional forms of the sexual traffic in women (by giving men absolute control over their female kin). Perhaps tired of providing so much nuance in his proclamations, he issued a blog-decree in language even non-sovereigns could understand: "Women Must Have Their Behavior and Decisions Controlled by Men."[6]

Sovereigns have often found themselves under attack, needing safe spaces like forts and castles. In 2016, Valizadeh faced his own grand battle, as his valiant attempt to hold court off the Internet was ruined by the threats of marauding hordes of women. Valizadeh had issued a call for nationwide in-real-life meetups for the many kings and kinglets in training. After hearing women were going to show up with the intent of disrupting these men's assemblies and squad roundtables, he canceled the event, declaring that he had been victimized by feminist harassment. His claim of victimhood only fueled his royal renewal project since it's embedded in what Sarah Banet-Weiser calls "the dynamic of masculine injury and capacity—the injury is that masculinity has been lost, and the role of popular misogyny is to find and restore it."[7] The king never fully arrives—his "return" is a renewal of capacities at the expense of women's capacities, via the further injuries visited upon them.

However, at least one woman provides something other than epic ordeals for Roosh V: his mother. The self-made Roosh-man makes himself thanks to the supportive infrastructure of his mom. His version of MGTOW (Men Going Their Own Way) involves going down the stairs to his mother's basement. His man cave—in good necrophilic fashion—is a simulated womb, now filled with things hostile to the bearer of its predecessor.

The self-made man is obviously impossible. Moreover, it is a *redundant* phrase. Valizadeh embodies—in a distorted simulated way—what I'm calling *autogenetic sovereignty*. This might seem like a more convoluted way of saying self-made man and to some degree that is correct. But the "self-made man" phrase has a contemporary sociological connotation that limits its explanatory power. "Self-making" goes much deeper into the history of social power than the modern entrepreneur or success story can convey. And it has to do with the long history of microfascism.

Autogenetic sovereignty harkens back to an idea that a subject can create itself *ex nihilo*, disconnected from material connections and contexts. This very separation, as we'll see, is part of a long-standing patriarchal form of masculinity that distinguishes itself from women, turns to abstraction, and grounds itself in its own fabulations *all at once*.

Masculinity as such, traced through notions of sovereignty, is defined by autogenesis, an absolute act of power to define and create oneself. The self-making *is* the primary sovereign act. The phrase "self-made man" is thus redundant, as to be a man is already to have the claimed power to make itself. This is key to our understanding of microfascism since autogenetic sovereignty only exists as a process of renewal (rebirth) and elimination (of women).

Roosh might be an exemplar but it's the regularity and norm of masculine subjectivity that is under investigation here. Why are self-made men so adamant about their separation? Why do they incessantly have to assert sovereignty rather than just be sovereigns? Why does the regeneration of sovereignty depend so much on managing others, and more specifically, on depleting the capacities of others?[8]

This chapter investigates these questions with an elaboration of ways modern and ancient selfhood is forged in autogenetic sovereignty. In addition to seeing this as hyperindividualization, we will explore how autogenetic sovereignty becomes composed into collective action as a network of black holes that resonate to produce life-destroying reality. Autogenetic sovereignty is embedded in the foundational philosophy and rituals of subjectivity. To put it bluntly, autogenetic sovereignty is microfascism in the subjective mode.

The circuit of flight and return: patriarchy and divine abstraction

The concept of autogenesis appears in feminist writings on modern subjectivity. For example, Judith Butler, drawing from Luce Irigaray's work, argues "that the subject, understood as a fantasy of autogenesis, is always already masculine."[9] Susan Buck-Morss calls autogenesis "one of the most persistent myths in the whole history of modernity" (and of Western political thought before then, one might add). Doing one better than a Virgin birth, modern man, *homo autotelus*, literally produced himself, generating himself, to cite Terry Eagleton, 'miraculously out of [his] own substance'."[10]

Buck-Morss traces autogenesis to myths that the "'birth' of the Greek polis [comes from] the wondrous idea that man can produce himself ex nihilo. The polis becomes the artifact of 'man,' in which he can bring forth, as a material reality, his own higher essence."[11] She also sees it in Machiavelli's "praise of the Prince who self-creatively founds a new principality and connects this autogenetic act with the height of manliness."[12]

The essential resonance of men with the *divine* becomes one of the earliest mythic operations that create autogenesis. Traditions claim that man was created by the gods, or God, as a special category differentiated from nature and animals. The prior existence of the male infuses the Genesis Fall of Man myth in which "man came before woman, created autonomously by the gods or God. Man . . . was a separate creation, set apart from nature, with a unique relationship to his creator."[13] The Greeks' origin story in the tale of Pandora also narrates the birth of men without women. In such stories, order and sovereignty are projected onto a transcendent sphere. Nature here comes second, after an initial separated, abstracted relationship that connects Genesis with autogenesis, masculine Creator with masculine created.

Through reenactments within initiation rites, men ritually repeat the divine act of Creation, thus authorizing their own project.[14] The autogenetic sovereign flees toward an abstraction, authorized by that abstraction. Autogenesis means being a self-made man, but only via the power of the invented relation to a god. Men, created by an abstraction they created, get to become a creator, giving "birth" to politics, aesthetics, and other world-shaping structures. There is therefore no patriarchy without a foundational myth of self-reproduction, of autogenesis.

Women are required to play a part in this "phallic phantasy of a fully self-constituted patrilineality, and this fantasy of autogenesis or self-constitution."[15] For one thing, the introduction of women severed the relationship between man and the Divine and "introduced into man's world all the features associated with nature."[16] Woman as original sin, a fall from transcendent abstraction, is a transgression primarily because her actions caused men's own fall.

Women's very existence is the disruption of the mythic order that established God in the first place. Women are positioned as the cause of all ills, including sin, severance from the Creator, and most importantly, death. Women become natural enemies of men because they resolutely embody nature itself. Women are not just seen as resisters to their roles, they are positioned, like Lucifer himself, as existential rebels, ones whose transgressions set in motion the *necessity* for order and the resulting status of women within it. Addressing women, early Christian lawmaker Tertullian proclaims, "You are the devil's gateway; you are the unsealer of that forbidden tree; you are the *first deserter of Divine law*."[17]

We can pause here to note a reversal. It's not that patriarchal order is established first and then women transgress it. Law only exists as a way of framing Eve's behavior as transgression. The Biblical God's mythic punishment for woman's transgression is twofold: the pain of birthing and the subjugation to men. Patriarchal order thus emerges *afterwards*, as penalty for original transgression. The need for punishment and control precedes the establishment of the law, with men becoming authorized to mete out the penance in the form of patriarchy. In the inaugural, primordial instantiation of order against transgression, autogenetic sovereignty mystically disappears as the inventor of order after inventing its rationale—the sinfulness of woman. Men give to themselves an origin—a relation to the divine, the autogenetic creation—while women are secondary and moreover tempt men downwards into nature (including death). Patriarchal masculinity is in this way *self-invented*, creating a system in which men are middle managers, interpreting their invented mythic divine figure while executing eliminationism based on those interpretations. The state of exception precedes the state, but now as primordial mythic violence based in gender production.

Of course, such autonomy is impossible. The gendered core of autogenesis positions women as the disavowed yet necessary realm of *materiality*, something that cannot be excluded once and for all. The efforts of pure flight are constantly thwarted as what subtends this sovereign is "a Gordian knot of interwoven dependencies, involving our very existence both as individuals and as a species."[18] The inaugural subject of autogenesis simulates creation as "a denial and cooptation of the female capacity for reproduction" and a disavowal "of its dependency on the maternal."[19] Renewal (the palingenetic repeating of origin stories) cannot banish this dependence, it can only highlight it.

Here we have the gist of the sovereign dynamic: the autogenetic maneuver requires that the original woman "be rejected and denigrated as the ambassador of the mutable world from which he seeks to assert his independence and over which he strives to establish his superiority."[20] Therefore, men must continually resist this pull by *reinaugurating* the foundational act of sovereignty. Because the autogenetic sovereign is ultimately an impossible project, it needs continuous renewal, and it recommences world-making via policing, punishment, and control. In sum, we are faced with a double move by the autogenetic sovereign: a flight from dependence while returning to depend on women (whether for reproduction or due to her position as stubbornly material cause for the flight).

Autogenetic sovereignty is not a successful and stable ground—it is predicated on a flight that *fails* to secure itself, resulting in the need to restart the autogenetic process again and again. A failed autogenesis generates a dynamic of flight and return, a circuit that casts abstractions back onto the world as ordering forces. Subjectivation takes place on this autogenetic sovereignty circuit.[21] The circuit of flight and return means flight is never able to operate on its own terms—it's a relationship that seeks to rearrange the terms of the relationship. It's this usurping of power that defines the microfascist relation. But we need to take another step, one that addresses the drive to autogenetic sovereignty. For that, we next explore the social production of fear.

Social desire: fear

Microfascism is the realm of producing subjects, which involves the *social organization of desire*. Desire is not a personal, psychological property but always an assemblage, a socially produced force that shapes reality through material investments of energy. It is not personal, but it forms persons. Thinking of fascism, Guattari foregrounds a "micropolitics of desire":

> We must abandon, once and for all, the quick and easy formula: 'Fascism will not make it again.' Fascism has already 'made it,' and it continues to 'make it.' It passes through the tightest mesh; it is in constant evolution, to the extent that it shares in a micropolitical economy of desire itself inseparable from the evolution of the productive forces. Fascism seems to come from the outside, but it finds its energy right at the heart of everyone's desire.[22]

Fascist production of desire has often been understood as repression and channeling. John Protevi posits that "desire, the movement of connection and immanence, is repressed by microfascism; in its place arises the strange cancer of a thousand 'cells' or self-contained units."[23] While Protevi pinpoints the generic operation, the repression is specifically directed at a material that is gendered. Microfascist desire is a fear of dissolution of an order; specifically, fear of a manhood in danger that gets actualized as misogyny.

One area where this fear appears is in the relation to the material realm called *mimesis*.[24] Mimesis is the repetition and imitation that foundationally forms human beings. Rather than presuming an individual with consciousness, mimesis proposes that, as Benjamin put it, "sentience takes us outside of ourselves."[25] What he called the *mimetic faculty* is an openness to particularity, a mode of receiving the world of concrete objects and sensuousness. We live not as self-sealed individuals but in relation to others and the world, primarily via mimicry.

The mimetic faculty involves copying but moreover refers to the "the visceral bond connecting perceiver to perceived."[26] Mimicry is not just a visual process of repeating an external form—it is transmitted and felt embodiment, a perception by feeling.[27] Mimesis is the sensuous connection to Otherness, whether other humans or the environment.

Mimesis has been fundamental to Western thought, but primarily as the threat of nature against all things human. As Horkheimer and Adorno note,

"For civilization, purely natural existence, both animal and vegetative, was the absolute danger."[28] Mimesis, it was said, was tied to the death drive, or the "the tendency to lose oneself in one's surroundings instead of actively engaging with them."[29] Mimesis is coded as the sphere of passivity, of pure absorption into an environment, an undifferentiated realm where the human's special qualities are de-activated. This was "a fearful confrontation of the consciousness with phenomena it could not control."[30]

Resonating with the archaic positioning of women as lures, modern philosophy positions the mimetic realm as a danger to be overcome. Mimesis always beckons, luring the subject towards undifferentiation, so "civilization" developed abstractions, erected structures, even imitated mimesis in the form of magic. Abstraction in the form of knowledge is a violence, as it "takes the place of the mimetic adaptation to the other."[31] These abstractions, often enacted through initiation rites, are designed to supplant the mimetic faculty.

First, autogenetic sovereignty *disrupts* mimesis—or sociality—through differentiation and fleeing (the development of abstractions). Second, autogenetic sovereignty *imitates* mimesis, a mimetic mediation through divine abstraction that then gets mimicked by/as Man the Creator. Third, autogenetic sovereignty then *imposes* those imitations (flights, transcendences, abstractions) onto the social by reducing and subjugating.

This dynamic of the flight and return embodied in autogenesis is spurred on by *fear*. Such a social desire inaugurates the modern subject primarily as *differentiation* from the feminine (coded as the overwhelming capacities of nature and mimesis). Autogenesis thus operates to position a subject via fear of dissolution and absorption, both classified as feminine. Microfascist mimesis comes through fear of, flight from, and simulation of primary mimesis. Hostility to "raw" mimesis forms the autogenetic sovereignty. It's not just that the feminine is associated with materiality, but also that "the feminine" is removed from the binary of form/matter, which is determined by the masculine autogenetic sovereign who places himself on one side of the binary while simultaneously acting as controller of both terms.

The foundational violence against women seeks to complete the project of flight from mimesis through vanquishing, even extermination. We can see the visceral fear and actions among the Freikorps. Klaus Theweleit notes that they were fueled by a desire for a "bloody mass" while fearing the "bloody mess" that comes from women's bodies. To avoid being annihilated in fear and horror over bio-sanguinity (menstrual blood) the troops were compelled to enact a relentless pursuit of necro-sanguinity (massacre, rivers of blood).

For Theweleit masculine subjectivity emerges from a primordial fear of dissolution, a dread of the engulfing potential of women's bodies.[32] For Kant this is the terror of the sublime. Origin myths, divine creation, man-god relations all stem from "the horrible danger that one may lose all connection with the sacred and be swallowed up by chaos."[33] All the abstractions are designed to keep this threat of chaos at bay. The circuit of affects and relations gets tighter: "Dependency, fear . . . contempt."[34] The social desire of fear (of the threat to the social order posed by women) generates the order and its maintenance.

The place or *topos* of "woman" is thus essential—she is the cause of the circuit (the nature that must be fled) yet a continual threat (to the order and abstraction produced through/as flight). The masculine autogenetic subject's compulsion to return is reframed as feminine (as seduction, as the dangerous allure leading to dissolution, as the terror of the sublime) which means returning *to* women via domination. The primary social desire of fear is blamed on women, which allows all sorts of subsequent blaming to take place.

When autogenetic sovereignty comes back to control its source, it displays its microfascism as the ongoing and ubiquitous process of gendered *eliminationism*. Eliminationism does not refer solely to absolute disappearance or extermination—it signifies a reduction of capacities *towards* the null. It is an annulment and nullification that needs to keep the realm intact as a source of social reproduction. The autogenetic flight extracts, enfeebles, and subtracts and is thus closer to the necropolitical "right to maim" or a "slow death."[35] The spectrum of eliminationism involves debility and decapacitation, belittling and diminishing; in sum, a negative relation to capacities. Autogenetic sovereignty reduces women through representation (what has been called symbolic annihilation) situated on a spectrum of eliminationism, including feminicide.

The flight/return loop of autogenetic sovereignty is also enacted through *substitution*. We'll see this more clearly in Chapter 3 when we analyze masculine rites of passage. The rites of subjectivity are developed in bands and warrior clubs, in what Celia Amorós calls patriarchal "pacted groups" who are "ratified" by the figure of woman.[36]

But the claimed "fear of absorption" by psychoanalytic, commonplace, and reactionary accounts only partially captures the dynamic of the autogenetic sovereign. More than the spell of the engulfment, what is feared is the *refusal* to be integrated into the systems of abstraction, the erected structures, the order produced by mythic violence. The primordial religious dimension of autogenetic sovereignty returns.

Women, refusers and rebels by definition, threaten to seduce consciousness, reject integrative conceptual systems, and upend narratives based on abstraction. It's the inherent refusal that needs controlling and renewed reduction. The fear that founds the order is fear of the loss of order itself.

Susan Bordo, in the tellingly titled collection *Flight to Objectivity*, traces themes of autogenetic sovereignty in Western philosophy, specifically in Rene Descartes. A philosophical ambassador of what Bordo calls "the seventeenth-century flight from the feminine," Descartes establishes the subject compulsively by "starting anew, alone, without influence from the past or other people, with the guidance of reason alone."[37]

Bordo situates Descartes in his era's "virtual obsession with the untamed natural power of female generativity, and a dedication to bringing it under forceful cultural control."[38] She notes the position of women as temptresses luring men to passion through a sexuality that "was seen as voracious and insatiable."[39] The material realm was not defined as passive, but a "common harlot" with "an appetite and inclination to dissolve the world and fall back into the old chaos" and who must be "restrained and kept in order."[40]

The patriarchal fears could not be assuaged in philosophy. The era required more violent means of pacification: the witch-hunt or the war on women. Witches were especially filled with desire, as they offered their "capacious 'mouth of the womb' the opportunity to copulate with the devil."[41] The witch-hunters' "nightmare fantasies of female power" were also directed at "female generativity," which in addition to sexuality, Bordo equates with biological reproduction.[42] The good witches (female lay-healers and midwives) were the main targets.[43] The witch hunts laid the groundwork for yet another violent substitution: the "male medical takeover of the processes of reproduction and birth."[44] A focus on female generativity need not idealize an equation of women with the maternal, as it involved a whole set of peer knowledges, skills, and technologies for health and well-being.

The autogenetic principle at work in Western origin stories and aesthetics (the flight from the body and material bios) thus depends on the reduction of women (keeping them at bay, into their own realm where they no longer create only procreate). With its focus on *birth* and *creation*, the masculine autogenetic sovereign thus seeks to make "females redundant in the very sphere where they are indispensable—that of reproduction."[45]

And the simulations start well before modern medicine, in the rites of passage for men in ancient times which imitate the material processes of birth and death, now cosmologically oriented as spiritual death and rebirth, with the aim of eliminating those material processes. Masculine subjectivity, formed in the secret societies, is a system of initiation that aims to replace bio birth and materiality with mythic subjectivity. The rite of passage for autogenetic sovereignty results in a transformed man through the elimination of women. Sometimes this comes in the form of specialized actors (Freikorps, incels, and manifesto-writing mass killers) while mostly the palingenetic elimination is distributed, immersive, and ordinary.

Contemporary misogyny can be seen as the policing and punishment required for the loop to go on. The 2021 Atlanta spa shootings, in which eight people were killed (most of them Asian-American women) were rationalized by the mass killer as his need to eliminate temptation by sex workers. The "fantasy of male autonomy" requires that women are "tethered to sexuality that keeps getting in the way."[46] It's this repetition that informs the palingenetic action.

Patriarchy's necessary protection schemes intensify when faced with feminism. Feminism challenges the masculine ability to self-seal and is therefore coded as an attack on sovereignty. Feminism, even its attenuated form as popular feminism, provokes men to feel threatened and claim victimhood as they launch their hostile counteroffensives.[47] One does not even have to be a feminist to elicit the backlash, as women's very desire is seen as a challenge to expectations and triggers hostile reactions. Autogenetic sovereignty cannot secure itself without managing reality, so any refusal of that ordering becomes a threat to the entire subjective circuit. Given that I am arguing that autogenetic sovereignty is at its root the subjective structure of fascist man, then feminism, insofar as its existence is a threat to that structure, is antifascist.

Self-preservation: a homi-suicidal act

While the loop of masculine autogenetic sovereignty is a form of life, it also generates forms of death. As Theweleit puts it, "Under certain conditions, this particular relation of [gender] production yields *fascist* reality; it creates life-destroying structures."[48] As hostility to life, autogenesis operates as a self-preservation that is *necrotic*. One might puzzle over how death and self-preservation coexist. Aren't they in opposition? Not when the *self* of sovereign self-preservation is rooted neither in *bios* nor in associative forms of life (for that's the realm of mimesis and particularity), but in abstraction and transcendence. The mimetic faculty based on the senses is geared towards "self-preservation of both the individual and the social group" which is then lost in the autogenetic reversal (the flight from sense and mimesis into abstraction).[49]

Social desire cannot fully invest in the flight without cutting off life, so it returns to control life/women mimetically. The reproduction of domination (via abstract schemas) becomes a substitute for the reproduction of life and sociality. This substitution is already necrotic. It supplants life with order, concreteness with abstraction, and the world with God. Simulation enhances the necrophilic character of autogenetic sovereignty.

The deathliness of the microfascist subject here does not just refer to the elimination of the Other but to something more "productive": a *will to preservation without life*. Klaus Theweleit goes so far as to call it a "mode of production" that continually transforms life into death and seeks to "build a new order from a reality that is devivified."[50] Autogenetic sovereignty is thus a doomed project of social reproduction through transcendence and flight. Instead of concrete social reproduction the autogenetic sovereign is a creator, in the image of a Creator, that is a "producer of life-destroying reality" or what will later be explored as necropolitical culture.

Kant and the aesthetics of the sovereign

Susan Buck-Morss zeroes in on autogenesis as a fear-based social desire in her assessment of Kant's aesthetics. In a nutshell, autogenesis for Kant is tied to sovereigns who get to produce reality and give "birth" to an order. Kant's inaugural question for the subject in facing the world seeks to solve a problem: How does one ward off the bewitching powers of the sublime? How can one not be absorbed by the world?

Like other thinkers, Kant is filled with the fear of absorption that has been the cornerstone of modern subjective flights. Gripped by a terror of being assimilated in the face of what he categorizes as the Sublime, Kant turns to what he considers to be the superior subjective models: the politician and warrior. "Both statesman and general are held by Kant in higher 'aesthetic' esteem than the artist, as both, in shaping reality rather than its representations, are mimicking the autogenetic prototype, the nature- and self-producing Judeo-Christian God."[51] Kantian aesthetics is based on a bounded and detached subject position responding to the terrifying uncontrollable sublime while modeled on men of action rather than contemplation.

Kantian aesthetics of abstraction and autogenesis once again allow us to see microfascism in culture as not just a flight *from* materiality but a *return* to it. Masculine subjective flight never really leaves the concrete, it must return to the source to reshape reality according to the sovereign subject's abstractions.

Let's take as an example Kant's position on judgment, which arises via the disembodied contemplation of abstractions (form, beauty). Any gendered perspective will quickly see that transcendent ideals of femininity and beauty never remain in a detached sphere—they operate as categories to *organize* reality. Representation (language, image, idealization) is a type of objectification, and judgment becomes the basis for sorting the world—and specifically women's capacities—through these judgments. Abstraction is a flight that ultimately cannot flee as it guides operations in a reality-shaping project. Making reality is performed through imagination, categorization, and differentiation, generating ideations that both found a "free" subject as well as empower that sovereign subject to control the "unfree" subjects yoked to their natures.

Julius Evola and the autogenetic sovereignty of the state

Plenty of critics of authoritarian state power discuss the works of Nazi jurist Carl Schmitt. Schmitt is of great value to understand the inner workings of totalitarian state thought. When it comes to sovereignty, however, he and his subsequent critics (such as Hannah Arendt and Giorgio Agamben) remain in the juridical realm. If we begin with microfascism, then the production of subjectivity as sovereignty asks for a different type of theorist.

If Schmitt is the premier fascist political theorist, then Julius Evola is the corresponding fascist cultural theorist and philosopher of subjectivity. Evola's devotion to cultural traditionalism and to the subjective existential foundations of fascism make him a noteworthy figure. Both Schmitt and Evola contemplate the state, but Evola roots it in mysticism and sacred foundations—war, masculinity, and selfhood. Evola has been cited by Steve Bannon, Richard Spencer, and others like them as inspiration, primarily for his justifications of traditionalism, elitism, and state authority.

Umberto Eco called him "one of the most respected fascist gurus."[52] Evola's work has appeared—often shorn of his political positions—in occult circles through his books on alchemy, yoga, Buddhism, hermeticism, and love. Evola has provided direct inspiration for Southern California masculine fascist groups, such as the Rise Above Movement and its successor Revolt Through Tradition.[53] While Evola was a proponent of an aristocratic rather than folk-based fascism, his US followers absorb his work like self-help motivations to "rise above," developing a peculiarly American version of sovereignty: a populism of self-made aristocrats.

Evola is the preeminent thinker of microfascist power: how to develop it, how to justify it, how to formulate authority, venerate war, and approach death, even suicide. Evola's importance to microfascism is that he grounds state authority in the production of subjectivity, in cultivating a new man, a sovereign subject. In his affirmative account, Evola provides the theoretical rationale for power via the autogenetic masculine self.

A sustained exegesis of Evola's work on the state, sovereignty, and masculinity will clarify the enduring parts of microfascism at work today. In the chapter on war, we will examine his claims about warrior bands being the basis of sovereign selfhood. Here we focus on the concept of autogenetic sovereignty through his fascist philosophy of the self.

In *Ride the Tiger*, Evola opens by asserting and elevating what he calls "*the principle of purely being oneself*. . . of living according to one's own law, the law defined by one's own nature."[54] Such grounding in nature is "not in relation to any other Being or the world, but rather on one's own specific being."[55] Such a person—always a man[56]—stands firm in turning "his own *being* into a *willing*, making it his own law. . . absolute and autonomous."[57]

In just a few assertions, Evola gives indicators of the circuitous logic he'll rely on throughout the book. For instance, we see it in his explanation of the above self-grounding by making duty derive from power. If you have strength, it must be exercised.[58] For Evola, a capacity must be applied because it's an imperative of inner-law. The *content* of that law is not to be established in advance, as that content is up to the sovereign himself to determine.

Already we see that the self-authorized man can only result via ongoing differentiation from life and women. The masculine subject "feels himself belonging to a different humanity and recognizes the desert around himself" and his actions require incessant defense of that separation.[59] In Evola's formulation of history (cited by Bannon and others), such a man "must stay standing as a free being, even in the epoch of dissolution." We see here an important topographical positioning: a subject steady and still, holding fast against absorption (linked to women). The goal is "transcendent confidence," Evola writes in a chapter called "Invulnerability."[60] Self-confidence is tied to abstraction as "the essential center of his personality is not life, but Being."[61] Such toughened subjectivity "prevents any intoxicated self-identification with the life-force."[62] It's this rigidity, coded now as freedom, which becomes the affective basis for armored fascist subjects in the context of decline.

In *Men Among the Ruins*, Evola elaborates his philosophical positions in *Ride the Tiger* by tying the sovereign subject to the state-form, warrior clans, and masculine rites of passage, among other things. Reconstructing his argument through both books will get us to the fundamental logic of sovereignty that infuses, and is renewed in, microfascism.

Evola opens a chapter titled "Sovereignty-Authority-Imperium" with a meditation on the essence of the state. For Evola, "the foundation of every true State is the *transcendence of its own principle*, namely the principle of sovereignty, authority, and legitimacy."[63] He cites Ancient Rome's doctrines around empire as his primary example. We can see the basic example of this transcendence when authoritative leaders are themselves the law and are not subject to it.

The foundational principle must contain within itself the necessary absoluteness of its power and authority. Any sovereignty requires a "meta-sovereignty," the ability (even right) to be able to invoke and apply sovereignty at will. Evola enacts what he seeks to analyze here by asserting this authority mythically (as the self-given essence).

Such authority exists prior to any state-form or hegemonic system. It is found best distilled in "the pure power of command, the almost mystical power and *auctoritas* inherent in the one who had the function and quality of Leader."[64] Such a leader is not simply a head of state; he is "the supremely realized person who represents the end, and the natural center of gravity, of the whole system."[65] Evola then gives us the chain of positions of patriarchal leadership, as a sovereign rules "in the religious and warrior order as well as in the order of the patrician family, the *gens*, and, eminently, of the State, the *res publica*."[66]

Unlike other thinkers who primarily analyze sovereignty in exceptional or emergency situations, Evola stresses that it must also appear "in ordinary functions, or wherever the State is a living organism."[67] Sovereignty must operate (as self-generated) in the *essence* of the state as authority, not merely in the ability to suspend those operations. Evola's state is a vitalist one, a life-or-death principle since its absoluteness is the "life-belt."[68] He distinguishes his version of the state from the juridical approach, which "refers only to a *caput mortuum*, namely the condition proper to a dead political organism."[69]

Putting the state into such an elevated biopolitical position tells us something about sovereignty's role. The sovereign doesn't just let live; it is a *life-giving force*. More than an adjudicator of worthiness of life and death, the sovereign is *creator*. Such a stance allows Evola to make claims about sovereignty as generative—as the making of reality, even of self-given life. We see here already the gendered quality of this creation, as the sovereign gives "birth to an Order" when he differentiates himself via self-given authority.[70]

Evola centers microfascism when he prioritizes subjectivity (masculine) in the claim that the "creation of a new State and of a new civilization will always be ephemeral unless their substratum is a new man."[71] He provides a progression of personhood that lays out the stages of producing this new man. The lowest form ("merely being a man") is yoked to humanitarianism and natural law, which is superseded by a more developed man who belongs to a given nation and society. This man, too, is still rather low on the chain of Being, and should strive to be a "person," a quality on a plane higher than the merely naturalistic and "social" one. But it does not end there. A person needs differentiation *vertically* among the political organization of "bodies, functional classes, corporations, or particular unities according to a pyramid-like structure."[72] At the top of such hierarchies there is an "absolute person," namely, the Leader.[73] Here we see Evola's key contribution: the substratum, the foundation, needs to be a type of self, a production of subject that can then be expressed in state-form.

And it's *sacred*. Evola goes on to recast the transcendent principle away from secular and juridical state powers to a spiritual domain of selfhood:

"Sovereigns differentiate themselves as elites "on a plane that is defined in terms of spiritual virility, decisiveness, and impersonality" and by breaking natural bonds.[74]

But giving life (to an order) is only part of the sovereign's authority. Evola takes some time to describe the sovereign power to *take* life. Perhaps surprisingly, taking life does not mean eliminating others. Instead, the sovereign's right to take life is best understood when taking its own. Even suicide is established through "sovereign right," Evola writes, which one "always keeps in reserve."[75] Not all suicides are expressions of sovereign power, however. He disdains suicides accomplished for "emotional and impassioned motives" as these signal "passivity and impotence."[76] The same goes for social motives, as the differentiated man has a dignity untouched by social bonds. The truly sovereign subject takes their own life not because life's ordeals and circumstances are overpowering, but because the subject sees those ordeals as not worthy of the will's actions. Sovereignty comes when a subject has a choice to "accept these ordeals or not."[77] Such a sovereign right, based on an already existing "detachment from life," preserves the abstract masculine subject in the moment of its demise.[78] Even a dissolving self is subsumed as a sovereign act rather than something that belongs to the human as material mortality.

Evola's importance to microfascism and sovereignty is multiple. As a fascist thinker of sovereignty, he ties state authority to subjectivity. The mystical foundation of the state rests on the substratum of the new man, an autogenetic sovereign. Sovereign power gives and makes "life," now redefined as an abstraction and a political order. It also operates even in the moment where the self is abolished (if done for sovereign reasons)

The new man gives life and controls death, even its own. Given that so much of his work is a study of "traditionalism," sovereignty emerges prior to the rise of the modern nation, in archaic practices such as Roman imperial action. Let's pause here to digest the significance of this when it comes to the usual equation of fascism with nationalism. Evola takes great pains to distinguish his idea of imperial sovereignty from nationalism. It's not that the two are merely different entities—Evola sees them as *opposed*:

> The 'nation' will always be a promiscuous entity . . . on the one side stand the masses, in which, besides changing feelings, the same elementary instincts and interests connected to a physical and hedonistic plane will always have free play; and on the other side stand men who differentiate themselves from the masses as bearers of

> a complete legitimacy and authority, bestowed by the Idea and by
> their rigorous, impersonal adherence to it. The Idea, only the Idea,
> must be the true fatherland for these men: what unites them and
> sets them apart should consist in adherence to the same idea, rather
> than to the same land, language, or blood.[79]

Rather than nation, ethnicity, or territory, what anchors and guides the sovereign is the "Idea," an almost Platonic abstraction that unites subjects. These are abstractions as "galvanizing ideaforce[s]," sometimes specified as duty or honor. For Evola, the tale of modernity is the fall of the empire into the nation. It is no wonder then that the restoration of sovereignty is a renewal of "man" in a spiritual sense, a tradition that is untouched by the "decline" into modern institutions, including nation and land.

The gendered essence of autogenesis becomes clear when Evola characterizes the state as being "under the masculine aegis, while 'society' and, by extension, the people, or demos, are under the feminine aegis. Once again, this is a primordial truth. The maternal domination, from which the political-virile principle subtracts itself, was also understood as the domination of Mother Earth and the Mothers of life and fertility."[80] Man's metamorphosis or progress from lowly man to leader is thus a subtraction, a flight. This differentiated ("reborn") man becomes the foundation of state authority as "the political-virile principle." Microfascism is thus profoundly tied to a flight from materiality into abstractions, even spiritual forms.

Our understanding of autogenetic sovereignty as microfascism has found itself in a fascist philosophy that is also a philosophy of gender. Evola lays out clearly the microfascist realm is the primary one, not an auxiliary dimension of state power or a stage in absolute authoritarianism. In masculine subjectivity as autogenetic sovereign, we have the fascist rationale for the spiritual foundation of power, one defined against women. Evola's characterization of the autogenetic sovereign that founds state order also relies on a cold, steely demeanor, one that draws from an older tradition of abstraction through desensitization.

Desensitization

As mentioned above, Kant looked not to the artist but to the warrior and the statesman as ideal subjects to emulate when it came to aesthetic judgment. In addition to their mimicry of the abstract divine, Kant's leader-models operate as *sense-deadened* subjects who can withstand absorption. Buck-Morss highlights this embodiment when she notes the "truly autogenetic is entirely self-contained. If it has any body at all, it must be one impervious to the senses, hence safe from external control."[81] To the aesthetic realm of senses the autogenetic sovereign brings an *anaesthetic*, a numbness to the corporeality needed for survival. Sense-dead while giving birth to society, the modern subject is "a manly creator, a self-starter, sublimely self-contained" and modeled in war.[82] The result of such an "asensual, anaesthetic protuberance is this artifact: modern man."[83]

Why would this anaesthetic be idealized? Buck-Morss cites Ernst Cassirer who attributes "the reaction of Kant's completely virile way of thinking to the effeminacy and over-softness that he saw in control all around him."[84] The autogenetic subject as anaesthetized man dreads and disavows women, specifically their material desires and biological capacities. In the place of life production and reproduction comes the "narcissistic illusion of total control" driven by "the fantasy that one can (re)create the world according to plan (a degree of control impossible, for example, in the creation of a living, breathing child)."[85] Instead, the modern subject makes worlds via numbness by fleeing to abstract notions.

The modern anaesthetic neutralizes those senses (that Buck-Morss identifies with self-preservation) and prevents the body from feeling pleasure. The anaesthetized subject pushes individuals to identify with abstractions that produce submission and conformity, working against the self-preservation instinct from which sensuous connection was developed. At the core of Western aesthetics is the production of an autogenetic subject as desensitized, setting the stage for subsequent operations of numbness.

Fascism's (an)aesthetics of embodiment and masculinity have been well documented. Falasca-Zamboni, also noting Kant's gendered anaesthetics, argues that "fascism relied on feelings and sentiments . . . [yet] strove to neutralize the senses."[86] Walter Benjamin sought to account for a range of embodied experiences and sensations resulting from World War I as well as the everyday upheaval brought about by industrial capitalism. Post-WWI popular medical discourse promoted the idea of "shell shock," inspiring Benjamin to identify a dynamic between numbness and shock as central to subjectivation at the time.

Mediated embodiment, Benjamin posited, was an effect of image-bombardments as well as the technologized experience that attempted to *manage* that assault on the senses. In a nutshell, the embodied subject was an interface of numbness and shock. For Benjamin, this was a result of modernity and not just fascism, which instrumentalizes the dynamic of stimulation and detachment to produce its collective mediated subject. He extended the experience of shell shock beyond the context of Great War veterans to describe everyday life under accelerating capitalist mass consumption, in which the phantasmagoria of culture distributes numbness and shock.

Technological environments, in addition to excessive work and sensory stimulation, shock subjects to the point where the outside world needs deflecting, resulting in subjective shielding. What emerges is an armored subject, one that refuses to be affected and to receive external social cues. The result is a stunted self, active in the world not by being "in touch" with reality but by blocking it out. This stunting "destroys the human organism's power to respond politically even when self-preservation is at stake."[87] The ordinary trauma of everyday life involves a subjectivation that becomes accustomed to shock and increased infosphere stimulation.[88]

Being numbed also means needing increasingly bigger shocks to feel anything, which forms the dynamic of fascism as elaborated by Buck-Morss, Falasca-Zamboni, and Koepnick. Through mass spectacle and a hardening towards others, fascist aesthetics incapacitated sentience and agency, forming a steeled self that refused to be affected, to receive the senses of others. Klaus Theweleit's analysis of the "body armor" of Nazis traces it to post-World War I Freikorps paramilitary culture, which developed desensitizing affects in its poetry, letters, and diaries. As Theweleit assesses them, these paramilitary and ex-military subjects roamed together and apart, assembling through each other's armored egos, and developing homicidal fantasies against women.

In sum, subjects resonate with each other through *receptivity*, not primarily of ideas and beliefs but through gestures, senses, and affects. Numbed interactors demonstrate that armor does not neutralize the capacity to act and react—it can stimulate desensitized action. Armor is *cultivated* and *maintained* through circulation into a collective body. This collective anaesthetized body is not inert, however. During interwar European fascism it was mobilized to operate as a mass, and now, as we'll see below, as a network. Let's examine how this desensitization finds its compositional forms in twenty-first century microfascism.

Digital numb troops

For Benjamin, the numb/shock dynamic was distilled in the Great War. Today, we note that war is immanent and pervasive: global civil war, holy war, global war on terror, dirty war, and cyberwar, in addition to the conjured ghosts of the US War of Independence and the Cold War. As this book foregrounds, the primary war is a "war of subjectivity," specifically a war on women.[89] And this war, with its shock/numb troops, thrives in online spaces.

Within digital culture, microfascist subjectivity is performed as freedom, irony, and fun transgression. The network plays a key role not just through education and information, but by initiating others and creating a *(de) sensibility.* This subject forms a body that is sealed, armored, and numbed in order to act against others. Let's examine this activated body of the disconnected through some of its familiar figures: the troll, the blackpilled, and the inspo-shooter.

A prominent subjective figure for interconnected desensitized subjects is the Internet troll. The troll is known less for its numbness than its social desire to shock. Shock is a long-standing value for fascists. "I want to shock a driveling Italy," Futurist F.T. Marinetti once wrote, welcoming absolute destruction through warfare. Their fascination with acceleration and technological disruption generated "a grisly puppet show that fabricates shock—alternately benumbing and inebriating."[90]

Trump was often described by analysts as a troll. Even his adviser, KellyAnne Conway, indicated as much when she described his political style: "POTUS is a man of action and impact . . . *a shock to the system.*"[91] Conventional right-wing media personalities such as Rush Limbaugh and Glenn Beck, who cut their teeth as radio "shock jocks," could be said to continue that proto-troll work when they became significant social media influencers. But the troll became an Internet subject par excellence, whose social desire to shock targeted those deemed outsiders along typical gender, race, sexuality, and ableist lines.

Microfascist trolls operate primarily via irony, defined here as the ability to act and then claim distance from the action's effects. The troll attacks and then, via irony, claims a nonserious stance. It undermines another's capacities and then departs while announcing that the attacked others are taking them too seriously. Irony is a subjective operation to affirm the subject which seeks to shock by generating distance and *disavowal.*

Trolls offend, and in common parlance, "push boundaries." They try to get a rise out of the social body to awaken it from slumber. Their targets are not as open-ended as they (or some of their more seduced critics) claim. Too often critics would position trolls as apolitical, in it for some "lulz" in a vacuum. This would often end up ceding to trolls the control over the meaning of their actions. Once we situate the troll as a variant of autogenetic sovereignty, we open a different orientation.

The troll's weapon of irony is grounded in a sovereign claim over the *self*. In these trolling operations, the subject gives to itself the principle to act without limits. The troll wants to determine when to assert its will (intimidating, undermining, policing) and when to withdraw (denying, disavowing, abdicating). It seeks control over the meaning of its effects and the suspension of its own accountability. Sometimes it invokes *freedom* as its overriding value. Joshua Citarella links troll freedom to "an underlying political nihilism, allowing one to disassociate from the real-world effects of one's own actions."[92] Rebecca Solnit calls it the "adolescent-boy glee" that accompanies disinhibition: "this is an art of disassociation—literally, in the psychological sense of disconnecting from one's own feelings" as well as "a philosophical disassociation: my acts should have no consequences; cause is unhitched from effect."[93] Freedom means evasion of their actions' repercussions.

Even irony, the seemingly "apolitical" stance, was already pervasive in postfeminist media culture, as Rosalind Gill argued in 2007.[94] From game shows to reality shows to lad magazines, the ironic tone allowed sexism to circulate with impunity in the 1990s. Such knowing sexism, enlightened sexism,[95] retro-sexism,[96] ironic sexism, and hipster sexism[97] created an environment that allowed trolls and other digital culture denizens to subsequently transpose the sentiments to its chans and forums. The rise of trolling wasn't an abstract, open-ended practice but was steeped in the patriarchal hostilities that preexisted it.

Resituating irony as an autogenetic sovereign weapon allows us to reconsider a fuzzy term that gets applied to trolls: transgression. When trolling's defenders employ the notion, transgression seems to mean pushing others' boundaries (especially those that would "impose limits" on freedom). But that topography of transgression already allows trolls to determine the spatial terrain. It's more accurate to say that trollish transgression involves operations against others who are perceived to be *out of place*, who themselves have crossed borders and become violators of sacred masculine space (e.g., gaming or the Internet as such). Even raiding others' online spaces protects the spatial order by keeping others in their places. Transgression is thus a vehement *defense* of boundaries and order which then gets glorified as the freedom to transgress other people's spaces. Trolls don't just violate boundaries—they primarily police them. Autogenetic sovereign freedom is a spatial practice, controlling public/private spheres within patriarchy, policing borders through common lingo like GTFO (Get the Fuck Out) and invading profiles, accounts, and posts. Microfascism is thus not primarily a matter of expression but of territorialization and protection. It defends a territory as property, especially the territory of its own subjectivity.

Trolling is neither apolitical nor abstractly transgressive: it seeks to shock, awe, and upset—these are specific forms of affecting others. It finds pleasure and fun in inducing those reactions, and vehemently defends a position of evasion when confronted. Karla Mantilla points this out when she coins the term *gendertrolling*, noting that it gets "lumped together with generic trolling, which covers up the unique characteristics of gendertrolling and obfuscates the fact that this is a pattern that happens to women."[98] One could even ask whether "generic trolling" ever really exists, given its particular targets and patterns.

The troll shocks and then aims to flee the scene and the damage. But, like the dynamic Benjamin examined, the troll is caught up in a shock and numb *circuit*. The troll already arrives as numbed through a variety of experiences online and offline. The troll then seeks to get a rise out of its (unwilling) target by shocking them, while exciting other trolls (who are also numbed). The troll stimulates its victim in order to stimulate themself while stimulating another troll (who applauds, criticizes, awards). Other trolls then reactivate the circuit.

But this escalation of shock and awe cannot continue ad infinitum, and thus there is a need to deflect from *overstimulation*. How does the troll shield itself from the shocks? Such a subject needs to escalate its border wall of insensate indifference. "Freedom" is tied to a callous numbing of the subject. Trollish shock is not always driven by active hate, but in its hardhearted, unfeeling, and indifferent subjectivity it acts on the world to reduce others. Manospheric microfascism creates a new man through such nonempathy and nihilistic composition, where autogenetic sovereigns gather in gleeful con(de)viviality.

This numbness takes numerous forms. Many in the manosphere cite Stoicism as their lineage, where virtue is tied to self-discipline and self-control. But what is controlled? Certainly not the deep patriarchal impulses of autogenetic sovereignty or the social desire to control women resulting from fear and resentment. Misogynist stoicism is a cultivated desensitization against all that is feminine. It refuses sensuous connectivity in favor of a masculinized abstract connection: collectivizing a disposition of numbness that then leads to collective action-challenges, such as "No Simp September."[99]

A prime example of dehumanizing numbness specific to online culture is the figure of the NPC, an acronym for the gaming term "Non-Player Character." The NPC refers to automated avatars in virtual worlds. NPC became a "gamer slur that channers deploy to dehumanize 'normies' as blank husks."[100] NPC is used against a swath of people who are linguistically converted from human adversaries to lifeless automatons. Opponents are put into a different existential category as fully programmed objects who don't qualify as human. Calling someone NPC is an interactional symbolic annihilation, an eliminationism not in representation but in *participation*. By defining interlocutors as mere tools and objects, the autogenetic sovereign seeks to shape reality where their adversaries—such as critics who are coded as Social Justice Warriors—are not just wrong but lack functional human consciousness.

This clear example of reduction and eliminationism is part of what Erich Fromm calls necrophilia (examined in Chapter 4), the desire to reduce others to the status of object, stripped of agency and life. The sovereign subject wields the term NPC, giving to itself the capacity to sort the world according to who is worthy of life/death, in this case by naming their status as nonliving from the outset.

In addition to the figure of the troll, *blackpillers* are the most intense subjective black holes resonating in microfascism. Blackpillers, unlike redpillers, do not see self-improvement and training as pathways to possessing women. Fatalists when it comes to their lot in life, blackpillers are found primarily among masculine incels who have hit a wall when it comes to believing in life changes. As Zack Beauchamp puts it, "The blackpill bundles the incel sense of personal failure with a sense of social entitlement: the notion that the world owes them sex, and that there is something wrong with a society in which women don't have to give it to them."[101]

Blackpillers take their desurgency into themselves, cutting themselves off from an exterior life. As though foreseeing the future, Guattari notes, "These black holes swarm and proliferate across the social field. The question is whether subjectivity is going to echo them in a way that an individual's entire life . . . depend upon a central point of anguish and guilt."[102] For blackpillers, the depressive certitude of being "Forever Alone" generates a subject ultimately indifferent to its own existence. Their isolation resonates with others, abyss-nodes in downsurgent networks. Digital culture intimately connects the isolated *through their isolation*. Forever alone, together.

The mediated collective of black holes

Often those troll subjects coordinate their actions. I examine this phenomenon more in the chapter on war (Chapter 3), but we can discuss here the ways collectives like troll armies are formed. Today's autogenetic sovereign subject is seemingly enmeshed in a paradox. It is both hyperindividualistic (the isolated, numbed subject) yet collective (connected in action). How do we think through this? Rather than the form typically seen in fascism (unified mass, individuals in conformity with each other through the leader) recent microfascist collectives are less regularized, though no less effective.

Filippo Del Lucchese's description of a population that seeks tyrants could be helpful: he calls it a "collection of disconnected, isolated individuals able to act together."[103] Guattari's description of fascism also gives us hints: "fascism, like desire, is scattered everywhere, in separate bits and pieces, within the whole social realm; it crystallizes in one place or another, depending on the relationships of force."[104] This roving mutating sphere of autogenetic sovereigns comprises what Gary Genosko calls "the cesspool in which microfascist forces connive and collide."[105]

Genosko examines 4chan around the microfascist combination of individual and collective, describing it this way: "extremely involutive black holes draw processes of subjectivation into themselves as their power increases with every iteration of them."[106] Such microfascism operates on social subjectivity, as "desire cannot extract itself from the echo chamber of emptiness that modulates its existence, making it lose its bearings, finding solace in distress, that travels surprisingly well along the bubbling resonances of social media."[107] Networked microfascism seals individual selves while encouraging resonance with (masculinized) others.

Prominent US right-wing movements—like the "sovereign citizens movement"—seek to form and unleash an entire wave of autogenetic sovereignty rooted in nationalist ideas under the sign of the "Patriot." But there are other less formed and less visible expressions that need our scrutiny in the microfascist realm.

The microfascist mediated collective moves from unity to networked performances which depend on transmission by autogenetic sovereign *influencers*. The most pressing example of these collective actors can be found when misogynist shooters mimic others. The disconnected subjects still resonate with each other through imitation, inspiration, and transmission. Online communities turn mass shooters into martyrs and saints, which becomes inspiration for others to act. The act inspires acts, but also the program of inspiration. The massacres under investigation here cannot be reduced to shooters and their imitators/copies—what's mimicked are *inspo*-shooters.

From Anders Breivik to Brenton Tarrant to John T. Earnest, from Elliot Rodger to Alek Minassian, these mass shooters are not traditional copycats. The term copycat needs updating for the kinds of mediated subjects in digital microfascism. Copycats imitate not just the act but the media package: the videos, lists, manifestos, and threats. The act that is copied is already an abstraction, a digital object in a media package.

Yet digital connective technologies produce a kind of intimacy in these mimics: some killers were in contact with their "heroes."[108] Tarrant was the most cognizant of himself as inspirational figure looped into digital and chan culture, developing himself as meme, troll, influencer, and shitposter.[109] He was harnessing "a well-established digital feedback loop where white male violence is uploaded, distributed, consumed, and remixed by others. . . . The Christchurch killer wasn't only trying to make himself go viral. He—with extreme self-awareness—was hijacking the white male violence digital feedback loop to spread and amplify his ideas and actions."[110]

The Internet becomes both a space of subjectivation (as a man of action) as well as social contagion (as influencer). The "visceral bond" that these autogenetic sovereigns develop, because it is born in a flight from women, is with a digital object—the memed killer. Mimicking with body armor, the autogenetic sovereign makes itself receptive to the inspo-shooters, to masculine goading, to further shocks to develop the numbness required for battle.

Simply put, numbness does not result in passivity or paralysis. It's a catalyst for increased alertness and seeking out thrills and stimulation. The network of isolates increases its collective numbness and callousness *in order to act*. Isolation does not result in pure individuation, as the loneliness is intensified by being shared. We have moved from lonely crowds to lonely social networks. The resonating black holes require the influenced as well as influencers, receivers as well as actors, who all become connected in their pain and numbness as a network of isolates able to act together.

These armored subjects are embroiled in a networked war primarily against women. Becoming-soldier means cultivating a receptivity to images not of the other, but of one's mirrored black hole of autogenetic sovereigns. Today's body armor is developed through irony/disavowal which both isolates and connects (to other isolates). This is the resonance of black holes, of the militarized body in formation with others: it is no longer amassed as in the Nazi orders but as *interactivated* and networked. The armored subject "has now become simultaneously an attacking machine and a funnel into which flows the contagion of fascism."[111] Horizontal influences magnify those connections. The self-sealed subject bonds to others to produce clusters of black holes, renewing themselves through war (specifically, the eliminationist war on women).

Masculine nihilism becomes homi-suicidal or really, *femi*-suicidal (a subset of feminicide). Combining irony, lulz, numbness and inspiration, the homi-suicidal circuit pushes others to action, to increase their status. A gleeful nihilism through disruption becomes the groundwork for subjects waging war, even a spiritual one, on others. As we'll see in Chapter 3, autogenetic sovereign action takes different forms: the lone wolf (individuals inspired and influenced by others); groupuscles (a term Roger Griffin borrows from Félix Guattari); and squads (in war as well as gaming contexts).

Microfascistic masculinity is now developed not through mass mobilization, but rather by irregular and distributed deployment of numbness and shock to the microfascist social body. Trolling and competitive shock form a network that induces numbness while inspiring necropolitical action (homicide and suicide). The result is a collection of desurgent disaffected nihilists indifferent to their own futures, ready to act on their autogenetic desire even if it results in their sovereign suicide.

Futures without worlds: sovereign ghosts and corpses

Autogenetic sovereignty gives to itself existence and therefore power. With this concept, we can trace what lurks in archaic form in the present. Autogenetic sovereignty is pivotal both in terms of its origins (patriarchy, state -orm, fleeing from the material) and its ongoing effects. It usurps powers of creation; it establishes and renews bonds while eliminating others.

Microfascism is the realm of the palingenesis of this subject, a renewal through reduction that preexists and founds the state, and now reappears as an ongoing civil war. Autogenetic sovereignty is a subjective structure that is *pactful*, generating coordinated black holes who determine spaces (public/private) and roles (subjective capacities). Ultimately, this operation continually engages in war, specifically a war of subjectivity upon women. And it tends to pursue this line of flight unto death, of itself and others.

The palingenetic project of masculine rebirth seeks a future without bio-reproduction. It populates the world with martyrs and myths, the ghostly squads of past and future. It is a replication without reproduction. Life-destroying reality involves specific acts of violence (shooters, harassers, eliminationists) but also a core/archaic eliminationism via the flight/return circuit. The flight from corporeality is not abandonment but returns to generate a dead corporeality, a corpse-reality. Due to its inextricable link with others, this flight returns as self-abolition, the homi-*suicidal* dynamic as the motor of microfascist subjectivity.

Autogenetic sovereignty has an ambivalent relationship to its own persistence. Conventional concepts of sovereignty presume that the subject is still invested in its own perseverance, that it acts in defense and preservation of its existence. Once we take the subjective foundations of microfascism seriously, especially as gendered, then we no longer have such a persevering subject. Sovereignty is more invested in itself as autogenerated through its abstractions rather than in life, including its own. It seeks to *persist* beyond life with its abstract values of sacrifice, honor, duty, and the divine sphere. It's a nihilism against this world in favor of an otherworld populated with ghosts and abstractions.

Speaking about Deleuze and Guattari, Genosko says fascism's internal catastrophe was because "it liberated the desire of the masses for their own deaths, in spite of themselves."[112] This collective subjectivity's necrophilic hostility to life no longer operates via the masses but by concentrated subcultures, niches, and networked actors, which are no less lethal or world- changing.

The autogenetic sovereign as homi-suicidal tendency begins to answer Spinoza's question "what can a body do?" Here it repeatedly *goes to its limit in the process of destroying others*. In that limit reality, it puts itself in danger to pursue the abstract glory of "absolute victory." It's here we can better glimpse Benjamin's understanding of the political relation of aesthetics to fascism, specifically as it produces a mediated collective body. What he finds is not the aesthetics of life, but of a core collective impulse towards self-destruction. A suicidal/homicidal mélange, in which "[s]elf-alienation has reached the point where it can experience its own annihilation as a supreme aesthetic pleasure."[113]

We are surrounded by autogenetic sovereignty, whether (dis)embodied in fully blackholed subjects that unleash lethal violence, or as elements within our own masculinized social desires. Judith Butler reminds us, autogenetic sovereignty only exists because "this subject is itself the effect of a genealogy which is erased at the moment that the subject takes itself as the single origin of its action."[114] Understanding microfascism means reinvoking that genealogy as the palingenetic renewal of fascist man via the ongoing feminicidal war of elimination. It's a genealogy of war bands, necropolitical flights, and masculinized sovereignty. The genealogy elaborates an antifascist stance articulated so well by Theweleit: "We need to understand and combat fascism not because so many fell victim to it, not because it stands in the way of the triumph of socialism, not even because it might "return again," but primarily because, as a form of reality production that is constantly present and possible under determinate conditions, *it can, and does, become our production*."[115] This production is more than the fascism in our heads—it's in our bodies, desires, and affects. With this concept, we can trace further the process where war, gender, and death converge.

2

Gender

Ancient Misogyny and the Microfascist Manosphere

On August 7, 2021, Matthew Taylor Coleman left the surfing school that he owned in Santa Barbara, California and drove across the border to Mexico with his two children (one aged two years and one ten months) without their mother. Two days later he was picked up by police trying to cross back into the US without them. He was arrested for killing them with a fishing spear and leaving their bodies buried in underbrush on a ranch. He quickly confessed to the murders but with what was in his mind a justification invoking a hero's tale. According to the FBI, Coleman said that he knew it was wrong, but it was "the only course of action that would save the world." From what, you might ask? Coleman declared he was "saving the world from monsters," and he knew this because he was "receiving visions and signs revealing his wife . . . possessed serpent DNA and had passed it onto his children."[1] News accounts of the garish event focused on his sources: Coleman claimed he was "enlightened by QAnon and Illuminati conspiracy theories."[2]

Three days later, Jake Davison shot and killed five people in Plymouth, UK, starting with his mother, before committing suicide. News accounts focused on his online videos and communications which indicated he was an "incel" (involuntary celibate) who had been frustrated with his inability to realize his sexual fantasies. His exterminationist revenge fantasies, however, could be fulfilled.

The cases were covered separately, each tied to a recently coined sociological phenomenon (QAnon, incels). These figures occlude as much as they render visible, namely the deep-seated and long-standing misogyny that gave men a context in which to kill. The "serpent DNA" uses genetic science to update the archaic hostility towards women as the Devil's consorts. From the Biblical Eve to the witch-burnings of the Middle Ages to the public murders of women suspected of being demonically possessed, Coleman's actions were a renewal of an old patriarchal violence now wrapped in the bizarre package of QAnon. In the Davison case, "incel" makes it seem that his act is somehow beyond the pale, a pathology rather than an acute expression of everyday sexism—the demand that women should obey men's orders and desires, and when they don't, violent retribution is easily accessible.

These are only two of the most visible cases that week. The same day as the Plymouth killer, a man in Indapur, India killed his wife for putting "excess" turmeric on him at a wedding (in fact, a quick Google News search resulted in at least ten incidents of men killing their wives that week in India). On August 10 in Saudi Arabia, a man killed his newly married wife of twenty-four hours with a rock and then ran her over with his car. Less than three weeks before Coleman's murders, a man killed his wife and child, then himself, in Venice, Florida.

In Texas alone we could register the following: hours before the Plymouth killings, in the Dallas area a man killed his wife and one-year-old daughter, then himself, ostensibly over a dispute involving her $2 million lottery winnings.[3] On that same day, a Memphis, TX man came to terrorize his wife and, while doing so, shot and killed her daughter. And, in a twist that ties individual acts with systemic brutality, on August 10 a man was charged with the death of his wife, who was in fact shot and killed by San Antonio police during a standoff. The well-documented sexism and misogyny of police meets the husband's version, and in the subsequent masculine eruption of violence, the victim is the woman. All of these were "local" stories, which prompts us to ask, when does something become national or even global?

This whole book could be filled with individualized accounts of feminicide and other gender-based violence during those two weeks. Alongside the rise of the alt-right and other ethnonationalist projects, the twenty-first century witnessed an increase in gender-based terror or feminicide.[4] Moreover, while the alt-right has waned in its influence since 2017, the everyday misogyny of gender norms has not disappeared with it.

At first blush, gender appears regularly in the writings on fascism, the alt-right, and the rise of Trump. Even mainstream US news regularly pointed out Trump's misogyny. Whereas his race-based messages were "dog-whistles," there was no need for such codes when it came to women, who were called dogs outright.[5]

When does gender appear in fascism? Is it when organizations draft doctrines about women's roles? When state policies around eugenics and reproduction are implemented? When auxiliary groups appear like the Proud Boys' Girls or the looser community of TradWives (women bloggers vehemently defending traditional gender roles)?

When it comes to fascism studies, a gendered analysis often subsides in favor of a race-based analysis. Antisemitism or white supremacy are taken as sufficient conditions for a *direct line* to fascism. These presumptions make sense when one's object of study is white supremacy, white nationalism, and ethnonationalism or one's antifascist practice begins with combating race and ethnicity-based oppressions. What if we afforded the same orientation to gender? Instead of making it a necessary but insufficient "stage" to fascism what would happen if we spent time tracing its singularity?

This chapter proposes gender as a long-standing and pervasive way of ordering the world, one that forms a microfascism expressed through a war on women that installs itself in, without being reduced to, state operations. In fact, this book makes the provocative claim that gender is the primary mode through which microfascism operates, as patriarchy's constantly renewable spectrum of reductionism forms the core of microfascism. Gendered microfascism is the ubiquitous and ordinary mode of palingenetic eliminationism. In the following section, we'll explore twenty-first century fascism's misogyny as not only a recruitment tool but as foundational in the production of microfascist masculine subjectivity.

Centering gender in antifascist critique

A feminist critique of fascism is not new; in fact, it was contemporaneous with the classic twentieth-century interwar version. Virginia Woolf's under-appreciated book *Three Guineas* was written in 1938 with "path-breaking insights into the patriarchal roots of fascism."[6] Unlike other critics of interwar European fascism at the time, Woolf explicitly compares the two: "patriarchy is to private life as fascism is to public life."[7] Picking up on the already well-established feminist critique of the patriarchal ordering of spheres, Woolf posits "the public and private worlds are inseparably connected; that the tyrannies and servilities of the one are the tyrannies and servilities of the other."[8] Woolf provokes antifascists to take up gender: "'feminists' were in fact the advance guard of your own movement. They were fighting the same enemy that you are fighting and for the same reason. They were fighting the tyranny of the patriarchal state as you are fighting the tyranny of the Fascist state."[9]

Inspired by Woolf, Mary Daly extends the entanglement of patriarchy and fascism even further. The only way to respect the severity of the Nazi genocide against Jews, she argues, is to understand its origins, which include patriarchy: "The Holocaust of the Jews in Nazi Germany was a reality of indescribable horror. Precisely for this reason we should not settle for an analysis which fails to go to the roots of the evil of genocide. The deepest meanings of the banality of evil are lost in the kind of research which shrinks/localizes perspectives on oppression so that they can be contained strictly within ethnic and 'religious group' dimensions. . . . The paradigm and context for genocide is trite, everyday, banalized gynocide."[10] Daly's unorthodox claim evokes overlapping systems of oppression that depend on each other, drawing on something broader than the long-standing entwinement of ethnic and religious violence.

Perhaps the most detailed and systematic cultural examination of gender and fascism came a few decades after Woolf, in the two-volume collection *Male Fantasies* by Klaus Theweleit. Theweleit examines a trove of archival material from the post-WWI irregular military units Freikorps. Theweleit found recurring images of women depicted as threats of dissolution, even a "bloody miasma."[11] The "soldier male" could only survive "by differentiating himself as killer, in opposition to whatever he perceives as threatening."[12] The soldier males roamed the countryside seeking "the conservative utopia of the mechanized body."[13]

Echoing our investigation in the previous chapter, the proto-fascist Freikorps compose themselves as armored lethal autogenetic sovereigns, carrying the microfascist impulses with them into the field. They position women as alluring embodiments of the threat to the self and respond by eliminating women (often literally) for the men's "self-preservation."

Because of this pervasive misogyny among proto-fascists, Theweleit posits that, "along with capitalist relations of production, a specific male-female (patriarchal) relation might belong at the center of our examination of fascism," as gender relations are also relations of production.[14] In this clear directive, Theweleit points to microfascism's sphere—of social relations, cultural expressions, media artifacts—as primarily gendered.[15] Microfascism involves a deadening of this "wilderness" within oneself, coded as feminine, a hardening that spurs action against others. As we'll see, this necrotic orientation turns on the self as a homi-suicidal line of flight and abolition.

Updating to the twenty-first century, Trump tapped into Freikorps fantasies and fears about dangerous "red women" when he said of Fox News' Megyn Kelly, "She had blood coming out of her eyes. Or blood coming out of her wherever."[16]

Trump's ascendancy was founded, almost invisibly compared to race and class-based analyses, on gender. For Carol Gilligan and David Richards, "Trump's election shows us . . . what happens when a patriarchal framework takes over—when patriarchy became the lens."[17] Gilligan and Richards argue that gender is not merely one among many identity-positions but takes priority (both in the sense of importance and precedence). They argue that "*gender shapes our way of seeing*" since "its binary and hierarchy . . . had become the lens through which everyone and everything were seen."[18]

Putting gender at the center of analysis does not mean women, specifically white women, are immune from participating in reactionary, even microfascist, politics. Patriarchy works on women through race and class to ensure that asymmetrical positions are established. Multi-demographic appeals were necessary in Trumpist populism, but what galvanizes Trumpism is the cultural production of a reborn *man*. The Trumpian restorationist project, which most often was identified as nationalist or white supremacist by its critics, was also a mythic resurrection of manhood with promises of sovereignty and control. Whether or not one considers Trump a fascist it was undoubtedly microfascism, steeped in misogyny, that swept him in and propped him up.

Capitalism and misogynoir

While this study teases out gender's singularity in the mesh of microfascism, it does so to strengthen a strand woven with others such as racism, capitalism, and settler colonialism. Capitalism's origins in primitive accumulation are founded on what Silvia Federici notes is a crucial gendered figure—the witch. Capitalism's precursors "destroyed a universe of female subjects and practices that stood in the way of the main requirements of the developing capitalist system," including confinement, control over reproduction, and systemic subordination within the patriarchal family.[19] In addition, women's sexuality and material desires were "both seen as a social threat and, if properly channeled, a powerful economic force."[20] The figure of the witch, which we mentioned as the foil of autogenetic sovereignty, now is systematically eliminated to make room for capitalism.

Witch hunts and burnings disrupt, eliminate, and neutralize the multitude of crafts and knowledges that composed *social reproduction* (specifically, healing, making, circulating, relationship-developing). What remained of these female knowledges and practices was consigned to the domestic sphere as "mere" reproduction. This violence reorganized patriarchy by adapting it to emergent forms of capitalism: differentiated spheres, labor roles, and expertise.

In addition to instrumentalizing women to inaugurate capitalism, the great burning was a *re-institution* of a founding violence that occurred in precapitalist religious formations and state violence and took the form of war.

Éric Alliez and Maurizio Lazzarato, discussing Federici, call the witch hunts a key example of a war of *subjectivity*, as "capitalism could not take hold without forging a new type of individual and a new social discipline . . . starting with the web of relations that tied the individuals to the natural world, to other people, and to their own bodies."[21]

Gender and capitalism's historical entwinement was also famously developed in the 1970s by Gayle Rubin. Rubin foregrounds the fact that patriarchy existed prior to capitalism and is irreducible to it: "Capitalism has taken over and rewired notions of male and female which pre-date it by centuries. No analysis of the reproduction of labor power under capitalism can explain foot-binding, chastity belts, or any of the incredible array of Byzantine, fetishized indignities—let alone the more ordinary ones—that have been inflicted upon women in various times and places."[22] Rubin prompts us to think materialism through gender relations, highlighting economies of circulation (the long-standing control over women as objects through kinship), as well as production and reproduction that come to position women in capitalist patriarchy.

The global machine of capitalism incorporates and reorganizes these prior patriarchal operations. But it would be a mistake to deduce that capitalism subsumes all forms of instrumentalization of women, including the preexisting ones. Capitalism draws on patriarchal resources (the subjugation of women) to ground itself, but it does not exhaust the forms of patriarchal control.

When it comes to microfascism, this means tracing and keeping attuned to gender materialism, meaning we move from patriarchal capitalism to *capitalist patriarchy*. This is important for understanding microfascism because it requires attention to how even challenges to capitalism may retain the patriarchal subjectivities. Autogenetic sovereignty can appear in *antimodernist patriarchy* (e.g., in atavistic religious movements) or *anticapitalist patriarchy* (e.g., in masculinized revolutionary movements or in some expressions of state socialism).

Racism and settler colonialism have also drawn upon and reconfigured primordial patriarchal orders to oppress populations more efficiently. In recent times, such an intersectional feminist analysis comes through most lucidly in the concept *misogynoir*. Coined by Moya Bailey and elaborated in collaboration with Trudy, misogynoir refers to the ways "racism and anti-Blackness alter the experience of misogyny for Black women, specifically."[23] Misogynoir's gendered anti-Blackness appears in the unique ways in which Black women are pathologized in popular culture" especially via representation of Black women as angry and hypersexualized.[24]

Most importantly, misogynoir entails a specific type of *dehumanization*.[25] While misogyny "dehumanizes women in general,"[26] anti-Black misogyny exists "to make Black women not just harmed, insulted, objectified and oppressed, but to reify the non-human status of Black women when juxtaposed to non-Black women."[27] Misogyny targets women as women, and misogynoir is a specific variation of it that carries extra dimensions of oppression that relieve white women of some forms of misogyny. An account of "general misogyny" in microfascism thus needs to recognize, if not elaborate, "that at the intersections, experiences differ; how oppression manifests differs."[28] When it comes to microfascism's gendered subjectivity, the war on Black women is indeed a specific entwinement, a pervasive and ordinary eliminationism that registers differently. I would offer a distinction here: the misogyny against Black women, especially with its dehumanization, is a type of *exclusionary eliminationism* (indifferent to the status of Black lives). For white women, the same necropolitical drive is not carried out, for they are more likely targets of *inclusive eliminationism*, in which the necessary circulation of women fosters a dependence and therefore ubiquitous control through reductionism. The overall results converge—though differentially distributed and experienced—in feminicide and other forms of gender-based palingenetic eliminationism.

Defining patriarchy: pack of the leaders

How do we make patriarchy a more essential lens for studying microfascism? Let's begin by explaining the choice of "patriarchy" as the defining term to understand gender and power. For one, it has become the commonly accepted way to name a social and political order grounded in male supremacy, so it works as shorthand.[29] However, it's important to delineate its specific ordering system. The term is contested by some, with Gayle Rubin's classic essay "Traffic in Women" being the exemplar. She prefers to call it "male supremacy" since patriarchy, strictly speaking, is the rule of fathers—a particular mode of gender oppression. Rubin focuses on kinship structures, examining them as a type of production, the power to transform "objects (in this case, people) to and by a subjective purpose."[30]

Gendered power is less the rule by father-leaders than it is an unequal control system whereby "men have certain rights in their female kin, and that women do not have the same rights either to themselves or to their male kin."[31] For Rubin, "the power of males in these groups is founded not on their roles as fathers or patriarchs, but on their collective adult maleness embodied in secret cults, men's houses, warfare, exchange networks, ritual knowledge, and various initiation procedures."[32] Rubin's mention of masculine bonded groups is crucial for an investigation of microfascist masculinity.

In "Thinking Patriarchy," Celia Amorós also highlights men's bonds, centering on the arrangement and proliferation of what she calls "patriarchal pacts."[33] She grounds her work in Heidi Hartmann's definition of patriarchy as "an ensemble of social relationships between men, grounded on a material basis, which establishes, while being hierarchical, some links of interdependence and solidarity which enable them to dominate women."[34] Patriarchy is less a stable order than "a practical ensemble"[35] made up of "real and symbolic practices."[36] Patriarchy combines the pacts into a "meta-stable ensemble of likewise meta-stable pacts between males."[37]

Amorós draws from Jean-Paul Sartre's concept of "the pledged group" to make sense of how pacts are bonded.[38] Pledged groups have a circular quality to their authority, as "the ensemble of males . . . sets itself up by means of a system of practices, and *self-designation* performs the function of articulating them."[39] Amorós argues that these auto-designations empower the pacts to be codifiers of spaces and distributors of women into them. It's this self-designation, a power to establish one's own subjective power, that I have been elaborating as autogenetic sovereignty. Patriarchal pacts are a stark example of collective autogenetic sovereignty—the assembled black holes of microfascism.

Groups enact their power as a way of authorizing it. However, these pacted and pledged groups cannot operate on their own as self-sealed units. A bonded group requires an *external* figure to define their boundaries and cohesion, so women become "a transactional object of pacts between males."[40] For Amorós, there are moments in history where the pledged groups are more violently patriarchal than others, while other times pact-making is normalized as everyday male camaraderie. Pacting against the "outside" woman ranges from "the ceremonial kidnapping of females in some societies, through group rape in war contexts (armies are institutionalized pledged groups), to the more everyday image of a sports team's cheerleaders."[41] Women are necessarily included in patriarchal pacts, but in a diminished state, as instruments.

Amorós specifies the central woman figure that "seals" the bonded groups: the "pacted mother."[42] Brotherhood bonds are no longer forged through a shared flesh-and-bone mother but a constructed common and emblematic mother that binds the pack. A gendered abstraction, the ratified mother comes to replace material mothers (who become objects to be fled and controlled). In fact, this new woman is "a figure re-instituted on the grounds of the symbolic death of the natural one."[43] We can point to the initiation ceremonies into secret societies as well as the routine rites of passage into manhood to locate the rituals of ratification.[44] Patriarchal pacts do not just "other" women—they integrate them as eliminated. Elimination is also palingenetic—the pledged group sticks together by periodically re-binding its "fraternity" with terror, including even "witch-hunting in a metaphorical sense" since the witch represents an absolute threat to the masculine pact due to her own pact—with the Devil.[45]

Recently, pledged group terror has risen in various forms of feminicide and misogynistic violence, often under the sign of the witch. Sometimes they are spectacular, as in Brazil, when prominent activist Marielle Franco was assassinated and Judith Butler's effigy was burned, or the more commonplace hunt for women healers in other nations.[46] In the US, Michigan Governor Gretchen Whitmer, the target of much right-wing ire, death threats, and at least one spectacular kidnapping plot, was accused (in tandem with two other Democratic women leaders) by her GOP opponents of being a witch to be "burned at the stake."[47] And these hunts can have more contemporary configurations, such as the "serpent DNA" rationale for the killings discussed at the opening of this chapter illustrates.

Two dimensions of defining patriarchy through pacts need highlighting to understand microfascism. First, the origins of these men's association can be traced back to war bands, or the Männerbunde (explored in Chapter 3). Women are central to Männerbund pacts since they comprise the realm (nature, home, even "society") that must be fled for the differentiated man to be reborn. Women thus need to be kept in that realm for the ongoing renewal of the bands, especially if it means activating the pacted group via a war on women.

The Freikorps were an example of a twentieth-century war band, as the troop was the main unit of masculine association, according to Theweleit. We see the patriarchal pact in its most acute form in the violent male camaraderie of street-fighting gangs like German storm troopers and the Italian *Squadristi,* but we'll also see the more diffuse but no less lethal forms in misogyny massacres.

Second, we need to move away from thinking about patriarchy, and autogenetic sovereignty, as an individual phenomenon and even as product of an abstract patriarchal system. Microfascism is the realm of composition, so examining misogyny needs to focus on the collective and assembling formations. The contemporary variations of these patriarchal pacts, specifically in networked warrior bands, will be key to understanding microfascism. These updated versions include Gamergate squads and more ordinary forms of coordinated harassment of women online.

Microfascism's production of autogenetic sovereign subjects sees patriarchal pacting in examples like the boogaloo bois, misogynist gamers, male tribalism revivals, meme warriors, as well as mass shooters and their fans. Even a lone-wolf shooter is pacted, having bonded with other masculine figures (even if highly mediated) through word, image, and sound. In addition to living campaign squadmates, this pack can include iconic inspirations from distant lands and times, a mimesis of lethal abstractions. An individual as such is already a pack, entwined with ghosts, martyred warriors, as well with future fans expected to deify them. These pledged groups operate at the intersection of gender and war and, to complete the microfascist triumvirate, are often steeped in necropolitics.

Using a word like "patriarchy," once embedded in pacts and group power, thus becomes more adequate than "male supremacy" which, like sexism, can often be restricted to the categories of belief, behavior, or attitude. While patriarchy technically only refers to *one* of the positions in the sovereign chains (God, leader, father, household), it seems apt because it names the rule of masculine "heads," a sovereign ordering principle. The concept of patriarchy also allows us to move up that sovereign chain to assess the mythic God-Father, whose divine transcendence is the "ur"-operation for autogenetic sovereignty, as elaborated in the previous chapter. To develop this distribution of sovereignty even further, we need to examine patriarchy's ordering system as fundamentally a spatial one.

Space and sovereignty

Patriarchy is an ordering force that shapes reality through "a system of attribution of spaces" which sets boundaries, blockages, and subjective possibilities.[48] Unlike accounts of colonialism or enslavement, there is no scene of "first encounter" to anchor gendered social relations in the imagination. Expansion, invasion, extraction: these comprise the topography of race and empire, typically around the axis of the West and the rest, or the Global North vs. Global South. But what would the spatial power imaginaries look like for gender?

Gender's topography needs its own specificity when it comes to fascism. We have already seen the most analyzed one with Woolf's essay: the public/private sphere.[49] This includes what Maria Mies famously called "housewifization."[50] In addition to this spatial enclosure, the house*hold*, we can add the distributed scenes of the witch hunts, especially their spectacular versions of public burnings.

Let's take another instance of this spatial dynamic, the familiar poem-cum-bumper sticker quote by Martin Niemöller about Nazi complicity. Known as the "first they came for. . . " poem, the list goes from socialists to trade unionists to Jews to "me." Such a precise series of abductions occludes the fact that somewhere, in some form, men are always coming for women.

This is especially the case for women who appear in public. More accurately, men rarely have to "come for" women because the kidnapping list presumes being *removed* from a home and taken elsewhere. Women are of course also Jews, socialists, and trade unionists and could be abducted for those reasons, and certainly women (especially witches) have been the targets of raids. But women qua *women* are more likely to be imprisoned in a home than snatched from it. The more accurate verbs would be "they went for" those women who dared to appear in public, chased out in order to be returned to their place. Take the Trumpist misogynist chant "Lock Her Up!" While it explicitly referred to a prison cell, its gender-sadism was rooted in the topography of the public hunt and domestic capture.

Patriarchal ordering takes place in micro, meso, and macro-aggressions. Patriarchy is a spatial operation that involves public masculine displays of *anti*-publicness against women, ranging from street harassment to online intimidation. As Jacqueline Ryan Vickery and Tracy Everbach put it, the cumulative effect of misogyny "is intended to remind women of their proper patriarchal place, one that is subservient to the interests of men; a place that is not powerful, public, nor political."[51] The war on women relies on both spectacular and less visible interpersonal spatial violence (in the home, in private messages). Gendered topography thus changes the terrain of the antifascist conflict, shifting the focus solely from public confrontations and street actions to the microfascist resistance against ubiquitous, private, and everyday expressions of misogyny.

Finally, a spatial analytic of fascism and white supremacy often assesses the genocidal process as a linear one moving from "hate rhetoric" to interpersonal violence to wholesale extermination (e.g., the Holocaust). This doesn't apply in the same way to the topography of gender power, which contains a micro, networked, and ordinary version of eliminationism. It is neither a phased passage nor a progression from micro to macro. Instead, patriarchy is persistent and pervasive, an ecology of policing and punishment shaping everyday life for women—a drawn-out and ubiquitous version of feminicide in the microfascist sphere.

Gendered microfascism is the intimate and everyday mode of eliminationism, eruptive yet environmental. Gendered power is not just an attribute of fascism (as gateway) but operates at the core of microfascism as production of subjectivity. While microfascism has required patriarchal topographical ordering for some time, its techniques of enforcement have come under scrutiny in the twenty-first century under the category of misogyny. We now turn to misogyny as both deep structure and recent mediated operations within the re-emergence of fascism.

Misogyny

During the second half of the 2010s, monographs, journal articles, and edited collections on the rise of gender violence flooded the infosphere. Concepts proliferated to make sense of the moment, including mediated, online, networked, or popular misogyny (as well as cultural sexism, everyday sexism, cyber harassment, Internet gender-based and sexual harassment, and digitally mediated rape culture). Terms such as "gendertrolling" and "misogynation" have been coined to describe the specific ways women are targeted online in the age of Internet and social media visibility. This outpouring has had scant dialogue with the works on fascism.[52] Notable exceptions include Carol Gilligan and David Richards, Tania Levin, and Alexandra Stern. Scholars and commentators have been pinpointing something both long standing and hypercontemporary, especially with its new (plat)forms.

Let's delineate some key features of misogyny, first by dispelling a common understanding: it is not an attitude or feeling. "Hate" as an attribute of a subject doesn't capture the way misogyny is a set of cultural operations rooted in a normalized system. Misogyny is a subjective orientation towards action, not a psychological trait.[53] Rather than define it as the property of an act or an actor, misogyny is the series of formal and informal practices that seek to undermine and unsettle women's subjectivity—a pervasive continuous effort at elimination. It's core to autogenetic sovereignty, which itself is not an attribute of a personality. Misogyny, to put it simply, is the action associated with a persistent and ubiquitous sexism.

Misogyny is obviously connected to masculine violence against women, a long-standing matter of feminist study and praxis. Violence can certainly take the most brutal physical forms, including the gendered necropolitics of Ciudad Juárez-style feminicide to be explored in Chapter 4. Misogyny's death toll is a result of lethal pacification campaigns against women's refusals of role, desire, and order. This includes a broad swath of "side effects" of reproductive control (not just medical procedures, but deaths resulting from evasion or resistance). We could also add here the deaths of despair, where women would rather die than be controlled, or to live with debilitating shame, or they simply collapse because of the depleting techniques brought on by neoliberal perfectionism.

Misogyny is thus not reducible to its most extreme physical manifestations. Lauren Berlant coins the term "slow death" to index the everyday attenuation due to "the physical wearing out of a population and the deterioration of people in that population that is very nearly a defining condition of their experience and historical existence."[54] Her concept gets us to the less obvious versions of misogyny: the networked, pervasive, ordinary slow annihilation, especially in the Global North. Sarah Banet-Weiser identifies it as *popular misogyny*—an everyday reaction to popular feminism, embedded in culture as an ongoing enforcement of bodies and expectations.[55] Kate Manne calls it the "the punishment of 'bad' women, and policing of women's behavior."[56] Misogyny's operations mostly involve eliminationism in the mode of actions *to diminish women's capacities.*

Misogyny is the practical expression of patriarchal eliminationism: an ongoing reduction of women to instrument, object, and resource. As a "war of attrition" and decapacitation against women, misogyny can be high-intensity (feminicide) or low-intensity environment deprivation (undermining confidence and constraining subjectivity).[57] Such an environment involves the following range of diminutions: "insults, leers, sneers, jokes, patronage, bullying, vocal violence and sexual harassment."[58] Everyday microfascism is enacted in everyday sexism. For instance, gendered microaggressions are the pervasive and usually unmarked efforts to undermine women, the ordinary operations in the ongoing war against women.

A "misogynist hostility" includes "infantilizing and belittling . . . ridiculing, humiliating, mocking, slurring, vilifying, demonizing, as well as sexualizing or, alternatively, *desexualizing*, silencing, shunning, shaming, blaming, patronizing, condescending, and other forms of treatment that are dismissive and disparaging in specific social contexts."[59] We could also add judging to this list, which as we have already seen is an auto-designated authority that comes from a particular circuit of flight and return via abstractions.

We encounter a spectrum of eliminationist control: from trivializing this composition (selfies, gossip, solidarities) to *demonizing* it (as signs of witchery, threat, temptation, even devil-consorting). This spectrum relies on the cultural production of images. Jack Holland argues that "there was no equivalent to the phantasmagoria associated with misogyny" especially the proliferation of witches, monstrous and devil women, and other demonic threats found in patriarchal myths.[60] Mary Daly recounts numerous patriarchal techniques of eliminationism including the "trivialization" of women.[61] Desire, knowledge, and practices are devalued to both marginalize them as well as *replace* them with masculine versions. For instance, gossip has been one of those trivialized forms of networked speech. Gossip forms community by making distinctions.[62] It was more than ironic, then, that when such gossip networks targeted male sexual abuse in the workplace (#MeToo), the accusers were turned into their opposite—no longer witches but witch-hunters. Men took on the role of victims, in a laughable yet cynical reversal, to become the objects of witch hunts that they instigated historically (and continue to enact as everyday sexism).

Misogyny generates an ecology of war waged by a masculine subjectivity whose differentiation is built on specific *hostility* towards women, especially their refusal (of role, order, expectations, performance, even identity). Misogyny operates against women's solidarities, disaggregating their gathering efforts. Misogyny is thus a kind of *decomposition* of forces and capacities for collectivity. Misogyny is an environment of operations that seeks to deprive women of their own environment of operations.

Misogyny is ordinary and normalized as patriarchal enforcement and subject (de)formation. Its continuous process means it is palingenetic (as the renewal of man) while its violence is eliminationist. Combined, we see that misogyny is microfascist in its core.

Microfascism in the gendered mode is the palingenetic project of reduction across spheres. The autogenetic sovereign is the subject that distributes people into spheres, then reappears as border patrol and gender security on the terrain of patriarchy.

Microfascist eliminationism in the form of misogyny is not a homogenous experience.[63] Eliminationism can be exclusionary (indifference to death, dehumanization, prevention of social reproduction) or inclusionary (requirement of subjugated status, liege-roles, forced social reproduction). It's often both. In Chapter 4, we'll see that such intersectionality is most foregrounded when it comes to making sense of microfascism's necropolitics.

The longue durée of microfascism and patriarchy means it preexists right-wing formations. The right only "weaponizes" it because the weapons are already being used and refined in the ongoing war on women. Even the seeming "peace" of the established patriarchal order was only a temporary settling. This peacetime patriarchal order, a specific moment in history of the war on women, provided templates and tools for fascism's own development.

Misogyny's tempos

Foregrounding gender means reworking the tempos and scales of microfascism. Temporally speaking, what are the origin stories told about settler colonialism? How does one tell those tales for gender? Throughout this book, we turn to religious (primarily Christian) narratives as well as spiritual martial ones (e.g., Julius Evola). We have already encountered the temporality of the witch hunts as foundational and cyclical moments. In this vein, misogyny is both backlash as well as a return of archaic forms of mythic violence.

Famously analyzed in the 1990s by Susan Faludi amidst a particular version of it, "backlash" has reappeared to understand the uptick in misogyny's reach, acuteness, and popularity. But backlash names a moment in a dynamic that does not always operate as a clear back and forth. As Sarah Banet-Weiser puts it, popular misogyny often flips this, being a "response and call" rather than a "call and response."[64] Feminism *responds* to injustices and oppressions, while antifeminism *calls for* a restoration, even with calls to arms. Backlash also works on anxious projections of future loss rather than just on past losses. Backlash simultaneously operates as a reaction to "achievements" as well as a preemption of potentialities, similar to how to Herbert Marcuse saw fascism as a "preventive counter-revolution."[65]

Backlash is a particular conjunctural configuration of the ongoing war on women. Silvia Federici reminds us the war on women is not a thing of the past: "From the spread of new forms of witch-hunting in various regions of the world to the escalation worldwide of the number of women daily murdered, the evidence is mounting that a new war is being waged against women."[66] As much as capital needs to produce new enclosures, so too does the war on women become more activated at different moments. Recent spikes in feminicide are a reminder and reinvocation of neoliberalism's birth in Latin America's 'dirty wars.' The newest version of the war on women turns on feminism as an "'internal enemy' that endangers the family, sexual, moral, and political order."[67] Judith Butler asks us to think "how the anti-gender-ideology movement is part of fascism," and Verónica Gago adds, "contemporary fascism detects and responds to our force as a feminist, anti-racist, anti-biologistic, anti-neoliberal, and, therefore, anti-patriarchal movement."[68] Misogynistic expressions of gender policing and punishment become more visible and acute—as *open* hostilities—in an ongoing "undeclared war" that stretches back to capitalism's preconditions.

Backlash as war on women stretches back even further, invoking prehistoric times, mostly through religious myths and anthropological artifacts, to name the *founding* violence of men against women. The primordial differentiation of masculinity via patriarchal pacts, the traffic in women, and the war bands establish this ancient ordering (the autogenetic sovereign power of naming and subjectivizing). Patriarchy is already a backlash against the unruly and rebellious woman *in advance*. Mythic patriarchal violence rests on a war that preexists the establishment of the order.

Any expression of misogyny is part of this ongoing cycle, a war on women that both carries the origins of capitalist patriarchy as well as precapitalist patriarchy. When the foundations are challenged, the reaction enables patriarchy to "reassert [its] dominance via harassment, violence, and intimidation" directed at women's refusal to perform their assignments.[69] Misogyny heightens violence to secure an order that is crumbling or recomposing.

While violence might increase in its acute forms during a decline, what is being reestablished is the foundational violence—the order and the norm mythically installed as domination. The misogynistic violence of a conjunctural backlash can be said to be seeking *revenge* against perceived proximate enemies (feminism, women) but also a *restoration*.[70] It is the *persistence* of order, not just its decline, that is violent. Patriarchy is founded on violence and continues its reign via further violence and eliminations.

When fascism is positioned as backlash in scholarship, it is as reaction to modernity or gendered progress. While this is conjuncturally grounded, it doesn't explain the violence that infused gender relations in modernity as capitalist patriarchy. The housewifization, traffic in women, continual witch hunts, and public/private ordering all were central to modernity, and continue in the everyday sexism of language, images, law, and interactions.

Misogyny as microfascism has a genealogy analogous to Ur-Fascism: it is both archaic and latent. Misogyny was there at the *emergence* of a patriarchal order (in mythic positioning; in subjugation within pacted trafficking networks; and, in capitalist form, the witch burnings), at its *peak* (normalcy, hegemony, stability) and at its *decline* (instability, contestation, crisis).

Misogyny is both the return of the past and preemption of a revolutionary future. Any contemporary misogynistic expression carries all these characteristics, which need analysis.

Backlash signals a deterioration of the violence through relatively stable enforcement of patriarchal norms and an unleashing of foundational violence in the return of the war packs/pacts. The result is a breakdown of the civil peace of patriarchy's reign (its mythic violence) and reversion to outright social war with a more scattered, eruptive, and volatile violence (everyday acts of revenge, rampages in public and online). Misogyny is enacted as activism for men's rights (MRAs), as harassment campaigns (Gamergate), as well as the more distributed coordination of male-supremacist mass murderers. Misogyny is not performed as an individual subject with beliefs and attitudes—nor as a state/institutional form—but as a *movement*, or better yet, an increasingly hostile environment. This is the microfascist war on women.

Misogyny media

We don't need to begin with the Internet to understand how misogyny has been mediated. The decades-long studies of gender and representation focused on early variations of mediated misogyny, which in terms of microfascism, can be defined as the palingenetic cultural production and circulation of images, gestures, and statements aimed at reducing women. Pop culture fantasies around the good life were oriented towards masculine fantasies of power and control, relying on the ordering of women (whether sitcoms with variations on housewifization, ads instrumentalizing women's bodies for male pleasure, or aestheticized visualizations of violence against women).[71]

Certain phases of patriarchal hegemonic media production contained what American sociologist Gaye Tuchman called the "symbolic annihilation of women."[72] Writing in the 1970s, Tuchman noted that advertisements, films, television programs, and music videos eliminate women representationally through "either condemnation, trivialization" or "absence."[73] Women are "symbolized as child-like adornments who need to be protected or . . . confined to their sexuality, their emotions and their domesticity."[74]

Changes in media culture resulting in "positive images" continued the symbolic annihilation, now by instrumentalizing women's capacities towards objectives that ultimately undermine them. Boundless can-do attitudes, endless labor on the self for brand value, anxious self-modification around ideals of perfection—these are all depleting activations.[75] From the 1990s onwards, consumer and entertainment culture represented active women and even "activated" them. Capitalist patriarchy took up the project of absorbing feminism, generating space for antipatriarchal positions up to a point (called popular feminism,[76] neoliberal feminism,[77] and postfeminism).[78] Such "activating" media forms reduce women's capacities to faux empowerment, consumer activism, and neoliberal parameters of subjectivity.[79]

The move from symbolic annihilation to active participation and interactive visibility brought its own changes in mediated misogyny. In addition to all the work that goes into keeping up with the demand for visibility and empowerment, women now must attend to the misogynist responses.[80] Such elimination is especially prominent at a moment when women are urged to express themselves, to speak up as part of digital public culture.[81] Women are caught up in a world of edicts to display and express themselves, only to face a variety of policing and silencing tactics against them.

Gendered microfascism found enhanced platforms in the twenty-first century, but the technological systems were already infused with patriarchal norms. Popular, networked, and mediated misogyny emerged from a preexisting history of a convergence of gendered power and technology. Internet-based misogyny, or what Emma James calls "e-bile" has been experienced as a defining feature of the early Internet, starting at least with "cyberstalking" in nineteen-nineties online communities.[82] Other names for this entwinement of media tech and misogyny include, "gendered cyberhate, technology-facilitated violence, tech-related violence, online abuse, hate speech online, digital violence, networked harassment, cyberbullying, cyber harassment, online violence against women, and online misogyny."[83] Mediated misogyny is neither sporadic nor individualistic but is rather embedded in the communication systems as a practical norm of interaction.

Microfascist misogyny appears not just in the most visible forms, but in its cultural formation and in the sociotechnical design. Mimesis in digital culture was poisoned at its root. There was never a tech that merely connected people; it was immersed from the outset in forms and assemblages shaped by autogenetic sovereignty.

Masculine microfascism, like misogyny in general, has a particular configuration—the most advanced tech—but is an extension and renewal of the ongoing war and the ancient differentiation. The misogynistic backlash reawakens the patriarchal topography of foundational gender differences. For instance, when it comes to online patriarchal topography, digital "manspreading" continues the masculinist expansionism found in physical spaces by harassing women out of a site to allow men to occupy it.[84] Another misogynist digital/spatial practice involves relentless public reminders of male domination. Take "cyberflashing," the act of forcing shocking images to appear on a target's device. "AirDrop bombing," as it's called, is most often "done by anonymous men to women in order to intimidate or provoke reaction."[85] This mostly involves pictures of male genitalia but can also depict gory death, graphic injury, and other shock-value content.

Natalie Gil relays the story by Rochelle about her AirDrop flashing experience on a London Underground train: "It made me feel shocked, uncomfortable, annoyed and quite sick as it kept popping up despite me declining the image." In a trenchant analysis of trolling rarely found in digital culture scholars, Rochelle posits, "I think men do it because they think it's funny to see other people's reactions, although I was far from amused. Perhaps they get a sense of power over others. . . . It seems predatory to me because it's subjecting people to unwanted and inappropriate images."[86] This was a double harassment—on a private screen and, given the insecurity she felt *in situ*, on public transit.

Like other examples of "technology-facilitated coercive control," AirDrop flashing seeks to intimidate women in public and push them back to the private sphere.[87] It is not as though the domestic sphere is a haven from similar mediated misogyny, evidenced by the rise of new technologies that are deployed by abusers to control women in households. We see a circuit here, as these home-based techniques of domination extend domestic violence into the digital sphere. Technologically advanced mediated misogyny reconfirms patriarchal microfascist spaces both through domestic violence and through the violence to domesticate women in all spheres.

In online spaces, a whole host of "new" microfascist eliminationist techniques have been developed.[88] Masculine patrols secure online borders through eviction, which includes the relentless utterance of the acronym GTFO ("Get The Fuck Out"). Elimination comes in the form of demanding that women consider trollish harassment as humor and then telling them that if they can't tolerate the "jokes," then they should GTFO. Milo Yiannopoulos announced, "the solution to online 'harassment' is simple: women should log off." He went on to boast, "I, Donald Trump and the rest of the alpha males will continue to dominate the Internet without feminist whining."[89] In the spirit of microfascism's contemporary affects, Yiannopoulos adds that this eliminationism "will be fun!"

Eliminationism doesn't always take the form of explicit violence, as it produces "*chilling, silencing, or self-censorship* effects."[90] In addition to acute and vitriolic forms of harassment, Heather Savigny invokes Berlant to remind us of the range of daily sexist experiences of "slow and steady shaming, depression around perfection, anxiety, sleeplessness."[91] Women in "digital publics" undergo similar treatment that they do in physical publics, now with the added feature where expressing disagreement with women effortlessly shifts into graphic threats against them.[92] The cumulative effect is silencing and disappearing women from online worlds. The ongoing containment of women in (house)holds thus has equivalents in online culture. Gendered microfascism found, or better yet founded, a technological system to expand the terrain of the war on women. And it eventually received a name: the *manosphere*.

The manosphere as patriarchal ordering

"Manosphere" typically refers to that part of digital culture devoted to developing "toxic" masculine subjectivity, especially the knowledge-production by and for men to restore patriarchal power in the social, juridical, and cultural realms (legal rights, education, dating tips, fitness advice, or sexual training).[93] To put it simply, the manosphere is a microfascist playground where masculine packs hone their weapons in the war on women, extending eliminationism both as expulsion from spaces as well as pervasive decapacitation.

What gets called the "manosphere" is less a specific Internet subculture and more a cultural norm across numerous sites. Manosphere names not a sealed space but the extension of harassment and gendertrolling into many online spaces, involving hostility towards intimate partners, ex-partners, potential dates, and strangers. "Manosphere" is thus a somewhat limited concept, as it names a particular part of online culture separated from the non-manosphere. I propose a more expansive version of it: manosphere names a part that seeks to turn *all* of the Internet into itself. The manosphere is inherently a manspreading project: it seeks to infuse the totality of the digital sphere with a technologically facilitated war on women.

The manosphere is feverishly defended by its proponents as a space of freedom while seeking to spread itself as a vast training ground for autogenetic sovereignty. The manosphere revives archaic initiation rites through what it has called "redpilling" (examined in Chapter 3). The manosphere thus signals patriarchy not just in content (men's rights, revival of patriarchal abstractions, claims of natural dominance) but in its autogenetic sovereign form as initiation and expansion.

For instance, take the way misogynistic packs crystallize in the intersubjective process of online trolling. Harassment does not just take place within a dyad (one-way from aggressor to target). For online trolling to work, harassment requires a *third* figure—a judge and/or applauder-audience. This is the bond formed with other masculine onlookers, who act as witness and cheerleader—a form of initiation. But there's more. The third subject is typically also a fellow harasser. This figure judges but also acts, competing with the first troll by either piling on or upping the ante. The bond formed by harasser and fellow harasser/witness, no matter how temporary, is the basis of the pacted group, now digitally reviving and accelerating the war on women.

When others (like women) take on the position of the third as a critic, the manosphere shrieks, "Political Correctness! Censorship! Social Justice Warrior! Canceled!" More than provoking a feeling in their target or even removing them from the space, patriarchal pacts ultimately want to preserve their power especially in the form of determining who can occupy the place of the witness, and how. The aim is for control over judgment itself.

The freedom that the patriarchal pacts invoke is really an autogenetic sovereign demand for license to enact whatever it defines as its eliminationist goal. Manospheric claims to freedom function not just to eliminate women from the scene, but to affirm and be affirmed about it. Ultimately, then, the desire for masculine freedom is really a maneuver to be authorized to control the terms of engagement, to impose space, and to order as a sovereign.

Manosphere thus names a digitally enhanced microfascism. Manosphere is the digital tendency of the *masculine* sphere, not in the sense of being just filled with men (though that is the patriarchal fantasy) but as escape/flight away from materiality into an abstract otherworld. Online culture, as masculine space, flees the material in search of disembodiment. More precisely, we witness a convergence of *disembodiments*: the flight from materiality for digital abstractions here meets the *aesthetic* flight (tied to judgment, especially beauty and value).

This escape is the primordial differentiation. The digital sphere, when infused with the autogenetic sovereign subjectivity of masculinity, is the latest instantiation of the microfascist production of subjectivity and reality.

We know, however, that the autogenetic sovereigns can never completely leave. Men cannot simply flee into the digital otherworlds; they need to incessantly *return* women to a private, offline, status. Microfascist man flees only to return as a mode of reshaping spatial and subjective conditions, controlling the territory of subjectivity.

Manosphere as terrain of the war on women

Most relevant for our investigation of microfascism is the way the manosphere (or patriarchal Internet) is the training ground that generates the patriarchal pacts. The language of war allows us to situate misogyny in a systematized and collective campaign, where online platforms can more easily facilitate *coordinated* misogyny, where packs of black holes organize as squads to attack on the platformed battle in the war on women.

Mediated misogyny as online operation was the form that *preceded* and *underpinned* alt-right strategy and organizing. Gamergate (examined in the next chapter) has been accurately established as the template for alt-right attacks. Gamergate's ability to take shape as a campaign of online hostile organizing depended on an already existing microfascist culture of mediated misogyny built into the patriarchal ordering of the Internet. The swarm-like movement of attacks across platforms, the use of irony and boundary pushing, the taunting operations: all have extensive roots in gender-based harassment, both on and offline. The slow, ordinary practices of violence and reduction were already in the composition, they just found a new way to get coordinated. Trolling, to echo our earlier assessment, was already gendered and in pack form.

The names given to actions emerging from the manosphere (operations/ops, raids, campaigns) indicate the origins in combat as do the coordinated efforts of patriarchal pacts. The war on women now involves digital weapons and terrains, but misogyny is an orientation to action, so it is important that we leave the Internet to note how operations and soldiers leap offline.

The most spectacular Western figure engaging in the war on women is the masculine-supremacist killer called an incel.[94] Incels are "involuntarily celibate," and while the term has a complex history, it has since at least 2014 referred to an online community of men united in their injury by their inability to convince women to have sex with them.[95]

Networked misogyny, formed over the years through online harassment, guided trolling, and mutual encouragement, turns into networked physical action. Resonating with the fatalistic monadism of the "Forever Alone" meme, incel violence often combines feminicide with suicide, a necrotic network of black holes.

Incel mass murderers' own words lay out their plan. In addition to Gamergate, the year 2014 saw another major turning point for hostile back-lashes against women. Elliot Rodger, who killed six and wounded fourteen people, expressed his hostility in his final video when he announced, "If I can't have you, girls, I will destroy you." This was after publishing his manifesto, which he titled "The War on Women."

Like other forms of warfare, networked misogyny develops a culture filled with martyrs and heroes. Alek Minassian killed ten and injured sixteen in 2018 by speeding his van onto a busy Toronto sidewalk. Before his mass killing, Minassian posted "Private (Recruit) . . . Infantry 00010, wishing to speak to Sgt 4chan please," in reference to his idol Elliot Rodger. Misogynist martyrs, soldiers, even saints comprise the war-based patriarchal pacts for a digital age. One doesn't have to be alive to be part of a war band—the invocation, imagery, and inspiration are enough.

Some incels and fans of the killers insist that misogyny isn't their motiva-tion but rather the jovial camaraderie with other men. This amounts to the same thing, as the humor is misogynistic: the patriarchal pact ratifies itself through the figure of the eliminated woman.

Incels declare war on women as an extension of everyday expectations and a violent response to women's own responses: their rejection of those patriarchal expectations. These are often micro-actions by women (e.g., a rejection of someone's amorous advances) connected to archaic refusals by women of their instrumentalization as well as expression of their sexual de-sire. Incels thus embody the misogyny of the backlash as restorationist war.

Incel murders are the starkest versions of techniques designed to incapacitate women, ranging from pick-up-artist negging to gaslighting to drugging. Incels have received an inordinate amount of scrutiny and coverage, as the killers have expressed their fusion of misogyny, necrotics, and war articulately. To dig into the broader context, we need to examine the overlap of misogyny and mass killings.

When motivated by racial and ethnic animus, mass killings are readily identified as such. Monotheist massacres (e.g., Christian attacks on synagogues and mosques) perpetrated for whiteness have certainly been mainstays of 2010s'spectacular killings. But we've also seen misogynistic massacres occurring before, during, and after the more overtly racialized ones. Sometimes these gender massacres take place in so-called "women's spaces"—e.g., yoga studios and massage parlors. But gender often informs the targets and the motives of less explicitly misogynistic attacks (school shootings, theaters, nightclubs). When misogyny is part of a killer's background, the massacre isn't necessarily considered a gendered one.

In Sutherland Springs, Texas, in 2017 a man shot and killed twenty-six people in a church; he had previously been convicted of domestic violence, and his wife claimed that "he once told her that he could bury her body where no one would ever find it."[96] In August 2019, Connor Betts—who had compiled kill and rape lists of his female high-school classmates—killed nine people, including his sister, with an assault-style weapon at a Dayton, Ohio nightclub. He was previously in a pornogrind band performing songs about sexual violence and necrophilia.[97] The Parkland shooter—who killed seventeen people in 2018—reportedly had committed domestic violence against his ex-girlfriend and her mother in addition to threatening his ex-girlfriend's new boyfriend.

When it's part of an explicit racist's history, misogyny is downplayed in favor of the racial motives.[98] Misogyny isn't just involved when women are exclusive targets (which would be something more akin to feminicide). It's tied to the targets, rationale, and unarticulated drives of microfascist autogenetic sovereignty.

Moreover, misogynistic killings are more distributed and pervasive than their mass shooter variation. Analysts have compared misogynistic mass violence to ISIS, since both involve online radicalization, penning manifestos, and spectacle-based terrorizing via mass killings. Most importantly, they share a common violent patriarchy, replacing the honor killings based on family (the more traditional patriarchal order) with ones based on ego and individual reputation. Militant misogynists, like other masculine restoration warriors, fixate on an abstraction like *honor* (the masculine abstraction that shapes sovereignty, according to Evola). Here that translates into control over women and makes the violence all the more rationalized (as dishonoring breaks the pact, triggering brutal retribution as a claimed justified response).

Honor killings are cultural expressions of a deep-seated patriarchal organization of desire embedded in the traffic in women. Whereas the US right wing persistently sounds the alarm about Muslim honor killings, American domestic honor killings abound. Murdering women as revenge for dishonoring the man's own ego/reputation are routines of *everyday* misogyny, both monotheistic and secular. While in some cultures being dishonored results in suicide, here that impulse is fused with revenge, resulting in suicide-feminicide operations.

Even if carried out by individuals, honor killings are coordinated operations in the war on women, if we think of these as *stochastic*.[99] Stochastic (as applied to terrorism) means hostile actions are decentralized and will inevitably recur, though the particular expressions are unforeseeable. To put it simply, rhetoric predictably leads to unpredictable moments of action.

As Gilligan and Richards put it, "The tribe that sacrifices love for honor is the patriarchy that will lead the world into war."[100] I would modify this to say that the love of honor has fueled patriarchal pacts and underpinned the war on women. This war is what feminist author Laurie Penny calls "cultural civil war. The context is two thousand years of violent religious patriarchy, five centuries of brutal capitalist biopolitics, and a decade of punishing austerity that has left a great many young men quaking in the ruins of their own promised glory, drowning in unmet expectations."[101] If anyone thought that the war on women was merely metaphorical or juridical, they might have a different perspective now that Rodger and others have explicitly declared that war, recruited others, and formed distributed units to enact terror.

The manosphere is thoroughly microfascistic—a production of autogenetic sovereignty *and* a collective of black holes (e.g., incels) that result in coordinated action (squads, campaigns). The coordinated autogenetic sovereigns are reality-shapers seeking to diminish women and produce a life-destroying reality. Manospheric war-based patriarchal pacts develop their weapons and terrains and tactics online, but they easily turn to offline action because the war on women has been enacted there for centuries. As expanded terrain of the long-standing war on women, the manosphere refers not merely to a part of the Internet, or the tendency to become the whole of the Internet but is an operation to expand the war on women everywhere.

From steppingstone recruitment to foundational war

With recent analysis of and organizing against feminicide around the globe, it is even more vital to give gender more prominence in contemporary accounts of fascism. Gender is not just a steppingstone but foundational: to the Internet, to coordinated action, and to war. If we center the war on women in our analysis of microfascism, we see a systematic patriarchal ordering, accompanied by policing and punishment when women deviate from their prescribed roles. Misogyny operates both as the policing of this circuit—e.g., putting women in their place—*and* the mythic foundation of it. Misogyny is the means for the palingenetic renewal of sovereign subjectivity, which is thus eliminationist in its essence. With technological developments, mediated misogyny can be seen as a new terrain with refined weapons in the longer war on women.

3

War

Männerbunde and Microfascism

EUROPEAN FASCISM IN THE 1920S AND 1930S HAD THE GREAT WAR as its reference point. About a century later US microfascism had its own mutation: the Great Meme War. It was "the grandiose name given—only half ironically—to the decentralized efforts of a swarm of anonymous Internet nerds to harass Trump's detractors and flood the Web with pro-Trump, anti-Hillary Clinton propaganda" during the 2016 campaign.[1] Soldiers in the Great Meme War generated digital objects in 4chan to then deploy in more official campaign media strategies. Pro-Trump meme war veterans include self-proclaimed general Charles Johnson and Matt Braynard, who led Trump's data team from October 2015 through March 2016 and who self-memorialized his service by buying a badge online. Then there was "Pizza Party Ben," a pseudonymous veteran of the Great Meme War who acted as a "meme-ology" consultant for Milo Yiannopoulos, and Anthime Gionet (aka Baked Alaska), who worked for *Breitbart News* while also summoning "vast meme armies" for Trump until his arrest as part of the January 6, 2021 Capitol stormers.[2] In this election/war campaign, humor and fun were organized by a trolling sensibility that put affects into action. As a participating former military intelligence officer put it: "It went from ironic to militant very quickly."[3]

Such coordinated efforts around war are certainly worth taking seriously rather than dismissing as frivolous pranks for political newbies fresh out of the College Republicans. The Great Meme War tells us something about how online coordination among strangers through trollish humor, harassment, and memetic production creates a collective temporary body through the masculine bonding of digital warfare. The Great Meme War can be seen as an extended squad effort, a particular campaign whose overall success was less about electing Trump and more about accelerating the revival of masculine war bands and generating a meme-based microfascist war machine.

It is no revelation to say fascism is tied to war, whether that takes place in 1930s Europe or in its prior colonial expansionism. But what about microfascism? We can begin with the linguistic and organizational sources of classic fascism. In the 1920s, Mussolini called upon veterans returning from the front to continue the spirit of combat, but now domestically. Mussolini asked them to organize as "*fasci di combattimento*," giving these men new purpose by finding ways of applying their training and solidarity into social and political life. As we have already discussed, in Germany around the same time, the Freikorps were war veteran units that roamed the land to intimidate communists and terrorize resisters, fueled by fantasies of feminicide.

These are the most obvious war bands: squads and other small troop formations. We need to update and expand the warrior compositions in line with our development of the idea of microfascism. Unlike the fascist collectives of 1930s Europe, the "mass" is no longer the primary mode of composing the microfascist body. Other compositional units thicken microfascism's relationship to war. War bands are a patriarchal primordial grouping as well as a recurring mutation in contemporary societies, so locating this long-standing recurrence can produce an antifascist perception to see the pervasiveness of these microfascist formations.

The twenty-first century restorations of fascist war machines are distributed at a mundane level of everyday misogyny while erupting via networked political violence. Microfascism's relation to war is expressed via war bands formed through masculine autogenetic sovereignty. Fascist mimesis is organized via mediated squad-based campaigns.

Shane Burley reminds us: "Violence is and remains a significant component of fascism, but much of this derives from the idea that the alienating effects of modernity must be smashed, and that mythic warrior societies show a path forward, especially for the veneration of 'masculinity.'"[4] Doing anti-microfascist work means tracing these mythic warrior societies as both patriarchal primordial force as well as mutating in contemporary societies, associations that have been called Männerbunde.

If we begin with microfascism, then we begin before the state can organize war. This means locating war elsewhere, in this case by focusing on patriarchal pacts, specifically warrior bands. Microfascist culture is the realm where patriarchal pacts are formed. This chapter delves into those pacts' composition more, especially as rooted in primordial forms of masculine initiation and war-based association. The stability of these groups is a result of the subjective structure of sovereignty often set up in the bands' initiatory structure.

In this chapter, we embark on an investigation into the heart of autogenetic sovereignty to examine initiation rites that control masculine metamorphosis, guiding it to war on women. To put it bluntly, the war on women is the bond that allows the Männerbund to arise (violent separation then violent policing of spheres). Groupuscules and squads are contemporary microfascist compositional modes, renewing the primordial patriarchal war on women.

Compositional styles: lone wolf, groupuscules, squadrismo

How do microfascist hostilities spread into the world? Let's start by elaborating the masculine pacted groups that Celia Amorós identifies as the operating system for patriarchy. We'll do so by focusing on the lone wolf, groupuscules, and squads. Then we trace their resonance with actual and mythified war bands, the Männerbund.

The lone wolf

The lone wolf has evolved into a conventional way of thinking about mass shooters and other political violence. It is often framed as "bad apple" individualism by centrist discourse. More recently, state agencies along with NGO extremist trackers and antifascist analysts of right-wing movements have identified lone wolfism as a deliberate strategy and a product of ideological radicalization. To put it simply, a lone wolf actor does not need a cell or a hierarchical structure—it acts on its own. However, the lone wolf is hardly an individual.

The lone wolf is a deliberate networked tactic, one that was developed in US right-wing insurgency strategies developed in the 1980s. The "new" Klan was concerned about state repression, so it borrowed a decentralized strategy from the US military to thwart government infiltration. Louis Beam, a KKK paramilitary strategist, called it "leaderless resistance." Leaderless resistance meant that while the organization cohered around a set of beliefs or even retained a hierarchical form overall, the operational process was headless. Commands need not be given down a chain, actions were not tied to specific roles (and roles themselves didn't require solid definition). As Beam put it, "No one need issue an order to anyone. Those idealist[s] truly committed to the cause of freedom will act when they feel the time is ripe." Beam adds, prefiguring the strategic use of peer influencers, "or will take their cue from others who precede them." Leaderless resistance could thus come in two forms: the "phantom cells" or individual action.[5]

Matthew Lyons describes the origins and rationales well. Leaderless resistance emerged at a moment when the US radical right was interested in waging armed guerrilla warfare against the US government. Leaderless resistance was drawn from state military cell-based operations, especially the Cold War anticommunism campaigns in Central America—such as those developed by Colonel Ulius Amoss, a US intelligence officer. Called fourth-generation warfare, leaderless resistance was taken up by many other neo-Nazis, as well as activists from the Patriot movement and the right-wing Christian Army of God.

Perhaps foreseeing the digitally enhanced modes of connecting and mobilizing, Beam's partner Robert Miles wrote of organizing as "a WEB, instead of a chain" of command, in which cells or even individuals would operate independently. Leaderless resistance gives us a context through which to understand lone wolfism. It is never an individual but an individuation, a *detachment* from a decentralized organization that acts logistically on its own as a one-person unit. But lone wolfism has mutated beyond even its function within such organizational forms. We have already examined the peer-to-peer affordances of digital communication technologies that help shape the collective of black holes. Networks rely less on a central ideological or organizational point (even a leader like Trump) and more on transmitting across nodes: imitation meets invention. Becca Lewis calls it an "Alternative Influence Network" in which right-wing ideas and information spread through decentralized media outlets whose connection is ideological (even if they don't all share common beliefs).[6] In the present variation of lone wolfism, one need not have a single platform, a named organization, or even a coherent set of beliefs. It is enough to feel an attachment to a particular hostility or a strongly felt affect (a feeling tied to action). Those affects (giddy nihilism, resentment, hatred, fear) push subjects to act. The lone wolf can be moved to action not from command or directive, but an identification with a war. In other words, a microfascist subject, filled with autogenetic sovereign feelings of confidence and entitlement, is moved to act with impunity.

The milieu for the lone wolf has changed; it no longer belongs to an organization (even as decentralized strategy) but to an ongoing microfascist composition in which the activated collective body is made up of peer influencers. But again, these are not isolated individuals—they are the subjective black holes formed through resonance with other individuals but moreover mediated through abstractions: images, ideologies, icons. We discussed incel killers in Chapter 2, noting how a pack can be formed through living and dead material (idols, peers, martyrs).

The lone wolf now engages in a participatory version of virtual reality, cobbling together simulations with fragmented ideas, memes, and convictions to become a mediated fighter. The lone wolf is now produced via transmission, imitation, mutation, and it's profoundly accelerated and densified by digital platforms. We'll take the most extreme, and obvious, example: the lone mass shooter.

The lone mass shooter

Anders Breivik set one template for alt-right shooters. His 2011 massacre contained a mediated manifesto: he emailed his thoughts on the Great Replacement and titled it, in good autogenetic sovereign flight, *2083: A European Declaration of Independence*. One of Breivik's fans, a rather conventional "white genocide" shooter named Christopher Paul Hasson—a forty-nine-year-old Coast Guard lieutenant—created a hit list of democrats and media figures. News analysts spoke of these as copycat shootings, and to some degree, they are certainly embroiled in a mimetic relation—even a poisoned mimesis that transmits lethal gestures, media packages, and modeling behavior. But I think we're in a new phase of imitation, one enhanced by sociotechnical conditions for microfascist action.

What I am calling *inspo-shooters* comprise a network of loosely linked participants who challenge, goad, and inspire each other to escalate their actions. They accumulate attention, generate fanfare, and even receive veneration as saints and martyrs. More than a model to be emulated, these are peer influencers, even peer players in the same microfascist palingenetic eliminationist game. The conditions include a "demotic turn" in popular culture, in which promises of a good life are transmitted to ordinary people *by* ordinary people (as seen in reality TV and in social media micro-celebrities).[7] It's also a branding strategy in consumer culture, where commercial entities (companies as well as individuals) seek to inspire others not just through uplifting cliches but through easily replicable practices of the self.[8] Finally, inspo-shooters draw from the decade-long ironic stances of trolls and other memetic production, as discussed in the previous chapter.

Another Breivik fan is Brenton Tarrant who could be considered the most well-known inspo-shooter. When Tarrant massacred forty-nine people in an attack on two mosques in March 2019, commentators called his bloodbath an act of "Inspirational Terrorism" and almost an Internet performance.[9] Tarrant was a special case of enacting and understanding the logics of online culture, as he embodied the figures of meme, troll, influencer, live streamer, and shitposter.[10]

Tarrant claimed to have been influenced by Dylann Roof and Breivik— even of being in personal contact with the Norwegian mass killer. Tarrant called Breivik's manifesto his "true inspiration."

Tarrant acknowledges his predecessors and announces his desire to pass this inspiration on to others. In his final 8chan post, he exhorted his peers: "Well lads, it's time to stop shitposting and time to make a real-life effort post," taking on the position of inspirer with his challenge. Tarrant's calculated efforts to become an influencer through his massacre and manifesto worked in at least a couple of cases. John Timothy Earnest (Poway, California synagogue killer of one in April 2019) admiringly announced: "Tarrant was a catalyst for me personally. He showed me that it could be done."[11] Tarrant demonstrated "relatability" through his act. Patrick Manshaus (Baerum, Norway Al-Noor Islamic Center mosque shooter in August 2019 who ended up killing only his sister before the rampage) had a more fatalistic perspective, announcing: "My time is up, I was chosen by Saint Tarrant after all. . . . We can't let this continue, you gotta bump the race war threat in real life . . . it's been fun." Manshaus references the meme that canonized Tarrant (typical for shooters) as well as Internet lingo ("bump" as in "make it trend") and the "fun" affects that accompany inspo-shooting.

Previous mass shooters often created media packages to accompany their actions, but Tarrant inaugurated a category of shooters who began to understand their own mediation as a core component of their actions. Shooters want to become memes. They don't want to just inspire others, they seek to become-meme as they copy memes' digital qualities, platforms, and affordances in their acts. To be "inspo" means more than just becoming a model; inspo-shooters turn themselves into a kit to be adapted and mutated.

Mimesis is key to the inspo-shooter, as the killers transmit and imitate each other *viscerally*. Mimesis is *a hybrid of* material life and digital objects, mimesis leaping from digital realms to act in the world. The flight and return circuit of autogenetic sovereignty is evident here, as subjects flee to digital realms to play among the abstractions (including memes), then return to the world infused by those memes, acting as memes to replace material life, specifically to eliminate women.

Like the Freikorps, these are contemporary shock troops or, more accurately, digital numb troops, circulating desensitization through ironic stances, sadistic humor, and callous goading. The result is a digitally enhanced armored male. Imitation is mediated through the meme and then the subject becomes meme, an abstract self-replication that then is incorporated by the inspired. What is absorbed is sense-deadening, a callousness that allows violence against others. The lone wolf is also microfascist in its social production of desire: it seeks not just to kill, but also fame, camaraderie, and fun. Sometimes the hero rewards are religious, as when inspo-shooters are given saint or martyr status.

We see the media difference from copycats. Inspo-shooters are no longer interested in getting wide public attention, reaching an unknown audience through spectacular news coverage. Rather, they are communicating to their community, subculture, online squad with in-jokes and community references. They are posting to their group, forum, or thread through in-real-life (IRL) actions. The news public then puzzles over the actions for their own communities.

The lone wolf as inspo-shooter is thus an influencer caught up in mimesis. The lone wolf might act alone, but as black hole it is interconnected. It contributes to the *stochastic* quality of microfascist violence: the dynamic between isolation and transmission. Stochastic refers to the idea that eruptive events will inevitably recur, but the concrete details are unpredictable. The unpredictable predictability of actions in the world means we don't know when or how the lone wolf will act or even how to identify one in advance (distinguishing from the milieu of trolls, boasting misogynists, and generic masculinist self-puffery).

Del Lucchese's concept of a network of the disconnected acting together is helpful here, again. We're also reminded of Guattari's notion of microfascism: "fascism, like desire, is scattered everywhere, in separate bits and pieces, within the whole social realm; it crystallizes in one place or another, depending on the relationships of force."[12] Stochastic eruptions are these crystallizations, a lightning storm that is peer produced rather than generated by a central authority figure.

The stochastic meets the mimetic—and memetic—as the prompts to act are transmitted and shared as affective composition, as unit-cohesion for the far-flung patriarchal pact. The lone wolf is an individuation produced from a milieu, one defined by mimicry and inspiration. Often the milieu is comprised of strangers, memes, images, and anonymous statements—all of these could be considered part of a pack. To put it simply, lone wolves are embedded in packs even when they logistically enact violence solo. Like memes, lone wolves are variations on a theme, mutations of the microfascist fragments in circulation through culture. Lone wolves crystallize the microfascist bits in the moment of action. To get closer to the modes of microfascist composition, we need to analyze another clustering, one that Roger Griffin says is endemic to fascism: *groupuscules.*

Groupuscules

For Griffin, groupuscules can be defined as numerically negligible "political (frequently metapolitical, but never party-political) entities formed to pursue palingenetic ideological (i.e., revolutionary), organizational, or activist ends."[13] Drawn from Guattari's understanding of desire and subjectivity, groupuscules refer to loosely auto-organized crystallizations of social desires-into-action. They don't have the same formal organization that we might see in groups or even cells. Groupuscules are not the small unit at the bottom of a larger pyramid; instead, they are active assemblages that operate provisionally and quasi-independently (while being bound by common dispositions).

Such a compositional clustering has been ignored in much of the studies of the extreme right which tend to focus on mass and/or party movements. When small groups are considered, it's as identifiable named units that visibly express their objectives (e.g., groups like the Atomwaffen Division). In other words, the state still determines the way we see microfascism. Groupuscules are treated "merely as embryonic Fascist or Nazi parties that simply withered on the vine long before they reached maturity and are thus consigned at most to the endnotes of modern history."[14] Griffin beseeches contemporary readers to pay attention to groupuscules as "myriad minute, and at times highly ephemeral and eminently unmemorable, grouplets" whose small numbers should not be viewed as "as abortive mass movements" but as "an incubator and reservoir of extremist energies."[15]

Groupuscules can be distributed across space but also across *time*. We are reminded again of microfascism's primary logic of "resonance": connections are made through invocation. A groupuscule reconvenes as a form periodically (but it need not have the same members). The gathering and dispersal can also form the core operational logic for years. For example, one might see QAnon as paradigm of this from 2017 onward.

Such assemblies have now found a decentralized home on digital platforms as their "qualities duplicate the very features of the Internet," leading Griffin in 2000 to offhandedly coin the term "cyber-fascism."[16] We saw some of this digitally recomposed microfascism in the Great Meme War. We could also point to the recomposition of right-wing media after Big Tech's Great Purge in 2020–2021. QAnon influencers, microfascist agitators, and Trumpist disciples sought to cobble together their own reactionary media networks through various minor channels. Corporate deplatforming (shadow banning, outright banning, demonetizing) triggered a counteraction: the creation of self-valorized "networks" across minor platforms (DLive, Twitch, Gab, BitChute), and subscriber/patron-based content communities.

For instance, the Warrior Poet Society network declared independence from big tech by announcing that they were going to gather influencers not to create a niche market or a micro-community but to expand into a new corporation. The project flopped, but such a dream was temporarily realized in Frank Speech, a platform funded by MyPillow founder and Trumpist devotee Mike Lindell in April 2021. Lindell, after being upset with the quantity and quality of his appearances even on right-wing news channels, decided to bring together various popular media agitators and influencers to his new network. It too flopped.[17] Gab founder Andrew Torba calls his platform part of a "Silent Christian Secession."[18] While these are still experimental, such reactionary recompositions in the face of a state/tech company decomposition generate a new communications infrastructure for parallel worlds.

But more often groupuscules appear and disappear without a stable platform life. We are reminded of Chapter 2's account of online misogyny, which Emma Jane describes as made up of "vast audiences of like-minded allies. Under the right conditions, these fuse into cyber lynch mobs, firing off near identical messages with the relentlessness of profanity-powered machine guns."[19] Groupuscules can coalesce around a single campaign to attack one statement by a person, an extended campaign on a series of statements by a person, or the entirety of their online presence. Groupuscles can appear as particular operations, such as the 2020 attempted kidnapping of US Michigan Governor Gretchen Whitman, or they can take the on-the-ground form of Trumpist boat and truck caravans around the 2020 election. In one case, a highway convoy blocked a major bridge leading to a US city and in another case, it ran a Biden/Harris bus off the road. The "group" thus assembles briefly and disappears, a swarm with constituent components able to reconstitute and remix in other ways in the future. As Jack Luna notes, these "were not 'just' a display of white pride but were intended to form the *operational core* of any call-to-arms tweeted out by an unpopular president whether or not he loses at the ballot box."[20] Such "nascent paramilitary exercises" were the compositional seeds for Trump's sought-after armed followers, including those that stormed the US Capitol in January 2021.[21]

One could say that the January 6, 2021 riot at the US capitol was a groupuscular action. Individuals from various elements of the extreme right (Proud Boys, Oathkeepers, QAnon, boogaloo, run-of-the-mill MAGAists) converged in Washington, DC to protest the Congressional ratification of the Electoral College votes. Among the thousands who gathered, a few hundred invaded the Capitol grounds and the building itself. A mix of co-ordinated action (especially by ex-soldiers in the groups) and spontaneous crowd movement, the reactionary riot presents an update to the concept of the groupuscule.

Rather than think of it as small in number (compared to what? one might ask), the groupuscule refers to forms of affinity, modes of gathering, and temporality. Groupuscules can be traced to tactical actions like flash mobs (temporary gatherings via minimal logistics and goals) and swarm operations (e.g., vigilantes who quickly mobilize through Facebook and WhatsApp groups to defend racist statues).[22] They can also refer to something broader, such as longer-term operations launchers like Anonymous. Platform-based groupuscules that make their way onto the streets sometimes have names (boogaloo, QAnon) and other times are events made up of named units ("The Jan 6 storming"). They converge and then scatter, and the afterlife of their connections can reform for future actions.

Like other packs, or even lone wolves, groupuscules compose themselves via a bricolage of myths and images from different eras. Groupuscules combine "fragments of archaic discourses, recontextualized images, slang and recycled codes" to form a consistency.[23] Groupuscular initiation rites are a hodgepodge of practices that get synthesized into "tradition" to create a fascist unity through time. And these are ultimately *fantasy* squads composed of friends, strangers, idols, martyrs, intermediaries, memes, comments, jokes, and images. Together these elements generate a groupuscule composed of simulations and interactions that result in an operationalized mythic otherworld that unleashes war.

Groupuscules develop as networked armed men, with variable relations to the state. Sometimes they self-organize as security (e.g., vigilantes that harass in the name of nationalism with a cozy though occasionally conflictual relationship with police). At other times, groupuscules detach from their state training and status (ex-military) as mimics (militias, boogaloo). Groupuscules do not act as small parts of a larger state or party organization, yet they do not act as completely independent units either. They compose themselves as temporary and cellular (though states and parties do attempt to organize them), in other words, as bands and packs.

Attention to groupuscules gives us a steppingstone to understand microfascism's composition. Groupuscules have been named by Griffin as the microfascist mode of composition par excellence.[24] The clustering of black holes is less identifiable than conventional political or social groups. Groupuscules might have common features but eschew proper names and identity over time.[25] Instead, they contain "minute bursts of spontaneous creativity" that circulate "in a web of radical political energy fueling the vitality and viability of the organism as a whole."[26] Key for microfascism, however, is how these molecular actions are drawn from war machines as well as patriarchal production of gender relations. To get to these, we need to examine a more distinct version of groupuscules rooted in war: the conventional Italian fascist types of affinity and action known as *squadrismo*.

Even before Mussolini's official call for the *fasci di combattimento*, brigades of Italian ex-volunteer assault specialists self-organized to attack their adversaries at meetings and on the streets.[27] This form of bond and organization became known as *squadrismo*. The Italian micrological groupings would terrorize civilians to prevent other forms of organizing (labor unions, socialist parties) as well as to harass opponents of fascism.

Squadrismo is not simply a thing of the past, even in Italy. It has been self-applied in recent revivals of Italian neo-fascist tendencies, such as CasaPound, a group with a social center headquarters, propaganda campaigns, membership, and public events. Their identarian movement includes what they call *squadrismo mediatico* [media squadrism].[28] We could also point to vigilante groups and gangs as contemporary versions of squadrismo.

Squads are perhaps most infamous in the past century in the form of paramilitary death squads, especially in Central and South America. Admiration for these death squads have been expressed by US right-wingers—from Larry Pratt's 1990s book *Armed People Victorious*, which celebrated the use of anticommunist "citizen defense patrols" in Central America, to alt-right microfascists in fashwave memes and jokes about "free helicopter rides."[29]

Roger Griffin distinguishes groupuscules from squadrismo, calling the latter "individual units of large-scale capillary organizations" and therefore should be distinguished from groupuscules, which are not attached even in cellular form, to a larger unit.[30] I agree that the 1930s Italian version of squadrismo does not operate as a groupuscule. The question is whether the difference is historically specific or "ineliminable," in Griffin's terms.

I would argue that it's the former and posit that under certain conditions squadrismo has been *groupuscularized*. Historical forces have complicated the distinction in a few ways. First, as mentioned regarding Klan recomposition in the 1980s, non-state reactionary structures have shifted from strict hierarchies to "leaderless resistance." The extreme right has promoted lone wolf and cellular actions without chains of command or communication, relying on provisional peer clusters for operational work. The squad in this instance would be loosely tied together, not a microcosm of a larger organizational structure. They would be closer to digital fascism,[31] "on-the-spot" fascism,[32] or cyber-fascism.[33]

Second, even conventional fascist squads weren't simply units of organized action. The Freikorps were a self-organized mobile band of war veterans that the state subsequently incorporated and deployed for official fascist violence. The patriarchal pacts were composed through microfascist spiritual abstractions: the "elevation of militarism, male comradery, and heroic youth to a virtual cult." Like the Freikorps, the Squadristi were veterans of WWI who continued the *mission* (duty, honor) without a formal war context. They were inspired by their bonding via *combattentismo* or *"arditismo*, the spirit that had driven young men who had fought as volunteers in assault units."[34] It's the informality of these men of action, composing subjectivity through experience, abstractions, and fantasies, that makes squadrismo relevant to understanding microfascism. Their formal relation to a larger organization is important but secondary to its cultural resonances.

Third, the more recent version of squadrismo has been heavily technologized and mediated to the point of blurring it with the digital affordances of groupuscularization. Squads have become less a military dispatch unit and more of a cultural unit of association. Whether as friendship circles (Girl Squads, #squadgoals), corporate teams, influencer crews, or most relevantly gaming campaign clusters, the squad has become a defining sociological unit of association in the US. This recomposition of affinities is a result of labor management strategies (pooling worker intelligence and skills to spur collaboration-based value extraction for capital), the militarization of culture (especially gaming, which we'll elaborate below), and everyday coping strategies for life under racialized capitalist patriarchy (e.g., friendship circles and support groups). Squadrismo has become groupuscularized, as has the lone wolf. Microfascism's mediated and compositional logics thus need to be updated to consider the economic and political mutations as well as the rise of decentralized platforms for coordination.

Militainment squadrismo

We could call any war-based temporary group a squad. And where do we find the immersion of war culture into everyday life more than gaming? Networked gaming, arising around the turn of the twenty-first century, allowed strangers to connect as teams to go on campaigns, often in war scenarios. *World of Warcraft* was a pioneer in this regard, taking live-action roleplay operations into networked simulated combat. Guilds were the featured unit of actions, but in other games the unit was less stable as connections were more provisional—involving coordination of actions with specialized functions and logistics—in war play. At other times, a campaign would involve only a "pickup" team (see the squad or team mode in gaming worlds like *Fortnite* and *Minecraft*).

Mike Wendling defines alt-right tactics as drawing from gaming worlds, particularly MMORPGs (massive multiplayer online role-playing games). In these digital otherworlds, we find "battles against teams, large-scale coordination of tactics, 'raids,' and various specialized characters and units performing specific functions."[35] Squadrismo, in other words, finds itself forming online as gamer groupuscules. These augmented reality otherworlds become the terrains where one gains wartime experience via high scores in war simulations like *Call of Duty*, team battles in *Fortnite*, or eventually as veterans of the Great Meme War.

The recomposition of squads via digital warfare is not an inherent affordance of digital technologies—it's steeped in the militarization of popular culture. Contemporary squadrismo is an unintentional (or maybe intentional) consequence of what media scholars like Robin Andersen and Roger Stahl have dubbed *militainment*. Militainment goes beyond the typical notions of lionizing representations of US imperialism on film and TV. Militainment generates decentralized cultural recruitment through games, ads, memes, and films.[36] The militarization of culture is a form of connection and subjectivation, shaped through interactive platforms and gaming protocols (in addition to performances around sports, cosplay, toys, etc.).

Culture has been a site of training, shaping subjects to be predisposed to feel victorious over enemies, to valorize honor, to heed the call of duty. These state and commercial culture efforts produce "soldiers" via peer interaction and military composition. Militainment sets up virtual worlds for lone wolves and groupuscules to train and provide actors with a sense of accomplishment, camaraderie, and fun in their violence. Transient packs and actions in militarized culture become less dependent on leaders or organizational structures should they want to move operations out of a particular game world and into other terrains, digital and otherwise.

Militainment sometimes focused on imperialist content for war, but more often was a training in "acting-together" in accordance with war logistics. Acting-together in this mode is decentralized and stochastic, nevertheless resulting often in visible and named actions. Moreover, squadrismo refers to the composition of the subjects, the bond through identifications, associations, affects, and tactical goals. Squadrismo resulting from militarized media culture has the intended goal of recruitment into state armies, but its microfascist dimension means it is irreducible to the state-form of war. Instead, it involves the formatting of subjects in continuous "wars of subjectivity"[37]—cultivating and binding through solidarity, morale, and guided dispositions of digital soldiers. In other words, militainment targets and intensifies the existing martialized subjectivities that constitute microfascism.

Gaming wasn't the only site for developing warrior groupuscules. Boards, chans, and forums were replete with shared statements and images about waging campaigns. Anonymous' mid-2000s actions were telling. Launched from 4chan, Anonymous used language drawn from war to describe their actions as "raids," "campaigns," and "ops." Clusters would self-organize as *operations*, not groups, while generating an ongoing and consistent collectivity as "Anonymous" which itself could be seen as a meme and meme-generating platform in addition to being a "collective." These mostly leftist squadrismo campaigns included doxxing, trolling videos, pranking platforms, jamming signals, as well as generating "sockpuppets" and bot accounts. More than these tactics and ops, Anonymous demonstrated a particular way groupuscules eschew traditional notions of membership: by naming a general ability to coordinate while allowing subjects to pop in occasionally for particular ops. This connective action gets us to the looser resonating structure of *groupuscularity*.

As mentioned previously, contemporary squads, especially when mobilized as trolling campaigns and meme wars, are composed within affective structures that include "fun" and "irony." Sahana Udupa observes that fun functions in right-wing online collectives as "group identification and collective (if at times anonymous) celebration of aggression."[38] Contemporary squadrismo is "a manner of gathering together on one's own will, chiding and clapping together, exchanging online high fives for 'trending' or pushing back opposing narratives, and making merry with the colloquial use of online language and vibrant visuality, which are distinct from a serious style of political pontification or cadre-based disciplining."[39] Having extended beyond game worlds, squadrismo now defines a whole host of operational and digital campaigns in which "achievement and hilarity intertwine and constitute one another."[40]

War in the mode of online squads is not bound to a large capillary organization. These groupuscules at times join movements or even electoral campaigns, but this is not what defines them. They form bonds as bands, through humor and humiliation. They share subjective power orientations against enemies they wish to vanquish. Some display their squadrismo fantasies through jokey T-shirts about Pinochet's death squads. From gamer units to Anonymous to the Great Meme War as well as broader movements like the alt-right, online culture is filled with experiments in militarized subjectivity and networked bodies.[41] It is easy to see how such squads launch their coordinated attacks on women, including Gamergate, which could be said to be the most prominent operation that fused militainment with everyday patriarchal policing of public spheres.

Gamergate

It is widely accepted that whatever fragments of the nascent alt-right were circulating online in the twenty-first century, they only found a sense of their collective power in an operation rooted in misogynistic militancy, namely Gamergate. David Neiwert narrates it this way: "Aggrieved MRAs from the 'manosphere,' white nationalists who shared their virulent hatred of feminists and adoration for what they called 'traditional values,' gamers, and online trolls all came together during Gamergate to form their own online movement."[42] It was eliminationist at its core. Neiwert, who had prior to this written a book called *The Eliminationists*, calls Gamergate communication "a language of dismissal and belittlement."[43] While most of Gamergate occurred online, the effects included real-life intimidation and some direct actions like bomb and assassination threats. It also turned into a flipped victimization, where gamers sought protection for masculine fragility and perceived marginality. Gamergate was a security campaign to make masculine spheres safe spaces to express anything—especially misogynistic impulses.

Gamergate was an exercise in mobilization via swarms, using multiple platforms to harass and threaten women while also composing an extensive and far-flung squad using inside language, jokes, and male camaraderie. It is difficult to ascertain just how many gamers and accomplices got on board with the misogynistic campaigns but suffice it to say that its recruitment, its pacting against women, and its coordinated violence give us an example of a digital, networked war band galvanized as a temporary groupuscule. Gamergate was hardly a movement, but it was a campaign in the long war on women, intensifying resonances among black holes and affectively bonding its misogynist belligerents through trolling violence.

Soon after their specific battle waged against women, Gamergaters mutated for longevity, morphing into elements of the alt-right. Its flips (of victimhood and of tactics), quick mobilizations, and self-affirming humor were established for future campaigns and movements, crystallizing the already pervasive but less organized online misogyny. While it's important to position Gamergate as a template for subsequent alt-right actions, it's also vital to note that its compositional formation was based on preexisting ordinary practices of trolling, gender-based harassment, and the policing of digital spheres as masculine publics. As discussed in Chapter 2, misogyny infused Internet culture's formation, so the pacts and trolling squads that eventually became Gamergate and later the alt-right was already gendered. Gaming also provides a sense of light-heartedness and "fun" when waging cyberwar on women. From Freikorps to Gamergate, squadrismo informs the masculine subject engaged in war on women.

Boogaloo movement and other Trumpist squadrismo

Other forms of squadrismo have become prominent. The aforementioned Trumpist caravans and flotillas are a case in point. In addition, the Trump 2020 campaign sought to raise a network of squads. Fundraising efforts included mailings from the "Army for Trump," which offered donors a camouflaged MAGA hat identifying them as "the President's first line of defense" ready to be mobilized against "the liberal MOB."[44] The Army for Trump called for its foot soldiers to become poll-watchers during the November voting and supplied videos and detailed instructions on their roles and missions. Is it any wonder that thousands mobilized to fill the Capitol grounds as agitated mobs who saw themselves on the frontlines of America's restoration? Or that that army continues its campaign via electoral recounts and fantasies of Trump's restoration?

While the Army for Trump still had some measure of integrating squads into a broader electoral apparatus, the on-the-ground actions were taken up by grassroots citizens empowered with digital tools, militant spirituality, and missionary zeal. We could see a more distributed version of squadrismo with QAnon's recruitment of a digital army. In June 2020, the QAnon community circulated an "oath" in which a person vowed to become a "digital soldier." Lt. General Michael Flynn, a hero among QAnon adherents, took it and started calling his followers "digital soldiers." Many happily embraced the moniker, mostly working in various media channels to spread their belligerent gospel, including the delegitimation of the 2020 election and the Biden administration. But that digital army was only a prelude. Many QAnon followers believe that mass arrests of politicians and celebrities is imminent and will take the form of a military coup. Many are thus preparing for an actual civil war.

A related, but as of this writing more organized and deadly, groupuscular movement is that of the boogaloo bois, an extended memetic squad. With its syncretic uniforms of Hawaiian shirts, guns, and MAGA hats, the boogaloo bois came onto the street scene from the Internet in 2019 (like Anonymous did a decade and half earlier). Their bricolage was easily identifiable: camouflage cosplay, meme-patches, coded phrases, and vaporwave imagery comprised the aesthetics. What bonded them, beyond the pastiche memes and in-jokes, was a fixation on social collapse and a thirst for renewing civil war. The boogaloo bois are not just weapons buffs; they are future war reenactors, no matter how glitched out and fantasy based. They imagine and then act on digitally enhanced virtual wars projected through time.

The boogaloo bois accelerated and guided lone-wolf stochastic action, including the fatal shooting by Steven Carrillo—an active-duty US Air Force staff sergeant and head of its anti-terrorism squadron—of a guard kiosk in Oakland, killing a sheriff's officer and critically wounding another. Carrillo also detonated pipe bombs while lying in wait to attack officers, in addition to assaulting a firefighter and three other law enforcement officers.

Boogaloo bois compose a war machine, often from ex-state military, that targets other parts of the state (e.g., the "soup bois"— federal law enforcement "alphabet" agencies). It's almost as though boogaloo bois were an experiment in reinventing Louis Beam's "Leaderless Resistance." Beam saw Leaderless Resistance as a sifting operation: "Those who join organizations to play 'let's pretend' or who are 'groupies' will quickly be weeded out."[45] While such a distinction might have mattered when Beam was writing, the new groupuscles are successful precisely because they can blur the lines between the genuine and the pretender through irony for stochastic action.

As a populist war band, boogaloo bois link themselves to existing causes to further their own: instigating and accelerating a multilevel US war. While misogyny and harassment don't seem to be expressed in their statements or images, the very reason for the existence of boogaloo bois plays into masculinist restorationist fantasies (even of a military without women). These are Civil War future reenactors, obsessed with pure war to the point of turning all innovation (memeing, joking) into its masculine restoration war. Neither meme nor movement, boogaloos embodied contemporary squadrismo, now spread out and connected via ephemeral digital culture. Their bricolage is an accelerationist machine that turns armchair warriors into armed street patrollers.

Certainly, there are US state-based squads (notably in the Department of Homeland Security). But the contemporary variation of the squad is immersed in a networked composition as part of the cultural, subjective, microfascist sphere. Forming in and then leaping from digital culture, contemporary squadrismo generates quasi-state war machines unleashed by militarized culture. While conventional European fascism's squads were more akin to conventional death squads as "individual units of large-scale capillary organizations," today's squadrismo has mutated to become more like groupuscules. Meme warriors, troll mobs, digital soldiers, gaming teams, raiders, temporary affinities around ops, and masculinized gangs harassing women: all of these comprise various dimensions of squadrismo. Troll armies, boogaloo bois, QAnon foot soldiers all become enrolled in a war machine that is now attached to some parts of the state while sometimes engaged in actions against other parts. They absorb the contemporary tools, affordances, and mythic fragments to bricolage themselves into groupuscular weapons. Meme warriors (shooters, spreaders, fans, meme-makers) are dedicated to restorationist victory. The new and reborn man is a soldier, only now detached from the state to kill and occasionally be killed.

These death squads are necropolitical groupuscules that produce a life-destroying reality. They are also revivals of archaic groupuscules called *Männerbünde*. Before delving into this further, let's examine masculine initiations as processes of metamorphosis that also contain the microfascist triumvirate of war, gender, death. But first, a note about the complexities involved in addressing fascism's own writings.

Taking on tradition

A question emerges when citing fascist and fascist-adjacent scholars, like Schmitt, Evola, and Eliade. How much do we take their assessments as empirically grounded or insightful into power systems versus being mythifications to ideologically justify those systems? With Evola and Eliade, we encounter this challenge when they analyze masculinity, especially through initiation rites and men's societies, as an unbroken "tradition." If tradition (for instance, the war band) is mythic then how are we to speak of archaic practices that inform today without buying into the mythification?

Donna Zuckerberg gives one response, when speaking of manosphere types who invoke a traditional past in order to restore it: "The men of the Red Pill who write about the ancient world would have their readers believe there is a straight line from antiquity to today, a continuity of male and female behavior. As I have been arguing, however, this illusion of continuity is actually an ideologically motivated strategy to *resurrect* ancient norms in the present day."[46] On a similar note, Courtney Burrell argues persuasively that Otto Höfler's canonical Männerbund Theory was driven by an ideological goal: to synthesize past scattered practices into a unifying tradition that would occlude any contextual or material account of contemporary fascism.[47]

I agree. We need to be wary of repeating fascism's own method of projecting itself into the past. We must be attuned to fascist mythifying efforts to construct an ideological unity that justifies violence (aka mythic violence that repeats itself). I would argue that we can keep the synthesis but not the motivation. An antifascist investigation constructs not a unity that ideologically justifies but a continuity that orients us to the fascist palingenetic efforts.

At the same time, we also need to account for the material power dynamics of microfascism, especially the way feminists like Amorós have positioned packs and groups as the origin of patriarchy. War bands and other men's associations existed, and their primary purpose was separation and control, flight, and return. Thus, we need to both recognize the power of mythifying Männerbund by Evolaists and incorporate long-standing war bands as patriarchal pacts into an antifascist analysis. Identifying some practices as primordial does not naturalize or ideologize them. A reminder of the method laid out in the introduction might help: microfascism is long-standing but neither an eternal nor natural realm. Guattari gives the rationale for this long view: "We simply don't want to miss the impact of this totalitarian machine *which never stops modifying and adapting itself to the relationships of force and societal transformations.*"[48] We need an antifascist development of longue durée and the archaic to prevent its return.

Microfascism operates via resonance. We have so far discussed this in terms of a network of black hole subjects that occupy the same "time" (in other words, are living subjects). Microfascist resonance also takes place *across* time, connecting the dead and alive, the waning and the waxing, the ebb and flow of forms. This means there is no unbroken line from the archaic to the present, but an ability to reactivate the past within the microfascist realm. In fact, this is what palingenesis does—it renews and reinvokes. Palingenesis is a "making-resonate" across contexts, including temporal ones.

When it comes to the specific discussion of war bands and masculinity, it means reframing their archaic status. What Eliade, Evola, and other scholars call "tradition" (the overarching value that synthesizes the initiations) we would call *patriarchy.* To be specific, patriarchy—like tradition—is pervasive, mundane, and systematic (if decentralized).

While war bands are romanticized and mythified as universal, the actual war on women is material, is long-standing, and has various terrains with battles over time. War bands are both an actual unit of the patriarchal pacts for misogynistic enforcement and a mythic abstraction that is invoked by those masculine subjects. In other words, war bands operate as and through autogenetic sovereignty, as subjectivity formed through mythic abstraction about itself.

What we'll be assessing as masculine war bands reside in between Griffin's poles, being both "ineliminable,' definitional components" of microfascism and "time- or place specific, peripheral ones." This seeming paradox means examining current and archaic practices, not to naturalize war or masculine violence but to trace a long continuity with specific eruptions. This critical reframing does anti-microfascist work by tracing mythic warrior societies as both patriarchal primordial force as well as mutating in contemporary societies, associations under the sign "Männerbund" (though not always explicitly so).

Initiations

While anthropologists have spent considerable effort studying rites of passage, we will home in on one that Julius Evola considered a contemporary, one who also supported Romanian fascist thought: Mircea Eliade.[49] Eliade wrote extensively on archaic societies' myths, spiritual practices, and rites of passage but it's his *Rites and Symbols of Initiation: The Mysteries of Birth and Rebirth* that lays out masculine metamorphosis rituals clearly and affirmatively. More than just acquiring traditional knowledge or entering a special group, initiation involves "a basic change in existential condition" in which a novice is "endowed with a totally different being from that which he possessed before his initiation; he has become another."[50] The teachings and the ordeals that a subject undergoes constitute a type of sacred instruction and spiritual transformation.

First, let's be clear about the material process. Masculine metamorphosis happened through rites of passage which were often preceded by a period of detachment and isolation, predicated on a raid on the household, "snatching the child from the natural mother."[51] Eliade universalizes it: "Everywhere the mystery begins with the separation of the neophyte from his family, and a 'retreat' into the forest."[52] Creating men meant removing sons from households and the matrix of relations with women to be taken into rituals involving isolation and harsh ordeals, and then reintegrated into a new social construct—men's associations.

Celia Amorós has situated these initiations in the rise and proliferation of patriarchal pacts. She finds the ritual of rebirth to be key to gender differentiation: "pledged liberty, fraternity, represents itself as self-engendering, in some kind of sovereignty myth where the beginning would not start with the natural origins."[53] As Amorós notes, the "pledged group . . . is a pact between masters, between quasi-sovereignties . . . [via] . . . the sacrifice of immediate life to legitimate it by rebirthing it in a new socio-cultural sphere."[54] Male mentors position themselves as divine creators (of the new man initiate), a power that now passes *to* the new man. The autogenetic sovereign comes into being not on its own but through and by other sovereigns.

Alongside the material dimension of metamorphosis, we need to pay attention to the symbolic and ritual elements of the microfascist metamorphosis of boy to man. It is a "magical flight" linked to sovereignty with a palingenetic dimension: "The genesis of the world serves as the model for the 'formation' of the new man."[55] Rites of passage invoke the original Creator via *recreations* of this original moment: "To become a new man, he has to re-live the cosmology."[56] The creation of masculinity is thus a recreation of the foundational act of divine Creation of Man. In other words, the origin is a renewal of a connection to the abstraction, the transcendent relation to the divine. The transformation through repetition is not a mere imitation of an act—it's a process of undergoing passage from chaos to cosmos.

Eliade lays out the recreation process in a particular way: "every ritual repetition of the cosmogony is preceded by a symbolic retrogression to chaos."[57] The retrogression requires a mimicry of physical birth resulting in the "candidate's regression to the pre-natal stage"[58] and "foetal condition." If the boy is masculinity tied to nature, then becoming-man means annihilating that aspect along with all the elements of that realm, including the feminine. Actual material elimination would require physical death, so this ritual death is symbolized "by darkness, by cosmic night, by the telluric womb, the hut, the belly of a monster."[59] The inauguration of the new requires a return to and overcoming of chaos-as-child. The desired result: "The neophyte dies: he dies to childhood—that is, to ignorance and irresponsibility."[60]

Metamorphosis initiations generate a mimesis through obstetric symbols "inextricably connected with germination, with embryology." Sometimes they are physical, for instance when the "initiation-cabin symbolizes the maternal womb."[61] Together, these images construct a simulation which replaces physical birth with the "second, initiatory birth."[62] The new life is a *substitution* for bios, a new mode of existence that is spiritual, abstract, and thus cultural. To be created anew, the old world must also be destroyed, since according to Eliade a "state cannot be changed without first being *annihilated*."[63] Rebirth follows a ritual death, and in good microfascist fashion we see palingenesis and elimination conjoined.

Women aren't merely excluded from this rite of passage; they are included as symbolic representatives of the chaos to be eliminated. As Amorós argues, this new woman is "a figure re-instituted on the grounds of the symbolic death of the natural one," one that requires elimination.[64] A brotherhood emerges but "brothers are not so because they are . . . children of the same mother, but, in their self-instituting as a brotherhood, they adopt a common mother and they set her up as emblematic mother to the pact."[65] The "pacted mother" symbolically ratifies the band of brothers through veneration and vilification, one fought *for* (e.g., in duty to the Motherland) and one fought *against* (e.g., the witch or temptress). In either case, women are integrated into the order as an abstraction and instrumentalization with material consequences. Elimination is not pure disappearance but a *displacement through symbols*.

To sum up, the masculine metamorphosis initiations contain at least three dynamics: *separation* (snatching, flight, seclusion), *simulation* (of womb, of birth, of materiality), and *sacralization* (invoking divine abstractions). More than a piecemeal set of rites, microfascism attempts a comprehensive networked "rebirth of man" as collective rite of passage via restoration. What Eliade and others universalize as archaic tradition for all humans can now be reframed as gendered transition rites to establish masculine supremacy. This is a gendering with three major implications for microfascism.

First, the rites don't just produce manhood but *autogenetic sovereignty*. Inauguration does not just engender a new social status for the initiate, it installs the power to inaugurate as such. The rebirth cuts ties with initial birth to ensure an autogenesis through relation to *other men* and most importantly to *divine men* (or really just one Divine subject). The material violence of snatching becomes justified by the mythic violence of men's associations as source of power. We see here the flight/return loop of autogenetic sovereignty: cycles of initiations across generations, appearing in various patriarchal societies across the globe, renewing the eliminations alongside the initiations.

Second, at various points the *necrotic* also permeates these gendered rites. Once separated from life, the subject can be tied to new life through abstractions including "joining the company of the dead and the ancestors." Like the Divine, these ancestors become abstractions who make him, replacing women and preserving a patriarchal lineage, now through ghosts.[66] In addition, the womb is symbolized by a tomb and the rituals often involve symbolic dismemberment and dying before resurrection. To be a man is thus to die, overcome death, and in doing so give life to oneself.

This passage to manhood could only happen through flirting with self-destruction (even as ritual performance). New life is anchored not in simple differentiation from other life, but in its replacement—a production of life-destroying reality. Man as such can only exist after a rebirth that eliminates/annihilates (through substitution and simulation) the previous birth and all things natural, including women. These death-oriented rituals make the necropolitical dimension of microfascism central to metamorphosis, as the homi-suicidal elimination is indispensable. One dies and kills to become reborn.

Finally, *war* is central to those everyday rituals of the masculine metamorphosis machines because mimicry of the act of creation is done through a reenactment of an original battle. This founding act often involves slaying a dragon or some other icon of the underworld, the preformed world ratified as the domain of women. Subsequent wars reestablish that initial mythic violence of sovereignty. Most importantly, one war in particular, the war on women, continues this renewal and re-inauguration.

Beyond the symbolic war found in the eliminationism and battle reenactments that found the new self and the new cosmos, war is central because one type of patriarchal pact stood out among the men's associations as the most withdrawn from society—the war bands, or Männerbunde. Eliade mentions the Männerbund primarily as a secret society with a special set of ordeals (and therefore essentially different from "ordinary" rites of passage).[67] The Männerbünd, as mythic and actual war band, becomes a central guiding image for microfascist composition.

War and the Männerbünde

Various translations of the German word Männerbund into English have included "warrior societies," "warrior bands," "military confraternities," or "men's societies."[68] Joseph Harris defines it as "a secret organization in a tribal society to which only men, but not automatically all men, may belong."[69] What's important is that the word *bund* points to both a mundane object (a "band" of individuals as empirical group) and a more spiritual quality (the essential binding principle) that belongs to masculinity as such (*Männer*). While *Männerbünd* refers to a single group and, here, to the principle of grouping, *Männerbünde* is the plural, referring to multiple masculine associations.

A small number of early-twentieth-century European anthropologists took up study of the Männerbunde, noting that the gendering of these warrior groups was done not just through exclusion of women but through profound hostility. Männerbunde formed "under the mantle of religious mystery and symbolically opposed to everything female in the tribe."[70] Männerbunde could have varying functions and goals, but "the preservation of male power" and "struggle for male authority over against women" were paramount.[71]

Like other masculine initiations, Männerbünde are developed through gendered displacement and substitution: "the symbolic male rebirths of *Männerbünde* are often explicitly births without female agency: the boy was born of the mother, the man of the father or of his own power."[72] This rebirth is a renewal, a simulation of birth. This simulation is eliminationist as it seeks to break up, reduce, and supplant concrete social reproduction as well as women. These are "primordial" rituals not in the sense of being ahistorical or natural but as emanating from the "prime-order": the inaugural moment of a social order and its sovereign subject. For microfascism, the principle of Männerbünd as the elevated concept of warrior masculinity is important because it distills autogenetic sovereignty as the source of right to rule.

For a better understanding of Männerbund, we turn again to fascism's preeminent cultural theorist, Julius Evola, who provides the reactionary philosophical underpinnings of this all-too-common phenomenon. Evola conceptually elaborates how the entry into the Männerbund is thoroughly masculinized against the feminine, resulting in a "higher man" who functions via war as autogenetic sovereignty and, ultimately, as the foundation of the state. Like Eliade, Evola sees separation from women as founding the initiations. More than the material separation from the household, however, the differentiation takes place on an existential plane. Simple man belonged to the same realm as "women, children, and animals" and the spiritual initiation resulted in "detachment from the naturalistic and vegetative plane."[73] Here is rebirth through a fusion of spirit and war. The process of separation and initiation results in a "Männerbund . . . that wielded the power in the social group or clan." This Männerbund was a specialized group, distinct even from the other men's associations, which allowed it a special status in the social order. The Männerbund's content or collective goal is less important than the *autogenetic* performance the rite provides.

Like his claims about autogenetic sovereignty described in Chapter 1, Evola presents a circuitous might-makes-right rationale as the Männerbund's "establishment occurred through conquests and aggregative and formative processes that *presuppose* the continuity of a power, of a principle of sovereignty and of authority, as well as the bond of a group of men sharing the same idea and loyalty, pursuing the same goal, and obeying the same inner law reflected in a specific political and social ideal. *Such is the generating principle.*"[74] The becoming-man through Männerbund contains within itself its own authorizing operation, giving to itself the principle of command. The rituals justify themselves through shrouds of sacredness to create the power group. The resulting Männerbund was authority *as such*, rooted in its self-given power to command with impunity, embedded in its own transformation rite, one that separated itself from women (natural world) to give itself birth.

Evola attributes all sorts of values to the Männerbund that are abstractions, numbness-inducing orientations, and affects of masculine bonding: "Love for hierarchy; relationships of obedience and command; courage; feelings of honor and loyalty; specific forms of active impersonality capable of producing anonymous sacrifice."[75] Such a sovereign subject seeks abstraction and develops "the faculty of subordinating the emotional and individualistic element of one's self to higher goals and principles, especially in the name of honor and duty."[76]

The "ideal without content"—in our times consisting of America, Donald Trump, patriotism, manhood, God—is valuable because it activates a *heroism* that can eliminate others while providing a rationale for evading accountability. Glorifying abstractions means that the war hero is not defined by its motivations, but "a cold, lucid, and complex heroism in which the romantic, patriotic, instinctive element is absent."[77] The anaesthetized Männerbund sovereign can claim not to be moved by 'lowly feelings' such as racism or sexism, but instead coolly and numbingly enacts its violence through love of abstractions.

We hear the echoes of the autogenetic sovereign's numbness and abstraction, a microfascist asceticism and affect-regulation primarily motored by cold detachment to develop the hero's necessary subjective armor. Evola's differentiated man is accomplished through an embodied indifference to the world, with the goal of action upon that world as command and control. Previewing our next chapter's emphasis on microfascism's homi-suicidal tendencies, Evola says the Männerbund sovereign has "a sacrificial disposition: man's capability to face, and even to love, the most destructive situations through the possibilities they afford. [78] The coldness of the abstractions prepares the way for a heroism that is not only tolerant of self-destruction—it welcomes it.

The content or cause for warring is less important than *love for the abstraction* (e.g., honor, duty) defined as an "intangible and inalienable thing"[79] and *the masculine pact itself* (the bond through separation). War becomes its "own" realm of experience; reasons for war become instruments for the development of sovereign power, a realization of capacity and will-in-action.[80] Turning the ignoble into the noble, the warrior subject removes itself from its material brutalities through an act of autogenetic sovereignty.[81]

As we saw with the circuit of flight/return in the autogenetic sovereign of anti-mimesis, the steely withdrawal (a differentiation from women) never fully leaves, it returns to reshape reality through order and domination, interpersonally and institutionally. The Männerbund thus brings its honor to the war on women. Evola finds roots of the state here: the "substance of every true and stable political organism is something resembling an Order, a *Männerbund*."[82] Modern state sovereignty is grounded in "the principle of the Männerbund, the *shaping force* of the State" the creation and then dissimulation of patriarchal warrior pacts.[83] Evola takes the Männerbund's mystical foundation as source of the divine right of kings and notes with particular favor the Prussian Order of Teutonic Knights, which later on became the structure and the "form" of the German *Reich*.

Several ramifications follow from this account of the Männerbund origins of the state. Evola, unlike other theorists, situates sovereignty not primarily in a state as a juridical matter, but in the material dynamics of culture, specifically in gendered rites of passage and wars. He also pays attention to embodiment and affects, whether that involves love of hierarchy or numbness and desensitization. Evola has bequeathed a lucid, if loopy, account of the martial roots of ideals. Fascism's cultural philosopher has laid out the source for authority, for the importance of abstractions, and ultimately has left us with the clearest articulation of microfascism as the nexus of war, gender, and death.

Ultimately, analyzing the Männerbund not only gives us a model for masculine war bands (groupuscules) that are active today, but explains how autogenetic sovereignty got its sacredness and mythic absoluteness. Given the gendered essence of the Männerbund (not just in its demographics but as the process of *making man*), we could say that the formation of the state represents a victory in the war on women. While autogenetic sovereignty clearly shows up in colonial zones of exception and continues to operate as settler and racial supremacist projects, it does so after a long-standing, pre-state version of patriarchal order and ordinariness, forged in initiation flights and rites that generated war bands. The state here is the result of cultural material origins in a war on women, one that gets invoked in constructing ideals like nationhood and inferiority of peoples.

Highlighting these archaic formations, especially as rationalized by fascist intellectuals, allows us to see the longer durée of contemporary microfascism. In a conjuncture marked by crisis of authoritative institutions and their benefactors, the twenty-first century revivals of microfascist war machines seek to restore the autogenetic sovereign subject through a renewal of war bands. We turn to some of these now.

Redpilling initiation and the contemporary Männerbünde

Microfascist culture today is replete with rites of passage and war band actions. Invocation and language of war permeates right-wing movements (and not only them—centrists do it too).[84] We have already discussed war bands as contemporary squadrismo. From these early rites of abstraction, we can eventually see how honor, duty, and sacrifice take on spiritual dimensions. The Proud Boys valorize their abstract values of Western civilization by initiating men via violence, becoming a network of street thugs in a cultural war to restore the West. Jack Donovan, a leading member of the Evola-inspired cadre Wolves of Vinland, pens alt-right and neofascist masculinity books in which he posits that "the way of men is the way of the gang."[85] He recalls the Männerbund when he says "male groups are the creators of political and social change" and that the "creative kernel of society and culture" exists in the "insular male group."[86] For him, the war band and tribal order is one upon which decentralized reactionary and restorationist zones can be built.

Meme warriors, online trolling squads, and homi-suicidal mass killers continue to take up these venerations in contemporary microfascism. The microfascist project seeks to expand through a variety of pedagogical and initiatory processes, and, as we often do in this book, we need to turn to the gendered basis of these rites of passage. When it comes to modes of initiation, this means going into the manosphere's preferred term for it: *redpilling*.

Since the mid-2000s, manosphere mentorship and misogynistic support networks have taken on the role of training, induction, and metamorphosis management. Some of these initiations emerge from the self-help and self-esteem movements from the last quarter of the twentieth century (e.g., some pick-up artist agitators self-identify as "gurus"). Redpilling was the name adopted for these initiatory educational experiences.

Taken from the movie *The Matrix*, the red pill philosophy draws on ancient and modern notions of demystifying, revealing, and becoming-aware or waking from a dream. The red pill worldview could be found among pick-up artist forums, Men's Rights Activist (MRA) communities, and incel threads on platforms providing a shared orientation and belief system for a decentralized "networked misogyny."[87]

Redpilling is a gendered rite of passage that claims to shake men out of their stupor by revealing to them feminism's pernicious effects, grounded in misandry. Redpilling from the outset sought to be a form of *masculine* consciousness-raising, a mimicry of feminist modes of decentralized education now turned against them. In this way, its initiation through knowledge imparted by other men specifically in hostility to women, recalls and renews the microfascist mechanisms of making Männerbund.

Redpilling is not reducible to a transmission of knowledge, information, or even misinformation. It involves a transformation, an awakening via knowledge, in which revelation is *experienced* as a passage to a new mode of existence—not just changing your mind but changing your life.

In the redpill networks, the patriarchal order is policed and revived through imposing violence via the *truth* of gender, both as epistemological claims around gender differences and the existential transformation—the true man, now restored. Redpilling is thus simultaneously conversion and reversion. *Gender conversion* is the primary transformation, given its roots in manospheric metamorphosis (even if it has subsequently been taken on by women). The subject now sees the world differently after gender conversion to traditional manhood; more than awakening, it's a journey.

Redpilling operations continue the classic microfascist project of the production of (new) man, a spiritual type that now results from *networked* rites of passage. Sometimes this is characterized as the passage from beta to alpha, but it is always about a restored and reclaimed manhood, one that up until getting pilled has been undergoing the ordeals of victimhood; being downtrodden, ignored, and rejected. Men have suffered the test of women's existence and overcome it by learning how to achieve a state where one can "no longer be submissive." The elimination of women, now under the sign of feminism, restores (via renewal) the archaic position of autogenetic sovereign.

Redpilling has roots in masculine pedagogy, but spreads beyond the manosphere to refer to any transmission of reactionary awakening as a mode of recruitment and initiation. The redpiller is a masculine subject imbued with neoliberalism's persevering, can-do attitude along with the encouragement to seek out expert training. The aim, in addition to getting women to align with the subject's sexual power objectives, is to produce a self-starting subject, perhaps even a "self-made man" or autogenetic sovereign. The red pill ecology includes YouTube videos that analyze culture and politics, such as the popular "Cultural Literacy" channel by Paul Joseph Watson. Redpilling involves DIY education and adult homeschooling as well as professional development using media sources ranging from Praeger University courses to an array of influencers.[88]

Redpilling is not just education of the mind, it's an education of the *affects*. Donna Zuckerberg characterizes the redpill community as a group of angry stoics. They draw upon ancient Stoic precepts to ground their newfound masculinism. They develop numbness and indifference under the cover of "reason" and "self-control" but with a specific objective—not virtuousness but a project of managing and controlling *others'* affects (tone-policing people of color, taming emotion in women). The subject is born out of masculine ressentiment and anger, and weaponizes Stoicism to impose those affects on the world.

Taking the red pill produces the shock of awareness, an experience which stimulates one out of depression and desurgent states into a transformed self. But affect refers to more than the feelings that seek out or result from redpilling—it also involves the *passage to action*. Once a new man is birthed through the passage from sleep to waking, a second passage takes place from knowledge to *action*. Like Neo in the Matrix, taking the red pill means not just seeing things differently but transforming into a subject that inhabits a parallel world to join a struggle, to engage in combat.

The first action involves transmitting the knowledge to others. The newly formed subject mentors and recruits others into a great masculine awakening, primarily against women's power (named as feminism but includes any rejection of sexual advances). Being redpilled inspires one to redpill others, an echo of the power to recruit that comes with masculine initiations. The initiatory red pill structure contains within it the instructions and urge to pass the rite on to others. Some of this transmission structure has roots in religious proselytizing, even multilevel marketing, in which one does not simply transmit content or a product but the *form of passing* to others.

Redpilling has taken off in part due to sociotechnical conditions: it emerges alongside the social media influencer, a peer leader and micro-celebrity whose skills of recruitment and persuasion of others become the means of achieving value (money, fame, survival). Redpilling as transmission thus depends on an active entrepreneurial subject that can only exist through finding and binding followers, *and* those followers who themselves operate as hopeful entrepreneurial subjects. Users using users: This is not the same dynamic as leaders and followers familiar to fascism. It's a peer distribution of attention (recognition, affirmation) and affects (hope, inspiration, resentment) that comprise the microfascist network of black holes.

This first action (proselytizing and conversion) means integrating newly acquired knowledge into a whole way of life, or at least into a lifestyle. With redpilling we especially find this production of lifestyle around health and wellness. The red pill archipelago of education and transformation include Red Pill University, Red Pill Resort (an "Enlightened Men's club"), and the Red Pill Roadshow. RedPillLiving.com is the best example of the way knowledge becomes embodied, concretized in health behaviors and developing forms of life. From supplements to age-defying cosmetics to coffee to exercise regimens to essential oils, the lifestyle is tied to a refashioning through techniques of the self for fitness and durability during chaotic times. It's worth examining excerpts from their mission statement to see how they tie belief to action:

> At RedPill Living . . .
> We Believe there is a war on Information (Freedom of Speech)
> We Believe there is a war on our Health (Medical Freedom). . . .
> We Believe that Mankind is undergoing a great awakening, . . .
> We Believe others will join us who share these beliefs. And Together, we can Right the Wrongs.[89]

With this list, we can see the spiritual crusade that comes with self-improvement. A set of moral principles, and a mission, RedPill Living is a biopolitical force ready to engage in a global war to bring a new world into being.

If the first action is to proselytize and catalyze others, the second type of action takes on various forms of *war*. Very quickly these redpillers' stony stoicism falls apart when challenged. At that point, the masculine rage returns, throwing out the cool demeanor and callousness for the enraged aggrievance that fueled the redpilling to begin with. The actions could be legal, as when Men's Rights Activist Roy Den peppered the courts with masculine entitlement lawsuits (until he decided to kill instead). But more often the belligerent acts are sexual: the pickup artist who uses psychological operations against his "targets" (until the technique fails and he kills instead as an incel), or everyday hostilities like street, workplace, and online harassment. The overall goal of redpilling is a vanquishing through reductionism, and this bellicose initiation can now accumulate on digital platforms like 8kun but continue a more dispersed and ordinary networked war on women in real life.

Redpilling is ultimately a *subjective preparation for battle* (complete with a mythic sword of truth, affective armor, and a pacted group). Redpilling is a recruitment and training for the ongoing war on women. Redpilling, as religious awakening, is inspiration to revive the earliest holy war, based in the West on the biblical story of Genesis and necessary punishment of women. Even when taken up by women, we are witnessing an attempt at renewing Männerbund by reimposing gender norms, a spiritual foundation of autogenetic sovereignty.

What redpilling shows us is that even something that seems to be simply an epistemological matter (knowledge) is an ontological one. Conversion, awakening, proselytizing: transmission here is less about information than transformation, one whose circulation is designed to form an active warrior body. The technologies of truth become weapons in, rather than settlements of, battles. Redpilling is recruitment for a man of action in an accelerated social war, now on an Internet-enabled much larger scale. Redpilling produces groupuscules as the revival of the warrior societies—a networked Männerbund against women and assembled through initiation.

Bound to loss, bound to lose: it's a Männerbünd's world

Microfascism's gendered subject, the autogenetic sovereign, has archaic roots both anthropological and in mythic construction. The recent eruption of microfascist war—exemplified by redpilling, Gamergate, boogaloo bois, and QAnon—is a revival of the Männerbünde at the heart of the Western order enacting a war on women. In addition, Männerbünd returns as a series of male supremacist incel mass murders (examined in Chapter 2) via vengeance and martyrdom.

Wars are declared everywhere by lone wolves and groupuscules. Contemporary Männerbunde include warrior groupuscules that come to assert themselves into the social as ordering forces. They're the shock and numb troops on the everyday frontlines of mythic as well as physical violence. Männerbund groupuscules push for action-based transcendence (based on principles like loyalty, duty, sacrifice).

While contemporary Männerbunde are most visible as the "enforcement" of patriarchy through packs and squadrismo, such an appearance is also the renewal of primordial patriarchy. To put it bluntly, the war on women is the bond that allows the Männerbund to arise (violent separation then violent policing of spheres). When masculine supremacy is in crisis, the war on women becomes more overt and, in the present, includes lethal reformation of Männerbunde throughout digital and material realms. Gilligan and Richards see the return of militant patriarchy in the twenty-first century, after a period of dormant normalization, as tied to honor and shame around American imperialist wars. They argue that the war on Iraq was "fueled by the promise to undo the shaming of American manhood by the attacks of 9/11, just as the attacks themselves . . . were explained by Osama Bin Laden as payback for over eighty years of humiliation and degradation that the Islamic world has suffered at the hands of the West."[90] Honor, shame, restoration through violence: this characterizes patriarchal masculinity from the macro to the micro, the affective structure of war band subjects.

As Kathleen Belew perceptively observes in *Bring the War Home*, the US right wing tends to draw on veterans returning from wars who are hungry, traumatized, and trained.[91] The recent paramilitarized white supremacists, libertarian patriot movements, and memefied militias join Italian squadrismo and German Freikorps as the figures of postwar shock and numbness, now eager for operational violence. Squadrismo today revives the spirit of those soldiers from *losing nations* (which Italy and Germany were in the 1920s). Masculine decline and loss are remembered as the fallen, glorified as the models to be restored, and projected into an accelerated future. This mix infuses the "new man" through war.

Contemporary microfascists ultimately seek to restore not any political system (e.g., a republic), economic structure, nor even a particular version of a race-based nation, but an order and sovereign process to shape reality. Through interconnected lone wolves, groupuscules, and squads, microfascism cultivates and expands its own lethal effects. It reinvokes Männerbund to unleash new men in patriarchal pacts, carrying the inherent life-destroying toxin of the Männerbund into social relations.

This is a trajectory towards permanent or total civil war, an acceleration of the war on women that seeks a final and collective separation from life in favor of a reunion with all abstractions. Decline, crisis, loss, and restoration: the interregnum's dynamic forms the revival of Männerbünde. And the revival invokes the necrotic, as its rebirth always entails a simulated death. What happens if simulation is an abstraction that substitutes and reshapes reality? It's a Männerbund's world: one that only binds via an accelerated demise, a restorative victory that brings the peace that only comes with death. This core tendency of deathliness—of others and of self—comprises the subject of the next chapter's investigation.

4

Necrotics

Death and the Microfascist

I T IS NO EXAGGERATION TO SAY DEATH FOLLOWED AND EVEN LED THE Trump regime. For critics of Trump, books like *America, A Farewell Tour* (Chris Hedges) and *Rendezvous with Oblivion* (Thomas Frank) reflect this end-time in their titles. For Trumpists, this appeared as Dinesh D'Souza's *Death of a Nation*. Chris Hedges, the tour guide of America's "death march," gives us this diagnosis: "A hyper-nationalism always infects a dying civilization. It feeds the collective self-worship."[1]

Numerous commentators defined Trumpism—especially the militant spiritualist movement QAnon—as a death cult. Trump's responses to Congressional attempts at impeachment prompted Judith Butler to write, "it is increasingly difficult to determine whether his reactions are suicidal or a means of triumphant survival."[2] The essay, succinctly titled "Genius or Suicide," asks us to consider both. As novelist Aleksander Hemon succinctly put it, "like other death cults, Trump's supporters are willing to kill and die in his name, believing it will lead to personal rebirth and glory."[3]

Trump was the CEO of the homi-suicide state. His ongoing gutting of the biopolitical infrastructure in favor of militarized repression seemed to fulfill former political advisor Steve Bannon's grand objective of "the deconstruction of the administrative state."[4] Trump set the stage for a death-driven "insurgency" when he launched his campaign, especially in the speech where he first uttered the phrase, "Sadly, the American dream is dead."[5] He tells his followers that he has seen the dead body up close, he has intimate knowledge of the corpse. But right away he alleviates his followers' anxieties by proclaiming a new magical power: "I will bring it back. Bigger, better, stronger than ever before." When visiting Poland in summer 2017, Trump announced a biopolitical anxiety when he asserted "the fundamental question of our time is whether the West has the will to survive."[6] Trump signals a decline and a siege, autogenetically authorizing himself to keep it alive.

When taking the oath of office, Trump placed his left hand on *two* bibles. The first was his own and the other was one that Abraham Lincoln used in his 1861 inauguration. Not only does Trump invoke the ghost, he touches the sacred relic. He substitutes his hand for dead Lincoln's, imitating his gesture to transmit the sovereign power of restoration (of national unity through civil war). A restoration of the restoration—the myth inaugurates this palingenetic presidency, reviving a ghost again and again. Such spectral imaginaries were a defining feature of Trump "fan art" as well, whether inserting him into otherworlds of the afterlife with dead sovereigns or into fantasized battlefields of the Crusades.

Trump is a leader among other sovereign coroners and morticians. The aforementioned D'Souza, an intellectual darling of the alt-right, used the title *Death of a Nation* for a documentary film he made in addition to his book. Failed presidential candidate Pat Buchanan resurfaced in 2001 as a talking head with a book titled *The Death of the West: How Dying Populations and Immigrant Invasions Imperil Our Country and Civilization.* White nationalist leader Brad Griffin boasted that he was "redpilled" by reading Buchanan's book. His revelation? "Western civilization as a whole was dying and . . . a great historical event was unfolding within my lifetime."[7] More recently, alt-right influencers like Paul Joseph Watson have posed the question "Has Our Culture Hit a Dead End?" As Hemon puts it, "the advantage of Trump and his movement is that they do not care about reality or the truth. They are a death cult. They are not afraid to die. The Trumpists and Republicans are excited and motivated by the possibility of remaking reality itself, because they are in revolutionary mode."[8]

In 2020, the COVID-19 pandemic triggered a viral explosion of morbid phenomena. When an Ohio lawmaker demanded that Americans stop getting tested for COVID, a telling response came from a Canadian poster: "Have a good time dying, it appears you all are determined that it is your freedom to do so."[9] Add to that, the predominantly white constitution of the anti-lockdown protests and we get a lethal cocktail, as succinctly stated by Brittney Cooper (@ProfessorCrunk) on Twitter: "When whiteness has a death wish, we are all in for a serious problem."[10]

None of this should be surprising. Take the gun-worshipping death cult of devotees to the US Constitution's Second Amendment, which authorizes citizens to bear arms. For decades they have declared that their totem-weapon could only be "pried from my cold dead hands." It's no wonder gun stores in different parts of the US were deemed essential, even "life-sustaining," during 2020's COVID lockdowns. The accelerated and acute circumstances resulting from COVID-19 are drawing out what will be described herein as the *necropolitical* orientations of the US radical and libertarian right.

How do we account for this Trump-era active and passive orientation around death and what might it have to do with contemporary microfascism? This chapter explores these questions with particular attention to the subjective and structural elements of necrotics. From one perspective, the death-orientation is obvious: like their Nazi predecessors, today's fascists seek domination over others, including genocide and extermination. Their most violent actors have indeed murdered, at times en masse. While acknowledging this work that has centered the state and leaders, we need to tease out the microfascist dimension of death-production, one that precedes that state. I will argue that *necropolitical microfascism* is based on the patriarchal autogenetic relation to the biophilic realm as one of life and social reproduction.

This chapter sets outs to develop the suicidal aspect as a key dimension of microfascism: a necropolitical sovereignty. How might we think of microfascist death-politics and culture that does not rely on a rather vague and broad notion of a collective "death drive"? What are the structures, encounters, and operations that produce fascist subjectivities? What kinds of realities are generated in this production?

Comprehending contemporary expressions of emerging fascism needs to be situated in an older process—the homi-suicidal impulses within capital, state, and patriarchy. This chapter traces out those elements of microfascism with an extended excursion into the theories around the necrotic. Drawing from these works, I examine how the microfascist tendency courts its own destruction and the destruction of others. Through these careful conceptualizations we can see microfascist necrotics, or how the production of subjectivity, entails renewal and persistence of the self via elimination, including of itself. We will explore a *spectrum* of microfascist necropolitics, displacing the binary live/die with the long tail of eliminationism: reduction, indifference, neglect, maiming, slow death. The result is a necropolitical culture which infuses a fascist state but can be lethal without it.

Ultimately, this homi-suicidal tendency forms the subjective core of microfascism. With an understanding of these multiple levels, we find microfascism's deathliness is less of a death drive (psychological phenomenon) and more a type of desiring-production that involves a creation of reality through the active shaping of social relations. Klaus Theweleit goes so far as to call it a "mode of production," one that results in "*fascist* reality; it creates life-destroying structures."[11] A focus on the necrotic is designed to help us understand an enemy that seeks to de-vivify at any cost. What we're presently witnessing is a downward-oriented movement, a surge that does not rise, but sinks and seeks to take others with it. It is what I call a *downsinking* and a *downsurgency*.

Sometimes the necropolitical actions comes in the form of specialized actors—Freikorps, incels, and manifesto-writing mass killers—but mostly as distributed, immersive, and ordinary (everyday sexism killings). The contemporary cultural production of microfascist subjectivity includes the anti-lockdown protestors (who form a network of COVID spreaders) as well as mass shooters who have leapt from online chan culture into streets, big box stores, mosques, and clubs. To this we can add manosphere-fueled "lone wolves" who attack women (partners, exes, strangers) at birth control centers, yoga studios, college campuses, and other spaces where women congregate. Necropolitical culture traffics in performative memories of the never-existing and the dead, invoking ghosts of the US Southern "Lost Cause," medieval and ancient warrior masculinity, and defeated empires.

Microfascist culture is not a lifestyle but a *deathstyle*: a subjectivity that gives to itself a mode of nonexistence. The revival of microfascism in response to COVID-19 as well as Trump's 2020 electoral loss foregrounds this deathstyle. Sometimes it manifests as the cruelty of indifference—individual maskless spreaders as well as a structural possessiveness in whiteness that disadvantages other people's social reproduction. QAnon's slogan, "Where We Go One, We Go All" or #WWG1WGA, is a call to arms for a US spiritual civil war to revive a "lost cause" and to valorize martyrdom. Ali Alexander, an organizer of the "Stop the Steal" movement that contributed to the January 6, 2021 reactionary insurrection, tweeted he was ready to sacrifice himself to defend Trump's alleged victory. The Arizona GOP retweeted it with the following question to their followers: "He's ready to die, are you?"[12]

Such a deathstyle is not inert—its participatory, peer-to-peer goading and incitements unleash lethal phenomena. Through the cultural production of contemporary microfascist subjectivity the necrotic dimension gives form to a world as *ruined*. As a result, microfascist culture develops a networked body—both individualized and collectivized—that is capable of killing and being killed.

Deathstyle fascism, suicidal war machines, and lines of abolition

When it comes to death and microfascism, we can take up Guattari's insight: "All fascist meanings stem out of a composite representation of love and death, of Eros and Thanatos now made into one."[13] To get at how this circulates today, let's initially note the more commonly recognizable fascist contexts. Nazis and death are frequently connected, though commentators often focus on the fascist valorization of vitality in a way that downplays the death-desires. One exception is Enzo Traverso, for whom Nazi "irrationalism was nihilistic, insofar as its eulogy to virile force also entailed a disregard for life and a death drive."[14] It's this indifference, even hostility, to life that will mark the microfascist subject.

Nazism and eliminationism were thus closely tied not just in the industrial production of mass death, but in their production of subjectivity. Nazis paired genocide with suicide as sovereign acts, looping death between self and state. Jason Stanley argues that there was even an intellectual jurisprudence that fused them.[15] Psychiatrist Alfred Hoche coauthored the influential book *The Release of the Destruction of Life Devoid of Value*, developing a psychological rationale underpinning an individual's sovereignty in determining the value of their own life and death. His work conflated voluntary death with forced euthanasia, as the sovereign decision around value could slide from the individual self to the state.

Lawyer Karl Binding added a juridical dimension, with questions such as: "Shall the right to the legal extermination of life remain restricted to suicide, as it is in current law (except in emergencies), or shall it be legally extended to the killing of others, and, if so, to what extent?"[16] Like Hoche's psychological justification, Binding's question removes sovereignty from an individual act and ascribes it to the state, but now with race at the center.

The result is that "many Nazis, including Hitler, shared the belief that the state and the racial body were the final arbiters of life and death, rather than the individual."[17]

Prominent fascists, over time, have tied their own demise to higher values. In 2016, Rolf Peter Sieferle, a neoconservative historian and promoter of Alternative für Deutschland (AfD or "the Alternative"), took his own life soon after publishing an essay titled "Finis Germania." Sieferle might have taken inspiration from Otto Weininger, who similarly committed suicide soon after publishing an influential misogynistic opus *Sex and Character* in 1903.

Federico Finchelstein identifies the fascist fixation on homi-suicidal dynamics in "the sacrificial death, regeneration, and salvation of their warriors." Among the Romanian fascists, he finds the popular saying that death was "our dearest wedding among weddings." He gives some insight into the subjective dimension of this death-culture, noting that: "Fascists connected violence and death to a radical renewal of the self. For them, it was a means of revelation of the true will of men."[18]

Death and fascism were linked by thinkers of the time as well. In 1936, Freud wrote in a personal letter, "The world is becoming so sad that it is destined to speedy destruction."[19] Theodor Adorno, who spent time brooding on the rise of the authoritarian personality, also noted that "destruction was at the center of the psychological basis of the 'fascist spirit.'"[20] For Adorno, the result was not only the death of the enemy but also of the self, as the structure of fascism was embedded in the "unconscious psychological desire for self-annihilation."[21]

Years later, Deleuze and Guattari pick up on this dual necrotic feature: "in fascism, the State is far less totalitarian than it is *suicidal.* There is in fascism a realized nihilism. Unlike the totalitarian State, which does its utmost to seal all possible lines of flight, fascism is constructed on an intense line of flight, which it transforms into a line of pure destruction and abolition."[22] For Deleuze and Guattari, this self-destruction finds its apogee in fascism, which produces "a flow of absolute war whose only possible outcome is the suicide of the State itself. . . . [one that] would rather annihilate its own servants than stop the destruction."[23]

The homi-suicidal tendency infuses but does not originate in the state; it's that a suicidal war machine "has constructed itself a State apparatus capable only of destruction."[24] The ramifications of this absorption and transformation into pure war are deadly. They note "that from the very beginning the Nazis announced to Germany what they were bringing: at once wedding bells and death, including their own death, and the death of the Germans."[25]

Fascism is a "reversion of the line of flight into a line of destruction" that was always co-present at the origins.[26] Writing on Deleuze and Guattari, Nicholas Michelsen elaborates the dynamic, seeing in fascism a "collective rebirth through fire and bloodshed generat[ing] a politics which had no horizon but destruction. The Nazi pursuit of palingenic total war, as a perverse state militarization of the molecular dynamics of desiring mutation, was a line of flight into abolition."[27] I would add here: the homi-suicidal abolition machine only happens because of microfascistic metamorphosis of the masculinized subject in the Männerbund.

Chapter 3 examined how the Männerbunde, or masculine war bands, operated as machines for pure war. The Männerbund is formed in subtraction from the realm of embodied associations (coded as nature and the feminine). Initiations disconnect initiates from life itself in order to simulate and control it. Warrior masculinity separates itself via a spiritual rebirth which now roams through and shapes reality as substitution for life. Chasing abstractions like honor and glory, nation and God, it not only acts indifferently to its own demise—it welcomes it as long as it *controls the terms.*

A suicidal state is a result of the Männerbund subject's own trajectories, hostile to life, to women in favor of abstractions. As we'll explore below, microfascist necrophilia has its own cultural production. For example, the Punisher skull, emblem from the fantasy world of Marvel comics, has become prominent in militant right-wing culture as a revived and bricolaged death's head. The culture involves mythic futures, statues, memes, and street performances. Microfascist culture has already constructed a future filled with memorials to its nascent war dead. It has already generated a spiritual otherworld for martyrs and ghosts. It has already produced a "life-destroying reality." To better grasp the scale and severity of the necrotic production of reality, let's map some major works that use the prefix.

The necrotic in politics, economy, culture

A theoretical focus on the politics of death has been on the rise. Concepts like *necropolitics, necro-capitalism, morbid capitalism, Necrocene,* and *necroculture* all attempt to capture something of the deathly orientation of modern Western systems. A brief survey of these works will give us a conceptual context for understanding the death-orientation of microfascism.

The necrotic is no stranger to capitalism. Death metaphors abound in Marx's work (spectres, vampire, zombie) to such an extent that his oeuvre has been called a "political economy of the dead."[28] *Necrocapitalism* has been applied to the narcotics trade as well as religious terrorism, which have the shared goal of extracting the maximum profit from "terror, horror, and death."[29] It also refers to the reliance on genocide and colonialism to develop the most acute forms of "dispossession and the subjugation of life to the power of death."[30] A related term, "morbid capitalism" includes "'deaths of despair," referring to rising rates of suicide, drug overdoses, and alcohol poisoning and linked to health deterioration and chronic pain that is raced as well as classed.[31] *Necro-economics* has been traced back to Adam Smith, demonstrating that a free market is predicated on "the demand that some must allow themselves to die" and, if they refuse, there's a state ready to compel them "by force to do so."[32]

At the grandest scale, the concept of the Necrocene complicates conventional understandings of our global ecological demise like Anthropocene. Justin McBrien also calls it Capitalocene, referring to capitalism's extraction of value from fossil-based resources, themselves residues of previous mass death. But this logic expands, turning the world into dead matter for abstract value. It includes extermination of species, including the human. Capital "is necrotic, unfolding a slow violence . . . it feasts on the dead, and in doing so, devours all life."[33] Production (regeneration) and destruction (elimination) are combined in a Necrocene: "Capitalism is the reciprocal transmutation of life into death and death into capital."[34] McBrien astutely notes that capitalism is a suicidal megamachine, since its only mode of existence is to destroy its own sources. This homi-suicidal core logic combines palingenetic capitalism with exterminationism, the core dynamic of microfascism. It is a system that can only exist by eliminating its outside, its own sources of persistence. We have already seen this with gender: autogenesis is auto-necrosis.

The best-known account of the politics of death is Achille Mbembe's *Necropolitics*. His famous essay (and book a decade later) lays out the roots of modern sovereignty in "the right to kill, to allow to live, or to expose to death."[35] Sovereignty here is determined by *the generalized instrumentalization of human existence and the material destruction of human bodies and populations.*[36] Someone like Trump flirts with such necropolitical sovereignty but he goes beyond the secular model articulated by Mbembe and others. With "Make America Great Again," his necromancy doesn't start with who must die, but *who must be resurrected.* Who must be made to die in order to be reborn? Such necromancy puts him in the place of a God-Creator and not just a secular leader. Adherents took up this deification, like QAnon media mogul John Michael Chambers' book *Trump and The Resurrection of America: Leading America's Second Revolution.*[37]

Mbembe finds the birthplace of death politics in the colonial peripheries of empire, where colonialism suspended the juridical order of the state to enact a special kind of violence against those deemed not worthy of life. Colonial war could be unleashed without regard for the law because it *suspended* that law. How? Because the enemy was no longer civilized, or even human: "savage life is just another form of animal life."[38] Colonial warfare is not one among states, but "an absolute hostility . . . against an absolute enemy."[39] It's a hostility borne of sovereignty, here as both the subjective capacity to suspend law as well as determine who counts as fully living. Ultimately, apartheid regimes, colonies, and the "plantation world" are all spaces of exception where we see "the creation of *death-worlds*, new and unique forms of social existence in which vast populations are subjected to conditions of life conferring upon them the status of *living dead.*"[40] Colonial systems are rooted in the sovereign capacity to make them a subjective reality.

For the most part, Mbembe's necropolitics involve a sovereign who can dole out death without themselves becoming exposed to it. He does acknowledge the self-annihilation potential when he says, echoing Foucault, that the Nazi state profoundly exposed its own people to violence and "became the archetype of a power formation that combined the characteristics of the racist state, the murderous state, and the suicidal state."[41] Mbembe also notes, when it comes to martyrs who oppose the necropolitical state, "Homicide and suicide are accomplished in the same act. And to a large extent, resistance and self-destruction are synonymous."[42] His primary example is the "suicide bomber." Mbembe uses Palestine as the case "where two apparently irreconcilable logics are confronting each other: the logic of martyrdom and the logic of survival."[43]

While tied mostly to monotheistic martyrs, I want to dislocate the homi-suicidal tendency from any particular religious belief or ethnic wars. We can see them in mass shooters who commit suicide-by-cop. More generally, microfascism's mythic otherworlds—whether of the future or past—guide war actors, allowing us to glimpse the autogenetic sovereignty's deep resonance with suicidal tendencies. Necropolitics creates these "death-worlds" that also find their way back to their creators, a proximity never fully banished by sovereign decision.

For Mbembe and his followers, necropolitics originates with colonialism. And while this type certainly persists today, the concept tends to prioritize state formations and their legacies (even as suspended). Less visible in ne-cropolitical studies is the way the necrotic elements are profoundly rooted in and formative of patriarchy. In keeping with the theme of this book, to study microfascism as necropolitical culture, priority must be given to gender relations. As we have been doing, this means focusing on feminicide not primarily at the macro level but at the cultural level of microfascism—pervasive and long-standing.

Necropolitics as feminicide/misogyny

In some feminist accounts, necropolitics exists without being named as such. Silvia Federici's influential *Caliban and the Witch*, published around the same time as Mbembe's article, could be read as an account of gendered necropolitics within primitive accumulation for early capitalism. She exam-ines the destruction of women's knowledge, communication networks, and bodies under the sign of the witch. What Federici calls "the war on women" thus moves the scene of necropolitics away from an exclusively colonial encounter into masculine orders of church, capital, and state.

Two thinkers have taken up Mbembe's canonical work directly by fore-grounding feminicide as a type of necropolitics. Melissa W. Wright locates necropolitics' roots in the way "wars over the political meaning of death . . . unfold through a gendering of space, of violence, and of subjectivity."[44] Through a brilliant assembling of feminist analyses of feminicide in Ciudad Juárez beginning in the early twenty-first century, Wright demonstrates that "gender politics are foundational . . . to the organization of states as the legitimate arbiters of violence."[45] Feminicide is pervasive and ancient, and thus "this kind of violence is constitutive of necropolitics: the politics of death and the politics of gender go hand in hand."[46] For Wright, feminicide's ubiquity but obscurity indicates that "feminist analyses are needed to illuminate the gaps in universalist depictions of the necropolitical and biopolitical forces at play in politics, economics, and culture."[47] Wright sets us on a path to take a more nuanced and concrete understanding of everyday necropolitics, especially as masculine violence against women.

Shatema Threadcraft builds on Wright's work by deepening the intersectional analysis of necropolitics as well as extending it beyond the state. In "North American Necropolitics and Gender: On #BlackLivesMatter and Black Femicide," Threadcraft draws on Mbembe while arguing that he overgeneralizes the bodies undergoing death and ignores gender. Like Wright, she takes "seriously the significant distinctions between homicide and femicide" to ensure specificity within the necrotic.[48]

Using Black Lives Matter as her primary example, Threadcraft's multilayered analysis suggests that we consider what is excluded when necropolitics is understood through the slain body, especially those who succumbed to police violence. Within such spectacular and mediated death at the hands of the state, only some Black dead are legible—primarily young, able-bodied, cis men. Women do not capture the public attention in the way men do, so Threadcraft importantly asks us to expand our notion of necropolitics beyond the highly mediated and public versions of police killing.

Threadcraft notes that the slow death that characterizes feminicide means women, especially Black women, are most likely to be "killed during an argument and not during the commission of a felony. Women are killed in private, without witness, or only witnessed by politically voiceless minors. They are killed in the home, that space long considered a man's castle. Their deaths are unlikely to register as threats to the public order. Their deaths are unlikely to register at all." Death at the hands of police registers as witnessable, while microfascism as Black feminicide is rarely captured by mediated spectacles. What would it mean, in parallel with the spectacular street deaths of Black men, to circulate technologically enhanced witnessing of the *private* sphere, of the primary domains where women are eliminated (as reduction and as death)? This puts necropolitics squarely in the realm of microfascism as the production of subjectivity, specifically the gendered public/private spheres.

Threadcraft situates Mbembe's necropolitics as a specific type of death: one that can end up excluding other forms of state and non-state produced death, as well as other forms of reductionism besides physical death. Instead of the mediated and eruptive spectacle, we have feminicide as slow death, distributed and occluded due to patriarchal spatial ordering. Using this insight, Threadcraft enables us to rethink and rework Mbembe's key concept of the "massacre": rather than tie it to bureaucracy as he does, we would situate it in war, specifically the war on women. The settlement of patriarchy, born in blood, is a war on women that continues as palingenetic eliminationism.[49]

Threadcraft cites Diana Russell's early use of the term feminicide to make her case. For Russell, feminicide includes many types of actions, including "the stoning to death of females . . . murders of females for so-called 'honor'; rape murders; murders of women and girls by their husbands, boyfriends, and dates, for having an affair, or being rebellious, or any number of other excuses; wife-killing by immolation because of too little dowry; deaths as a result of genital mutilations; female sex slaves, trafficked females, and prostituted females, murdered by their 'owners,' traffickers, 'johns' and pimps, and females killed by misogynist strangers, acquaintances, and serial killers."[50] Russell notes that feminicide's breadth of manifestations is matched by its duration in history, as it ranges from "the burning of witches in the past, to the more recent widespread custom of female infanticide in many societies, to the killing of women for so-called honor."[51]

In sum, gendering necropolitics results in a few perspectival shifts. The most obvious one would be to *start* an analysis with feminicide as patriarchal necropolitics, rather than with state, capital, or colonial necropolitics. The first context here is the war on women. Unlike the state of exception in the colonies, gendered necropolitics' spatial arrangement (public/private policing) has never been peripheral—it is a pervasive and punctuated sovereign act in the heart of modern (and ancient) social order. Gendered necropolitics includes massacres such as spectacular mass killings but also involves the slow steady death that feminicide signals. It is this extension in both space and time that mark a wider context for necropolitics into patriarchal gender orders, the primordial realm of microfascism.

Political and ontological necrophilia: escape, Fromm, gender

The necrotics examined above were for the most part (save for the non-state versions of feminicide) embedded in large-scale systems. What would it mean to take necropolitics into the modes of subjectivation? It would entail the social production of desire. For a more sustained understanding of subjectivation under capitalist patriarchy, we now turn to thinkers that addressed the social desire called *necrophilia*. From the outset, it bears noting that these thinkers reflect on necrophilia not primarily as a desire to have sex with corpses. While that ghoulish figure periodically appears in societies, it is only the distilled version of the ways desire is socially invested in the negation of life. The microfascist social production of desire, specifically around gender and elimination, is key to broader conceptions of political necrophilia.

Decades before Mbembe introduced the notion of necropolitics, the existentialist analyst Eric Fromm sought to understand elements of capitalist society through "necrophilism." Fromm identifies the "necrophilous character" as "the passionate attraction to all that is dead, decayed, putrid, sickly; *it is the passion to transform that which is alive into something unalive*; to destroy for the sake of destruction; the exclusive interest in all that is purely mechanical. It is the passion to tear apart living structures."[52] Such passions, according to Fromm, can be seen in the social fixation with technology, war, and capitalism's alienation.

The necrophilic character is marked by a type of sadism, one that seeks to make its victim into a thing, a "living corpse."[53] The objective, whether against the world or the people in it is the same: to transform what is living and uncontrollable into something dead and controllable. More than just biological death in the form of a corpse, the necrophilic tendency refers to a subject's desire to renew itself through the elimination (reduction, instrumentalization, substitution) of others. This is the microfascist desire as a social production of others into things, of the living into the living dead. The result is a *continuum of necrophilia*: an ongoing transformation of life into objects and a substitution of the dead for the living. Fromm finds at least one necrophilous character exemplar in fascism: the Nazi Adolf Eichmann, who as obedient bureaucrat "transform[s] all life into the administration of things."[54] He also tied the necrophilous character to war (mainly as state wars with increasing capacities for total destruction). But again, we need to take up a neglected war in most of these discussions of necropolitics: *the war on women*.

Fromm's most relevant update for these times is done by Charles Thorpe, who elaborates this character orientation to coin his own concept—*necroculture*. In a book of that name Thorpe argues that capitalism produces "a culture that aggrandizes the dead and non-living over the living."[55] Thorpe situates pornography and the reduction of women to commodities and objects as part of a media culture oriented towards death, what we could identify as a *necroculture microfascism*. Thorpe makes an important contribution by adding gendered media reductions to the necrophilous character. It updates but challenges Fromm's own gendered logics, which tended to repeat masculinist frameworks. Fromm saw fascism as a kind of regression to a feminine-coded realm of bondage: an authoritarian attraction to an imagined time of comfort and nurturance framed as the "Motherland" and away from freedom.[56] Fromm's setup is reminiscent of how we have been characterizing microfascist masculine subjectivity as autogenetic sovereign.

Mary Daly, after acknowledging Fromm's "useful insights" for her own notion of necrophilia says that "he himself displays the necrophilic mother-blaming tendencies common to his profession."[57] Daly also defines necrophilia "not in the sense of love for actual corpses, but of love for those victimized into a state of living death."[58] However, this living death is not some generic victimization (such as Fromm's "alienated humanity") but is profoundly gendered. While Daly sees Fromm's definition as insightful, she says he avoids the difficult position that "[w]oman hating is at the core of necrophilia."[59] The binding of misogyny and necrophilia at the center of microfascist subjectivity thus becomes more pronounced once we follow Daly's extended work.

Necrophilia and gender

Mary Daly's feminist reading of Fromm is part of her trenchant critique of patriarchy and culture, which, she argues, is necrophilic at its core.[60] Daly's concern with a masculinist suicidal culture shapes her two-component definition of patriarchy. First, patriarchy is a "society which is characterised by oppression, repression, depression, narcissism, cruelty, racism, classism, ageism, speciesism, objectification, sadomasochism, necrophilia, joyless society ruled by Godfather, Son and Company; society *fixated on proliferation, propagation, procreation, and bent on the destruction of all life.*"[61] Second, "[p]atriarchy is itself the prevailing religion of the entire planet, and its essential message is necrophilia."[62] Necrophilia appears in both definitions, as one in a series of features and as a core feature.

Daly posits that necrophilia is rooted in masculine dependence on female energy, "a parasitic relationship to women" in which man "eternally attaches himself by a male-made umbilical cord, extracting nutrients and excreting waste (as he does also with 'Mother Earth')."[63] Daly notes that this necrophilia defines patriarchal forms of reproduction, or really of self-generated forms and abstractions. The infinite renewal of abstractions undercuts social reproduction and survival: "patriarchal future *has* no future—it's dead. The patriarchal future is repetition of the same, always." Self-made, technological, extractivist yet dependent: this constellation crystallizes the autogenetic sovereignty of gendered microfascism.

We have covered gender and elimination in Chapter 2 and here Daly gives us a clearer combination of microfascism and misogyny as they relate to sovereignty and necropolitics. Daly and others have focused on human origin stories, especially ones embedded in Western religious imaginaries, to grasp the core logics of patriarchal necrophilia. These mostly revolve around two poles: man as separate self-production through the Divine and woman as rebel and cause of ills. In creation myths like Genesis and Pandora, women are blamed for the world's troubles, for the fall of man, for deathliness itself.[64]

In response, the necrophilic patriarchy requires the constant elimination of women as a matter of policing and punishment. This happens with Eve's legacy, a twofold curse: "Unto the woman He said: 'I will greatly multiply thy pain and thy travail; in pain thou shalt bring forth children; and thy desire shall be to thy husband, and he shall rule over thee."[65] Thus, the menstrual cycle and the traditional agony of childbirth do not comprise the full punishment—patriarchy itself is the other half of that ancient curse. Necrophilia and patriarchy are tightly bound, as the founding reality-shaping is based on reduction. Order exists to eliminate potentials of transgression and refusal as well as other capacities. Subsequent recreations and regenerations thus carry this inaugural element of reducing the power of women.

However, two things must be noted: first, this diminution does not always take the form of degradation. It can take the form of exaltation and veneration: "misogyny can push a woman upwards as well as downwards. In either direction, the destination is the same: woman dehumanized."[66]

Second, while gendered necropolitics operates primarily to reduce potential in a slow death, it is not averse to more literal extermination.

Gendered necrophilia finds its apogee in the ongoing eliminationism of women. Necrophilia is primarily directed from men to women and incorporates a whole range of techniques of elimination (including and especially the ongoing practices of objectification, sexual and otherwise). Based on a fear of defection and refusal, the necropolitical is part of an ongoing war on women. The patriarchal killing we've witnessed at the sociocultural level for years accompanies the state-machine, whether in the form of the colonial state of exception or the fascist states of the twentieth century. Such a war founds states as well as subtends them, a war of subjectivity that orders subjects' capacities, systematized, and individualized without public visibility. Whether in state-forms or in the microfascist sphere, gynecide and feminicide reign. Because of this, an analysis of necropolitics needs to center the gendered dimension to make sense of microfascism.

The necropolitical sovereign tendency is on the rise, collectivized in cultural operations. We have already discussed the most obvious expressions in previous chapters, namely through how mass and/or misogynist shooters transmit their necrotics to others. The Christchurch killer Brenton Tarrant, for instance, clearly articulated homicide with suicide when he posted on 8chan: "If I don't survive the attack, goodbye, god bless, and I will see you all in Valhalla!" Tarrant's was a gamified massacre linking suicidal ideation to mass violence. In his manifesto, John T. Earnest (the Poway Synagogue shooter) expressed the homi-suicidal dynamic around lofty abstractions of duty and honor, now tied to race and survival (aka "The Great Replacement"): "They can't fathom that there are brave White men alive who have the willpower and courage it takes to say, 'Fuck my life—I'm willing to sacrifice everything for the benefit of my race.'"[67] Mass shooters, almost always men, don't have the decency to just off themselves—they demand that others join them. And since these microfascist individuals, even as lone wolves, belong to a patriarchal pact, we could say the Männerbund is a collective version of these homi-suicides. Let us further delve into the necropolitical culture that fuels microfascism today.

Necro-material: The Standing Dead

Jeffery Schnapp noted how Nazism constructed a separate mythic space and time through its cultural imaginaries. He finds this distilled in the 1932 Exhibition of the Fascist Revolution, especially the final room where "the climax of the entire exhibit . . . simulated a Fascist rally."[68] This was "a rally of the living dead, a rally taking place in some indeterminate secular otherworld, 'immortal' yet of this world, where history's victims are forever present to each other."[69] This spiritual sphere, an "ill-defined after-life," found expression in art exhibitions, films, posters, as well as the rallies assembled to induce mass transcendence.[70] Such otherworlds can be expanded to various microfascist cultural imaginaries, including one that predated Nazism: the US mythology around the Southern Confederacy. During and after the nineteenth century Civil War, the cultural production of the "Lost Cause" (as it is known) continues in fantasy and reality-shaping, especially as necrophilic culture.

It is no exaggeration to say that the Lost Cause of the Confederacy was born among the dead. The now-popular Confederacy myth existed in scattered form for the nearly three decades after the end of the Civil War, but it was only with the United Daughters of the Confederacy (UDC), founded September 10, 1894, that it congealed into its current coherent form.[71] After locating and exhuming the remains of Confederate soldiers from local battlegrounds, the women of the UDC invoked the fallen men. The ceremonies were pure necromancy, now with a reunification of corpse parts. Calling upon ghosts within their own territories, the group gave birth to Southern palingenesis by mythically reviving the dead soldiers. Their own reenactments involved cosplay as war widows who sing renditions of "Dixie" as mourning rituals.

That it was mostly women who founded the Confederate ghostly otherworld speaks to a patriarchal perversion. To put it bluntly, this was necromancy as social reproduction: to perpetuate the spectral abstractions across generations, or more accurately a forever afterlife. These "daughters" of ghosts resurrected the dead to fight for a future—a *necrosocial* reproduction. Moreover, these ghost swarms are no ordinary dead: they are the defeated and fallen, making the Lost Cause an ongoing project of constructing a battlefield otherworld.

The Lost Cause is a never-ending (re)creation of an otherworld through spiritual values (honor, glory, duty). Sacrifice, martyrs, heroes:

these comprise the death cult of Southern heritage and resurrection of Männerbund. This was seen as "a doomed, but honorable fight for the "Immortal Confederacy.""[72] This otherworld thus imparted the transcendent values of honor, nobility, and duty to the Lost Cause. This civil religion constitutes the microfascism of necrotic warfare palingenetically imposed, in this case occluding the social death required for enslaved populations.

They raise the fallen to preserve a tradition that was ultimately *unable to found a state, so its mythic violence requires perpetual retries.* We see this in battle cries like "The South will Rise again!" Here we have a necromantic prophecy: both raising an army and way of life as well as a collective corpse and way of death. Resurrection and insurrection combined— a re-insurrection.

And how did these necrophiliac memorializers create a resurrected world? As one writer quips, "Corpses cannot speak for themselves, so the UDC gave them words, and the method of their ventriloquism was memorials."[73] The Confederate statues, or as the title of one documentary astutely called them, "Stone Ghosts," became proxies, promises, and sentinels. Michael Taussig speaks of the "faith in marble" that comes with memorialized figures who now function as raising the dead (erecting a simulation of the corpse).[74] Confederate statues are immobile zombies reminding us that they're losers. But the standing dead do more than memorialize—they make a *promise.* "The South Will Rise Again" is one of them. Another can be found on one of the first memorials (at Cheraw) in the form of this inscription: "Fallen, but not dead!" The question arises: If not dead, then what? The upright statues seem to modify, even reverse, the phrase's necrologic: dead but not fallen or, more precisely, dead but risen.

The res-erection conjures the dead in order to unleash action in the world. For one thing, these were stony sentinels, concrete signals of surveillance and warnings to Black gatherings.[75] Often placed in town squares and public parks, these were less reminders and more minders, or marble proxies of the slave patrols. Statues are less a remembrance than a reanimator, a regeneration that can be viewed as a petrified palingenesis and a concrete imposition of abstraction as mythic violence. Another action restores, in eternal form, a familiar power: one of the inscriptions on a memorial by the UDC reads: "Dead, but Sceptered Sovereigns who still rule us from the dust."

The statues and other martyrizations could be said to populate what we have discussing as an "indeterminate secular otherworld," now expanded to a broader cultural production: a phantasmagoric realm where people find themselves surrounded by mythic images and projections. Microfascist culture becomes the realm of civil necromancy as well as the imaginary for civil war. In today's microfascist culture such an intermediate otherworld is dense with digital replication and networked simulation. Its Internet home means the otherworld is more pervasive, immersive, and participatory. Much like the Lost Cause imaginary, memes of martyrized and canonized shooters populate this otherworld, as does the bleak dead futurism of fashwave. For now, we'll focus on how this microfascist necrotic otherworld is *performed*. To understand the density, ubiquity, and ordinariness of the microfascist sphere, we need to delve into popular culture, especially with the costumed performance of necropolitical alt-right protestors.

Cosplay and the performance of necrotic otherworlds

In 2016–2017, pro-Trump street demonstrations surged and took the spotlight. Commentators noted that Trump's street "army" emerged from troll-based online cultures, as when some sharp-tongued antifascists during a protest yelled, "Go back to 4chan!" Observers of one alt-right gathering noted that it "had adolescent play-acting aspect of 4chan's culture, wedded, bizarrely, to the military dress up aspect" of more militant groups.[76] The often-awkward performances had older cultural references as well. CrimethInc. analysts noted, "They are the fan-boys of tyranny . . . a kind of cosplay: they can only be a pathetic imitation of the tyrants they look up to. They ape the Spartans, the Romans, the Nazis, who themselves were pathetic imitations of an idealized image of manhood, mere cogs in a military machine."[77]

The visual palette was reminiscent of Trump's cultural background in entertainment wrestling and here the wrestler characters were mythically drawn from dead regimes. Roman Gladiators, Spartan fighters, medieval knights, and Nazi troopers are all remixed into a costumed fan club of ruined empires. The scene was haunted in the way Elias Canetti spoke of invisible crowds: "wherever there are men is found invisible dead."[78] This was protest as cosplay spirit possession, the kind we saw (and still see) in civil war reenactors.

The collective necromancy of these street actions was infused with a gleeful affect. They had a classic carnivalesque feel, but with a twist. Since their future is dead, these teens and twenty-somethings walk as simulations not of victorious warriors, but ghosts of the defeated in a necropolitical carnival whose stakes are life or death. Necropolitical microfascism is cheered by some in their costumes and public-health indifference, while others operate on the more violent end of the homi-suicidal spectrum, creating a stochastic supply of killers (by gun, car, spit, and other weapons of networked destruction). The wrestling ring might be in the streets, but this time the blood is real, as evidenced by what happened in Charlottesville in August 2017. Trumpist reality reenactors' social desire is a necrophilia of empires. They are infused with a giddy Thanatos with their last gasps, now dangerously networked and stochastic across the terrain of everyday life. For all the talk of the West's need for preservation by Proud Boys and their Proud Papa, the suicidal impulse among these failed empire fans dominates.

In these necro-carnivals we see a colorful and less-regimented version of the Nazi *Totenkult*, or cult of the dead. As Meghan O'Donnell astutely observes, the Totenkult "[was] a powerful civil religion that ultimately ended in an ideological national suicide and widespread immolation at the end of World War II."[79] O'Donnell notes that this necrophilia writ large included the Nazi veneration of Wagner, especially the *Ring Cycle*, in which Brunhilde cries out, "Laughing let us be destroyed; laughing let us perish . . . let night descend, the night of annihilation . . . laughing death . . . laughing death."[80] The Totenkult also required veneration of dead heroes and "The Cult of the Fallen Soldier."[81]

Frederic Spotts finds that the Nazi death cult found expression in architecture, including necropolises, sacrificial altars, "forests of flags and banners, [and] the solemn music and flaming braziers [which] all added to the necromantic mood. Thus did ideology, melodrama and architecture complement one another in the self-sacrifice of the nation."[82] Nazi designers were fascinated with ruin value [*Ruinenwert*] including how future decay was intended to mimic Roman ruins as well as transmit Hitler's spirit in perpetuity. Through "hero-worship, glorified struggle, operatic suicide and artful destruction," the Totenkult sought its self-directed final solution: national suicide.[83]

What happens when that suicide cult gets resurrected in the cosplay crowds and online war bands? The Totenkult that dominated Nazi Germany returns here, but with some twists. Solemnity is replaced by irony and glee. Instead of a mass scale, the contemporary microfascist necroculture develops via networks and groupuscules. This takes the extreme form of the massacre, no longer contained within enclosures but distributed across territories.

The contemporary Totenkult thus aims for reality shaping. The microfascistic goal of these operations is to create reality, an act of metamorphosis harnessed to an autogenetic subject in the service of war. Once we include mediated misogyny and technologically-enabled everyday eliminationism, this war is primarily the war on women. We could say that the manosphere itself is a necrophiliac otherworld, in the sense of reducing living women to instruments for pleasure but mostly for vitriol. Like fascism and monotheistic afterlives, this otherworld is never simply elsewhere. It is constantly being imposed on this world as the mythic violence of reshaping reality, and often involves eliminating a woman's life completely, such as the Jake Davison case in Plymouth, England in August 2021.

Ultimately these performances are ones of decline and debilitation, an acute expression of the necropolitical foundation against social reproduction. They seek to *nullify* capacities in order to preserve themselves, an embalming process. Mythical embodiment is not a vitalist one, but a spectral one. This performance is a subjective detachment mixed with psychopathy and a nothing-left-to-lose sensibility. The refrain "kill or be killed" goes down a black hole: *kill to be killed.*

Overall, the contemporary Totenkult's cultural imaginary is oriented primarily around myth as resurrecting the dead and projecting them into an eternal future after life. The necromancy of the past is turned into dead futures that enact a global corpse-politic. This is the otherworld that is actively imposed on reality. With the rise of COVID-19, we saw yet another expression.

"Give me liberty or give me COVID!"

In mid-to-late April 2020, anti-lockdown rallies proliferated across US state capitals, with "pro-freedom" demonstrators apparently casting paralyzing spells on cops with their displays of armed resistance and weaponized spittle. The rallies, which featured Proud Boys, conservative armed militia groups, religious fundamentalists, and the boogaloo bois, directed their anger at state governors for requiring citizens to wear masks as well as shuttering businesses as public health measures to mitigate the pandemic.

How can we characterize these anti-lockdown protests as necropolitical microfascism? At core, these libertarian notions of freedom (to not wear masks, to enter buildings and businesses without restrictions, to open the economy) emanated from hyperindividualism. Masks were coded as speech mufflers, not as public-minded pandemic reducers. But selfishness is not a sufficient explanation. The ideology of individualism is the still the seat of sovereignty but now it's done in the name of a sociality—a homogenous one. Take for instance, the Texas lieutenant governor's infamous line, "There are more important things than living, and that's saving this country for my children and my grandchildren and saving this country for all of us."[84] The "us" here is an extension of "my," invoking blood (family) and soil (nation). Autogenetic sovereignty, as the determination of *who should be exposed to death*, is an individual act of protecting one's black hole network: a homogenous sociality of family, race, and nation. The anti-masker cries of "individual freedom" are in fact passionate protections of the homogenous, of a whiteness that articulates itself through an active *disregard* for the lives of others, an *indifference* to those who are different (in a pandemic that disproportionately affects communities of color). The eugenicist tones of the Tennessee anti-lockdown sign that said "Sacrifice the Weak" thus announced a microfascist sovereignty that determines who is unworthy of care and security.

Anti-lockdown and anti-masking protests continue a long American tradition of death-driven liberty. The mottos so beloved by libertarians now find COVID clarity. The canonical rallying cry "Live Free or Die" always seemed to be directed to other citizens as a call to arms, inspiring even martyrdom. In the hands of mini-sovereigns, the phrase now gets a necropolitical makeover, à la Mbembe. It is a demand directed at the government for freedom from it at the expense of others' lives: *to let live free and to make die*. A similar false binary was found on one sign's new twist on another old motto: "Give Me Liberty or Give Me COVID!" Translation: *give me liberty AND give me death (and throw in some death to others as well)*. Death-oriented freedom becomes a command to kill others, as evidenced by ethnonationalist Jeremy Joseph Christian shouting "free speech or die, Portland!" upon entering court for fatally stabbing two bystanders who intervened in his racist harassment on a train. The very founding of freedom is on the death of others (the Indigenous, the enslaved) to the degree that Russ Castronovo calls it "necro citizenship."[85]

The necropolitical dimension of microfascism with COVID-19 is less focused on gender and war as our other examples. Its more macro-focus and race-based eugenic nationalism has become more visible. However, the documented rise in domestic violence by men against women also factors in here, adding these feminicidal deaths to the overall "necropolitical body count rising in real time."[86] COVID-19 has brought to the foreground these long-standing traditions in addition to exposing ways neoliberal capitalism "can coexist perfectly with death machines."[87] To this end, the revolutionary anticapitalist collective M.I. Asma has compiled its COVID-era blog entries into a collection called *On Necrocapitalism: A Plague Journal.*[88]

Necropolitics and fear

We have been examining necrophilia as social desire: a subjective orientation to reduce, to objectify, to render inert, to pacify and diminish. It's this combination of Eros and Thanatos that Guattari placed in the dynamics of microfascism. But the social production of necrotics is not simply love. We have discussed in Chapters 2 and 3 how the social production of fear imbues the autogenetic sovereign. This is only heightened when it comes to the death-oriented dimensions of microfascism, especially when it comes to the reshaping of reality into death-modes. In *Male Fantasies*, Klaus Theweleit eschews a strictly psychoanalytic understanding of the drives at work in Freikorps masculinity. He delves into their words and images, finding that "the particles of reality taken up in their language lose any life of their own. They are deanimated and turned into *dying matter.*"[89] Eliminationism through culture takes over reality, as the masculinized war bands "find 'pleasure' in the annihilation of reality. Reality is invaded and 'occupied' in that onslaught. The language of occupation: it acts imperialistically against any form of independently moving life."[90]

Why is there such animus against the animated? What pushes such eliminationism? It is "the aliveness of the real that threatens these men. The more intensely life (emotions) *impinges* on them, the more aggressively they attack it, rendering it 'harmless' in extreme cases."[91] This eliminationist campaign occurs because, as we have noted in previous chapters, such microfascist soldiers develop psychic (and physical) armor through a numbing effect.

In addition to the destructive side, Theweleit sees a particular kind of reality-shaping, or creative aspect, to the Freikorps. In a resonance with our flight/return circuit, Theweleit says, "Reality, robbed of its independent life, is shaped anew, kneaded into large, englobing blocks that will serve as the building material for a larger vista, a monumental world of the future: the Third Reich."[92]Autogenetic sovereignty creates and recreates, even (perhaps especially) if it requires widespread eliminationism of the most material kind. In an echo of the way the Capitalocene/Necrocene relies on fossils as an ecology of death, "Empires can be built only on, and out of, dead matter. Destroyed life provides the material for their building blocks."[93]

The threat of the living, embodied in women, spurs such cultural production: "the monumentalism of fascism would seem to be a safety mechanism against the bewildering multiplicity of the living. The more lifeless, regimented, and monumental reality appears to be, the more secure the men feel. The danger is being-alive itself."[94] Homi-suicidal tendencies can be found in shooters who are on suicide missions. But martyrs don't always need such spectacular glory or mass death. The pervasive death brought by networked sovereignty is an everyday eliminationism, especially in the form of misogyny. These distributed acts of feminicide are the gendered mode of what Mbembe first locates in colonial wars: the "massacre."

From uprising to downsinking

The microfascist subject, ultimately, is a death-oriented one. While it installs itself as arbiter of life/death, it does so only through a substitution for life. It inaugurates itself via a separation from women (in origin stories and initiation rites) who are said to be the cause of all ills, including death itself. Sovereignty continues to institute its "production of life-destroying reality" today, while deeply embedded in the archaic war on women. Microfascism intertwines gender and death in the production of a subject removed from life in order to control it. Microfascism is thoroughly necropolitical. Moreover, necropolitics is more fundamental to the production of subjectivity than can be captured in an abstract "death-drive" but instead organizes the gendered order.

While necropolitical sovereignty pervades the colonial encounter, it does not find its origins there or on the outskirts of state-forms. As I have been demonstrating, sovereignty preexists that instantiation by being borne out of autogenetic logistics, particularly a gendered one. This autogenesis preexists not only the state of exception, but the state itself. It has been developing via a war on women and within patriarchal orders that found themselves on mythic violence.

By foregrounding the composition of microfascism and its mediations as necropolitics, we confront a particular kind of enemy, one that is indifferent to its own persistence. While the necrotic seems mostly directed at a renewal through elimination of others, the sovereign too puts itself at stake. Sovereignty seems to rise above the necrotic as a self-sealed foundational power to dole out death.

But when sovereignty is infused with suicidal directions, and a nihilistic indifference mythified as freedom, then it too becomes swamped by the necrotic. Like capital's Necrocene, a constitutive decline is indifferent, ultimately, to its own demise. The downward vortex (a *downsinking* rather than uprising) takes the "sovereign self" along with it. Such necrophilic sovereignty becomes embedded in everyday microfascism to the point where Wendy Brown, citing Marcuse, refers to nihilism's normalization where "individuals are getting used to the risk of their own dissolution and disintegration."[95]

Necropolitical microfascism is a nihilism formed in the spirit of defeat, disillusionment, and deflation. This networked minority acts desperately to guard a patriarchy and white supremacy increasingly losing legitimacy in the interregnum. These passionate defenders of servitude to ruins seek unwilling participants during their collapse (especially women and people of color). As Brown puts it, "If white men cannot own democracy, there will be no democracy. If white men cannot rule the planet, there will be no planet."[96] This is the twinning of palingenetic renewal and eliminationism. With its self-immolating death networks and techno-subjective ruination, autogenetic sovereigns hold tight to abstraction and forms even if they take all futurity with it.

Our conventional political terminology needs to capture this process better to understand the logics that undergird the anti-lockdown protests and other deathstyle operations. The homi-suicidal tendency disorients contemporary discourses (e.g., populism or democracy) that continue to invoke a persistent "people" even when the enemy is not ultimately attached to its own survival. This "populism" is lacking a *bios*, much less a *demos*.

Given the suicidal dimension of the fascist war machine, the twenty-first century expression of microfascism is not best encapsulated in a term like *resurgent nationalism*. Resurgent indicates something rising again, to new life and vigor, which is certainly what contemporary fascists would like to proclaim. The death-based actions defending and accelerating the suicide state do not have an upward movement. A profound *desurgency* (affectively bottoming out in despondency and despair) becomes the basis for shaping reality. Its war accelerates its decline—that is, it is less an insurgency than a *downsurgency.* They bring wedding bells *and* funerals. Given its trajectory and speed, this downsurgency is accelerating rapidly and must be stopped.

5

Platforming Micro-Antifascism

So far, this book has been an exercise in identifying an enemy. That enemy fears the material world, initiates through redpilling, and kills when rejected. It flees at the thought of dissolution, so it substitutes a simulated world for it. It appears spectacularly and in the most hidden spaces. It's there during initiation rites where transformation seeks transcendence to flee the feminine. It's in the moments of imposed judgment and imprisonment. It desires trolling and it trolls desires. That enemy is always closer to us than we think.

The enemy identification requires a change in collective perception. How do we sense the emergence and renewal of microfascism in "the interest and urgency of the micropolitical antifascist struggle?"[1] For an effective antifascism today, we need a keen perspective in the cultural and subjective realm lest microfascism returns in revivals explicit and unconscious. Autogenetic sovereignty, an archaic and modern production of masculine subjectivity through war, haunts even antifascism, so the project of perception looks around us (not always at others, but at the boundaries that surround us as fortresses).

Telling the story of microfascism's ubiquity and longevity should not be confused with a tale of its total victory or permanence. Microfascism might be latent and long-lurking, but it is never guaranteed to arrive. It pervades but never completely fills the time/space of its terrain. I want to propose here some sketches toward developing an anti-microfascism and a micro-antifascism. What would it mean to be antifascist before the appearance of the signs of fascism as we know it? Let's first lay out the more familiar types of antifascism.

Mark Bray provides a capacious definition: "antifa can variously be described as a kind of ideology, an identity, a tendency or milieu, or an activity of self-defense."[2] It ranges "from singing over fascist speeches, to occupying the sites of fascist meetings before they could set up, to sowing discord in their groups via infiltration, to breaking any veil of anonymity, to physically disrupting their newspaper sales, demonstrations, and other activities."[3] In addition to listing particular actions, we can also map different antifascist political positions and tactical orientations.

For openers, liberal and state versions of antifascism seek to manage an enemy through techniques forged in security and war apparatuses. Efforts by centrists to target right-wing extremism have primarily been *carceral* or focused on police criminological solutions. Fascism becomes one in a string of categories created in a discourse of "domestic terrorism" and "extremism" in which both problem-definers and problem-solvers reside in the state. Bray warns of the dangers of such a potential alignment: "Militant anti-fascists disagree with the pursuit of state bans against 'extremist' politics because of their revolutionary, anti-state politics and because such bans are more often used against the Left than the Right."[4]

A related approach (at times specifically focused on antiracism and antimisogyny) has been ripening within a broader therapeutic apparatus which also prompts the question: how antifascist can a state really be? NGO-based policy recommendations often feed into a carceral solution, under the guise of therapy. It involves intervening into everyday psychosocial relationships and individual psychologies to alter undesirable behavior. These techniques *could be* developed within and implemented by communities (with the goal of restorative justice, for instance). But the fact that they have been funded and deployed by state agencies (e.g., the FBI in the US) should make us pause before embracing these methods, no matter how tempting it is to mollify violence in the short term. Well-resourced institutionalized therapy operates in a *preventive carceral* mode, a state security form that attracts and displaces more immanent abolitionist and movement processes.

Movement-based antifascist responses have mostly been grounded in confrontational and intolerant tactics, and for good reason. Perhaps the most well-known signature antifascist tactic is known as *deplatforming*. Deplatforming prevents the composition of a fascist body by disrupting its ability to recruit, build a base, and gather momentum. Deplatforming commits to removing the technical and media conditions for fascist speech, thought, and performance. It prioritizes survival and community defense over uncritical commitments to abstractions like "free speech." Antifascism is determined to deny the legitimate standing of fascist opinions since "we may not always be able to change someone's beliefs, but we sure as hell can make it politically, socially, economically, and sometimes physically costly to articulate them."[5] The goal here is to push beliefs away from public sites, to get those perspectives to move into private and secret shadows.

Recently, social media platforms, especially YouTube, have been targeted as misinformation spreaders and channels for fascist recruitment. Algorithmic reworking and account banning have done their own version of deplatforming fascist composition from major social media sites, but those right-wing forces have created and occupied minor networks for a micro-platformed regrouping. Receding from popular media channels might curtail some info-spread, but we've already witnessed how inspiration to mass violence no longer needs mainstream channels. In an era defined by mass fascism, perhaps such deplatforming sites of amassing could be strategically central. But in the age of what we'll examine as groupuscular action and networked squadrismo, such mass action might never appear.

Deplatforming has historically involved praxis against public demonstrations of white supremacy, whether in the long history of Klan marches, neo-Nazi demonstrations, or fascist skinhead punk concerts. Antifascism tends to favor street organizing as its topography of deplatforming. But for whom are streets an easily accessed and preferred site of confrontation? Town squares and music clubs are not the primary places for *microfascism*. This book's centering of gender in microfascism now needs to be applied to micro-antifascism.

This is not to say women do not protest in the streets or engage in militant direct action, including the long-running revolutionary actions of warrior women.[6] The incredible massive demonstrations in Argentina, Spain, Chile, and Italy from 2015 onwards are but one example. Streets have been important for mass expressions against rape culture and feminicide (such as *Ni Una Menos* [Not One Less] and Sisters Uncut), as well as for living wages and reproductive rights. Unlike the more confrontational antifascist deplatforming efforts, feminist street actions are employed but not *fetishized*, nor are they separated out as a "leading edge" of a social body's innovations. The classic antifascist tactic of "meeting the fascists where they appear" has a different topography for gender-based microfascism.

We have already established how gendered microfascism's topography of elimination is ordinary and pervasive. The coronavirus pandemic has rendered more visible the terrain of struggle connecting streets and homes, as pandemic microfascism intensifies the gendered eliminationism in domestic spaces. Feminist antifascism (sometimes called *fantifa*) gives us a practical guide to micro-antifascist collective defense and transformative efforts through gender.[7] Antifa without antifeminicide ends up creating a scene with militant associations fighting it out over (and as) raced subjects in street and other platforms.[8]

We also need to expand deplatforming beyond ideas and beliefs. Information-based antifascism has a role to play but it reduces "platforms" to message delivery devices. Micro-antifascism is less interested in epistemological claims and speech statements and more on the shaping of reality through memory and myth, initiation rites, mobilizations of desire, self-sealing subjectivities, desensitized bodies, and affective investments. The cultural sphere, as the production of subjectivity with all the ways we have been examining here, attunes itself to something more subtle, such as affects and other micrological interactions. Micro-antifascism deprives microfascism of the conditions of becoming compositionally activated.

We find new challenges. For instance, conventional deplatforming has been effective by making nascent fascists feel embarrassed or shunned. But what does that look like in times of ironic shitposters and armored trolls? As Natasha Lennard puts it, "[t]he desire for fascism will not be thus undone: it is by its nature self-destructive. But at least the spaces for it to be nurtured and further normalized will be withdrawn."[9] A true enough starting point. We might also see that the desire is a *social* desire and locate its roots both in archaic traditions and contemporary media production. How might we think about deplatforming desire? Receding from a social site is a first step, but the broader project is defusing the social desire of subjects that coalesce, seal off, and activate each other. It means not only intervening into already-visible behavior and speech but abolishing the elements in the *pre*-subjective compositional dimensions.

To reframe it in terms of gendered microfascism: what would it mean to deplatform sexism? Reducing sexism and misogyny to mediated statements and expressions ignores the ongoing compositional development of patriarchal subjects. We might as well say we want to deplatform dominant subjectivity. Misogyny and patriarchy are not opinions, expressions, or spreadable information distinguishable from the platforms—they infuse the platforms' very existence and structure.[10] Information-based deplatforming can also easily feed into the carceral approach, as the problem is defined as individual users and their expressions. The same goes for an antifascist deprogramming, which would at least be closer to the ontological transformation needed. While this tactic is a valuable thought experiment, deplatforming needs to be tied to broader projects of destitution and abolition of the very forms of microfascist subjectivity that compose themselves.

This final chapter will explore such abolition. But first, we need to lay out some vulnerabilities and maneuverability within microfascism itself that generate exploits for antifascism. We begin by thinking through the idea that the palingenesis of microfascism always carries with it a shadow, a double—that which it attempts to replace.

Repetition and vulnerability

One way to think about this book is to note its deconstructive orientation. Here this means outlining a system to demonstrate its exclusions and its fragilities. We could say that this orientation is part of Guattari's project of tracing "the *genealogy* and the *permanence* of certain fascist machineries"[11] in order "to refuse to allow any fascist formula to slip by, on whatever scale it may manifest itself, including within the scale of the family or even within our own personal economy."[12] Unlike deconstruction, however, we need not have faith that the instabilities of a system will lead to its implosion. We exist in a world already filled with concrete contestation and antifascist struggle. It's amidst this conjuncture of crisis, the interregnum filled with morbid phenomena as Gramsci put it, that I gather a compendium of insurgent and resurgent theories and actions that are unsettling and challenging microfascism, even aiming to abolish the microfascist subject.

Let's begin with microfascism's instability. Microfascism is rife with vulnerabilities, even when it is as acute and "hardened" as patriarchal autogenetic sovereignty. As James Martel puts it, "fascism's requirement for a display of its violence . . . means that it only *survives from moment to moment*; *each moment could be its end*. It could vanish in an instant because its power is entirely mythic and not based on any collective decisions."[13] While I'm not as optimistic about the likelihood of an instantaneous disappearance of microfascist subjectivity, Martel astutely pinpoints the logic of fragility.

Microfascism's precarity is visible especially for two reasons. First, since microfascism is based on flight and abstraction, the repetition inherent in palingenesis is one of abstract *form*, specifically forms *against* life (aka material mimesis). As we have discussed, microfascism's own perseverance is tied to a "self" that is already an imitation, a simulation of that which it both needs and condemns. As flight-based abstraction, its form-based control is inherently ungrounded and fragile, so it needs to repeat its violences. Microfascism thus renews itself reactively because it relies on the very realm it reduces. This necessity undermines autogenesis, which cannot actually create itself (even within its own terms) as it is dependent and therefore vulnerable.

Second, its mythic renewals always carry the traces of the original impositions against refusals. Each revival is not guaranteed to result in a smooth reproduction—it conveys a *non*-reproduction as well (the primacy of refusal). This is because it's rooted in a war, specifically a war on women. As Michel Foucault notes, any political order is only a provisional truce of a war that was settled, not a fixed state of domination. Its precariousness becomes all the more apparent because it relies on the enforcement of abstractions, including forms of knowledge, rationality, and truth-telling. The crisis means a reversion to the original war. Applying this to patriarchal order we would pinpoint that "rationality which, as we move upward and as it develops, will basically be *more and more abstract, more and more bound up with fragility and illusions.*"[14] I would add other abstractions to this rationality like nation, civilization, honor, duty, and beauty; values belonging to autogenetic sovereignty which then escalates the war on women.

The temporary victory, the control through increasing fragility and illusion, has become unsettled in the twenty-first century. Internal crises to capitalism's ability to accumulate, exploit, and expand have been met with direct challenges by populations, along with resistances to their accompanying regimes of racialized and patriarchal systems. A decline in the smoothly effective hegemony of dominant ideas and practices has resulted in more explicit violence from those victors in the historical wars (economic, gendered, raced, colonial). The inability to secure consent has given way to all sorts of morbid phenomena, including reactionary ones that defend the institutions while claiming to oppose them (e.g., the modern state). The collapse of illusions has been reframed by centrist forces as a crisis of truth and trust brought on by reactionaries. But reactionary powers also see a crisis (in their privilege and power) and become violent.

The crumbling of hegemonic abstractions forces sovereign subjects to revert to the *origins* of those abstractions: the subject who forges abstractions in *war*, specifically here the bands in the war on women. Patriarchy's foundational and preservationist violence becomes acute, clarifying its war origins and its necessary violence. The terrain and the combatants become specified. Palingenetic eliminationism becomes more directly warlike, it is therefore more unstable, and the war is not guaranteed to continue in perpetuity. Rather than consider patriarchy as a reified and solid system, it is strategically important to revive these origins to unsettle them—the deconstructive gesture.

As Mary Daly puts it, these seemingly settled orders generate "clues which, as they are recognized, disclose the living process which has been hidden, caricatured, captured, stunted, but never completely killed by the phallocentric Sins. These clues point to a force which is beyond, behind, beneath the patriarchal death march—an unquenchable gynergy."[15] Archaic microfascism repeats itself only by re-ushering in this *threat* to it. It's therefore more precarious and fragile than its adherents would like us all to believe.

Verónica Gago updates this archaic counterinsurgency process in her examination of what she calls the "Ecclesiastic Counteroffensive" against feminism.[16] The Catholic Church has targeted "gender ideology" in order to eliminate gender-based critique in schools, homes, and in subjectivities. But this is already a response to something growing as "an offensive, a *prior* movement" which is feminism "*as a constituent force*."[17] Laurie Penny calls it a new "Sexual Revolution" and similarly sees fascism as a response.[18] The Ecclesiastic Counteroffensive is both very recent and a revival of the Church's own origins: the reduction of women's material existence as punishment. Feminism is the latest version of the original generative, rebellious, constituent force that is associated with the category "woman." In other words, the crisis in capitalist patriarchy is coming from an anti-microfascist force: feminism as insubordinate subjectivities and the social production of desire that is not fear.

Each return of mythic violence brings an overcoming: a production and refusal. Every instance of palingenesis brings its other, a doubling that prevents microfascism from being a completed "system." It's haunted by its exclusions. It also means we can see appropriations, contestations, and variations of many of the features of microfascism. One possible way to think of this is as the *pharmakon* of micro-antifascism with microfascism. As writers like Jacques Derrida and Bernard Stiegler have noted, pharmakon names a condition in which there is no pure distinction between cures and poisons. In other words, many of the features that seem to belong to microfascism are in fact ambivalent, as microfascism captures and contains micro-antifascism within it. When remedy and poison coexist, analysis and praxis work on the root to determine the overlaps and bifurcations as a project of disentanglement.

Let's survey some examples when it comes to tactics and terrains. While deplatforming microfascism on social media does work to move it into smaller platforms, a *platform pharmakon* would be something different. It could take the seemingly innocuous form of the ex-Nazi video confessional microgenre. Former recruits and believers tell tales of their metamorphoses into and out of fascist subcultures. The pharmakon takes the platform poison to create a copycat conversion, an inspo-exodus. More than a recruitment for "us," these are preemptive non-recruitments, preventing initiation into a fascist Männerbund.

Humor also has pharmakon qualities since it belongs exclusively to no social body. We can see this in the playful and cutting *Contrapoints* web series, in the way Black Twitter uses wit to point out power's machinations while composing a community of analysts, or in feminist street protests. Debbie Ging and Eugenia Siapera observe that "tactics of irreverence, humour, and shock borrow from the tradition of the carnivalesque" and point to performative feminist interventions like slut walks and demonstrations featuring *Handmaid's Tale* costuming.[19] We could also add #MaleTears, feminist joke lists, and feminist Twitter to a long-standing practice of feminist Internet humor.[20]

Groupuscules are not inherently fascist, though they have been most strategically used by fascist forces. Antifascist groupuscules include street-fighting affinity groups, intellectual production projects, and polycules devoted to experimental forms-of-life. Named projects like Revolutionary Abolition Movement, CrimethInc., It's Going Down, Feminist Anti-Fascist Assembly, and Making Worlds coexist with innumerable informal others who write and live antifascism.

While squadrismo was a tactical grouping in 1920s fascist Italy, even it cannot contain all the types of squads. The squad has recently become an object of fascination and cultural production, from corporate team dynamics to friendship circles with #squadgoals. We easily situate the origins of squads in war, but we can also trace them to affinity groups and social trust-circles. The research group Other Internet has written a cultural report on squads, noting they are associative forms "enacted by fictive kin" whose "playful exchanges produce trust, reciprocity, and VIBES—the ineffable group energy that squads value most."[21] They are archaic and hypercontemporary: "While ancient squads were brought together by the struggle for survival, always-on group communication sets the scene for contemporary squad culture."[22] I would say these are now fusing, as trust and survival are becoming necessary values again. With the prevalence of militainment, squads are increasingly turned into war machines, but squads are also machines (re)inventing for perseverance.[23] In other words, squads are ambivalent—microfascism cannot own them.

How does the groupuscule seal itself or open to others? What would squads without flight-driven abstractions look like? Squads can delink from a necropolitical dynamic and reground in mimesis. Antifascism's history has squads in it. Micro-antifascist squadrismo would take place in groupuscules who now fight a different war, groupuscules like the coven and sisterhood support squad networks. I leave this to others to investigate more thoroughly, but for now I want to stress the ambivalence of those elements that seem firmly embedded in fascism.

Even the invocation of tradition, long articulated with fascist imaginaries, has micro-antifascist vectors. Shane Burley argues that the "far-right does not own the right to reclaim ancestral religions or organic communities, thus it requires an active reframing by the left so they are not the only purveyor of ancestral memory."[24] How to invoke ancestors in antifascist manners? In that neglected early antifascist book *Three Guineas*, Virginia Woolf tells us that tools for resistance "may be staring us in the face on the shelves of your own library, once more in the biographies. Is it not possible that by considering the experiments that the dead have made with their lives in the past we may find some help in answering the very difficult question that is now forced upon us? At any rate, let us try."[25]

Incantations of ancestors can be micro-antifascist at the moment fascists try the same thing. The Black Angel of History "has traveled across beyond time and space to prepare us for a future African Zion beyond this place of wrath and tears," write Reynaldo Anderson and Tiffany E. Barber to envision an Afrofuturism that recognizes transhistorical traditions.[26] *Rethinking the Apocalypse: An Indigenous Anti-Futurist Manifesto* offers another way of invoking ghosts and ancestors when it comes to end-of-the-world narratives: "We are the actualization of our prophecies. This is the re-emergence of the world of cycles."[27]

Displacing and decolonizing the "end-of-the-world" narratives means death does not have to be tied to necropolitical sovereignty. *Rethinking the Apocalypse* responds to the question "whose collapse?" in this way: "Capitalists and colonizers will not lead us out of their dead futures."[28] Noting those homi-suicidal dynamics, they posit "[a]pocalyptic logic exists within a spiritual, mental, and emotional dead zone that also cannibalizes itself. It is the dead risen to consume all life."[29] Theirs is a militant existential refusal of the Capitalocene and its necropolitical subject: "These systems are anti-life" and they should not be allowed "to recuperate." Marcello Tarì locates in apocalyptic scenarios a revolutionary potential: one existing world dies for others to bloom, and this is "the only logical way to confront the West's insane desire for the apocalypse."[30] In other words, palingenesis as such does not belong to microfascism, only the version based on the repetition of abstract forms and belligerent orders to control life and death. The poison of autogenetic sovereignty comes with the remedy of transmutational survival—another way of living as well as dying.

Anti-microfascist orientations repeat and revive the past differently. What are some ways survival and reproduction compose themselves without replicating white patriarchal restoration? The Malcolm X Grassroots Movement calls their project a "movement for survival" and is organized through self-defense networks. The Black Youth Project 100 (BYP100) houses and incubates community-building praxis operations.[31] One project that is especially relevant for gendered antifascism is the "She Safe, We Safe" campaign, which seeks "to put an end to the different forms of gender violence that Black women, girls, femmes and gender non-conforming people face everyday."[32] The dual strategy includes countering "the patriarchal violence of the police" while developing communal bonds to ward off dangers of *internal* violence, the misogynoir that arrives in non-state garb as everyday sexism and microfascist feminicide.

The Agenda to Build Black Futures orients the BYP100 to a compositional and survival strategy that wards off the homi-suicidal ethos of fascism. Xenofeminism, as we'll see, appropriates contemporary technologies to reframe and renew second-wave feminist political and social impulses. Micro-antifascist projects are redefining futures as well as pasts. Afropessimism combats necropolitics as social death, pointing to irrevocable loss to develop a just future. Afrofuturism and the Black Speculative Arts Movement are making aesthetic-political worlds, ones "aimed at re-imagining both the past and the hotly contested present in order to catalyze the future."[33] They invoke the Black Angel of History, the "messenger of an African worldview in response to the COVID-19 pandemic and mass death within a post-U.S. world order, marked by twenty-first century Necrocapitalism."[34] To the bleak future, a different restoration. The Black Angel is called upon to understand and overcome "extreme economic and environmental collapse, mass death, and destruction" as part of its project of "Curating the End of the World." Black transfeminisms fight for a future of *unknown subjectivities*. Protecting the conditions for mutations is future-oriented while honoring a past filled with "what could have been" but was *prevented* from emerging in a world defined by microfascist autogenetic sovereignty.

Contesting and displacing autogenetic sovereignty

In addition to pharmakon-based repetitions, we also need to examine how autogenetic sovereignty is contested conceptually and practically. Much thought and action have been proposed to decenter and displace the seat of modern sovereignty in the individual. The long project of feminism has placed relationality at the core of being human, including recent work that centers vulnerability.[35] Here I'll mention a few tendencies that gather *potencia* for anti-microfascism: deindividualization, solidarities, and mimesis.

Deindividualization

How do we think of selfhood without the poison of autogenetic sovereignty? What kinds of *auto* and *sui* are possible? We cannot simply fetishize *autonomy*, as it can unthinkingly bring with it the line of flight that forms autogenetic sovereignty and individual black holes. Spinozist economic and social theorist Frédéric Lordon warns us against "a liberation in the sense of the sovereignty of a perfectly autonomous ego. Passionate exo-determination is our irremissible condition."[36] Any *auto* needs *hetero* or *exo* or *xeno* within its composition.

One approach comes from Laura U. Marks, who in contrast to fascist modes of mass conformity proposes another type of deindividualization. Her approach to the masculine subject urges us to examine subjectivity "perhaps built not on an individual, but some kind of open network or ecosystem."[37] This connectivity prioritizes vulnerability, including a receptivity to *death*. Marks sees a particular historical Western subject formed as enclosure: a necrophilic subject that actually *refuses* its finitude and thus generates eternities and fantasy futures. The antifascist subject, in contrast, "identifies with dissolution, or more positively, with the creative destruction of desire."[38] Instead of a self-as-fortress against mortality, she encourages an aesthetics of self that includes the introjection of "broken-down, demagnetized, glitchy images."[39] Her proposal thus repeats necrotics, but now detached from autogenetic sovereignty as it does not eliminate but instead embraces "a state of near-dissolution some of the time."[40] And, in a nod to the social reproduction work we'll examine below, such a self is "oriented to others with care."[41]

Another angle on deindividualization comes from Sylvia Wynter who wards off autogenetic sovereignty by grounding subjectivity in a concept borrowed from Frantz Fanon: *sociogenesis*. Sociogenesis names the dual character of being human: the fusion of stories and symbols with genetic tendencies. Sociogenesis begins with power relations, specifically the capacity to position any individual into the "governing code of symbolic life/death."[42] Specifically, becoming a Black subject operates in a society marked by racism and colonialism by first passing through the codes of subject/object and of life/death determined by an autogenetic sovereign white subject.

Sociogenic codes are neither fixed nor sealed. Retelling those stories differently interrupts the myths and identifications of existing sociogenesis and opens possibilities to other ways of creating selves. By taking over those codes and narratives, we reaffirm the "hybridly human."[43] Finding one's kin or kind becomes part of this reworking of the self, as part of what Black feminist thinkers have called "self-possession" and "self-definition," as "the power to name one's own reality."[44] This power has been usurped by the autogenetic sovereign, a subject that tells the stories in which others are denied stories. The autogenetic sovereign mimics sociogenesis to implant its version of being human as the only kind. Naming power and telling new narratives for the hybrid human is the first step in reality production that wards off the autogenetic sovereign tendency to produce a life-destroying reality.

In another register, Elizabeth Freeman draws on queer world-making to offer the idea of the "hypersocial" which "is not just excess sociability but sociability felt and manifested along axes and wavelengths beyond the discursive" or even the immediately sensual.[45] For her, "the synchronization of bodies does not require their physical touch, but rather a simultaneity of movement in which the several become one."[46] Rather than privilege collective bodies in time/space (e.g., mobilized in streets), her activism rethinks forms of being beside each other or being together. "Hypersociability" offers a way of thinking the collective without abstract unity, and in the historically organized material compositions of *kinship*. While antifascists have affirmed friendship and finding each other, this needs to be done with an eye towards preventing homophily and the love of the same. In other words, this requires a reworking of kinship.

In all three of these thinkers' works, living an antifascist life means revisiting and becoming hospitable to *heteronomy*, or at least delinking autonomy from autogenesis. Such an *auto* is not sealed, not separated, not fleeing. The deindividualizing operations (heteronomy, sociogenesis, hypersociability) do not just resist fascism and the autogenetic sovereign. These socialities are *primary* because autogenetic sovereignty comes later, *intervening* into subjectivation to flee, simulate, and control it. The micro-antifascist operations defend this primary social production against the usurping and settler powers, who seek to take over subjectivation to monopolize being human, even if it is homi-suicidal. These three thinkers unravel a sealed subject into the social, displacing the microfascist modes of individualization and coordination.

Solidarities

As mentioned above, squads are not exclusively Männerbundian forms of patriarchal pacts. In *Girl Squads: 20 Female Friendships That Changed History*, Sam Maggs documents the ways women's friendship and sisterhood circles invented and prevented forces in the realms of art, war, science, politics, activism, and sports.[47] Squads in the feminine mode became the focus of lists and media attention in the 2010s, especially as featured in books and popular culture.[48]

"Text me when you get home," a phrase familiar to many a woman at the end of a night in public, became the title of a book by Kayleen Schaefer who recounts the stories from over a hundred women "about their BFFs, soulmates, girl gangs, and queens while tracing this cultural shift through the lens of pop culture."[49] The phrase went viral after the abduction and murder of Sarah Everard by a police officer in South London, in March 2021.

With #YouOkSis, *Ni Una Menos*, #MeToo, and *Tranquila, hermana, aquí está tu manada* [It's okay, sister, your wolf pack is here] women found their networked solidarities on streets, around tables, and in WhatsApp chats. The last slogan, in response to a gang rape in Madrid, reappropriated the "wolf pack," the patriarchal pact name that the rapists—who included cops among them—gave themselves.

Olatz and Marian Abrisketa use this case to prompt us to rethink and revisit sisterhood outside of its blood-family sibling connotations (with its 1970s white-feminist baggage), and towards an explicitly feminist invention of sorority or women's association.

Of course, not all women's solidarities have anti-microfascist tendencies. Patriarchal capitalism already organizes women's friendships for its own purposes (e.g., what Alison Winch calls the *gynaeopticon*).[50] Let's also recall the United Daughters of the Confederacy, who popularized and materialized the Lost Cause mythology. Their *squadrismo* could be considered a Männerbundian auxiliary group—women bonding to preserve dead autogenetic sovereigns.

But those disaggregating and recomposition techniques do not finally determine the range of socialities and solidarities. Existing care networks developed in popular culture as well as mutual aid projects rooted in disaster capitalism now find themselves in accelerated acute mode to ensure survival and health for a "post-pandemic future."[51] The Care Collective challenges us to rethink and rework kinship through "promiscuous care."[52]

Xenofeminism has provided some new ways to reimagine feminist solidarities, especially around kinship as they call for (and provide) "imagination, theory, and action to unravel the ties of both genealogy and kin, and kin and species."[53] One of their major provocations is that we delink kinship (and being a woman) from bio-reproduction and to a technologically infused social reproduction. Kinship is created, not given in biological function, and thus "[k]in making, over and against baby making, makes sense when understood as a means of prioritizing the generation of new kinds of support networks, instead of the unthinking replication of the same."[54] Care and support are central, with the nuanced feminist goal to conduct "better care of kinds-assemblages (not species one at a time)."[55]

For micro-antifascism, these are examples of affinities without homophily. These are squads as antifascist kinship forms. Another way to get into this sociality is by revisiting our discussion of mimesis, and then finding it in a sphere where codes and narratives are invented: popular culture.

Mimesis

How do we begin reintroducing mimesis as a mode of micro-antifascist living? To recap our discussion in Chapter 1: mimesis is an "openness to particularity" and to the world of concrete objects, sensuousness, and materiality. Mimesis forms the basis of sociality, as Being is shared, passed on, and imitated. It's the realm where we exist as material and sensuous beings, a *sine qua non* of being a human animal. With the autogenetic sovereign, we have already seen a microfascist organization of mimesis: an operation that first seeks to halt mimesis by sealing itself from alterity. Microfascism then organizes mimesis by simulating it for its own sovereign purpose, then imposing it through substitution.

A different subjectivation based on antifascist mimesis would mean recomposing the people's mimetic faculty, or "their desire to connect with or be transformed by others so as to develop sympathetic, noncoercive relationships between nonidentical particulars."[56] Feminist scholars of mimesis note its power to undermine gender essentialism and promote feminine agency.[57] More recently, mimesis has been investigated for its relationship to empathy, including a specifically antifascist version by Nidesh Lawtoo's Homo Mimeticus project.[58] Mimesis has been extended to processes that are not exclusively human, such as with what N. Katherine Hayles calls "microbiomimesis," a strategy for survival that is pervasive throughout the bacterial world.[59]

On a more praxis-oriented note, at a micrological media level we see a kind of antifascist mimesis in the imagery associated with *Ni Una Menos*. Counter to fascism's unity via abstraction (individuals replicating and conforming as parts in a whole body), *Ni Una Menos* fashions itself through a body of interlinked arms, an embodied collective touch whose representation embodies hypersociality. This collective body-shelter is forged as a counter to shock and numbness, a re-*corpore* and recuperation that proposes a mimesis of healing; in other words, recomposition as a *repair-composition*.

What we need is a *palingenetic mimesis* that introduces instability (non-repetition of flight and elimination) while also proposing new modes of connective composition (solidarity, sociality, autospeciation, social co-operation). We can see this happening in the most micrological spaces of culture, in what is usually trivialized as "popular culture."

Micro-antifascism and the trivial

Mimesis in the antifascist mode appears in the micro-expressions of cultural habits. What would appear as trifling distractions from real politics (organization, state-based, street visible) takes on new importance. To put it simply, the micro is the *trivial*. A reminder that the *trivium* was a meeting point, a convergence associated with feminine deities that became devalued along with the goddesses. Whenever pop culture is trivialized, we bear witness to both its devaluation and its powers as *confluential* composition.

This means no longer thinking of popular culture as capitalist escapism or ideological mystification and distraction. Popular culture is the site of contestation and composition. It's the sphere, as Stuart Hall and others articulated decades ago, where a "people" are formed in variegated ways. The metapolitics of the alt-right is the realm of antifascist material as well. In addition to memes and humor, there is potential in innocuous things, which can contain potentials in hidden areas. Here is another moment to reconsider how we perceive mediated phenomena.

Popular culture in 2020 became highly visible for its trivial mediated moments, often associated with youth.[60] Black US popular culture composed itself in the twenty-first century through typically devalued forums like celebrity gossip blogs as well as humorous videos. Taken together, these Black cybercultures[61] include what Sarah Florini calls "an assemblage of podcasting, independent media, Instagram, Vine, Facebook, and network of Twitter users" that compose the everyday social media practices crossing platforms and platforming crossroads.[62]

Catherine Knight Steele, Sarah Jackson, Meredith Clark, among others, all give elaborate analyses about the innovative cultural politics of Black technocultures.[63] The signifying and creative vernacular of Black online communities is composed of skillful humor, analytic precision, rhetorical sophistication, and affective nuance. These Black technocultures are a leading force for accountability in pop culture, for the refinement of community values, and for innovations in cultural political interventions. These are compositional movements, developing resilient Black futures through connectivity, mimesis, humor, and memetics. Micro-antifascism arrives not just when self-designated, but when we see the production of subjectivity that works to ward off, even abolish, structures of domination while strengthening the survival and preservation of the social body. Composition pushes back, undermining the dominant order as it contains Black creativity. These technospheres develop a digital composition that resists and works around the "intermediate otherworlds" brought on by a variety of microfascist wars of subjectivity (US Civil War, settler colonial war, war on women).

One example of such inventive acts is the collective working-out of accountability through popular culture. While often labeled by elite panics as "cancel culture," in terms of compositionism we can recode that "canceling" to mean the social body had reached a threshold of tolerance for unacceptable behavior. Operations to "cancel" someone were developed in, and helped strengthen, the feeling of collective power-in-action through community norms including antiracist and antimisogynistic values. New networks develop, setting up the conditions for future uprisings through cultural play and joy mixed with precise formations.

In other examples, tactical media mobilizations by fan cultures included social media operations against the right wing (e.g., the queering detournement of "Proud Boys" hashtags). The musical act BTS and other K-pop fans famously even led a logistical campaign against a Trump rally by swarming the ticket sales to secure seats only to leave them empty when the curtain lifted. These are not the well-planned demonstrations when streets are the primary site of fascist collective expression, nor do they confront and deplatform an enemy. Instead, they reappropriate humor, play, and platforms to preempt forms of microfascism from crystallizing. They decompose capacities rather than deplatform opinions. Again, these need not be explicitly antifascist—their ephemerality and potentiality are prompts for analysis of what an anti-microfascist body would look like.

Perhaps the most valued (as lucrative) yet devalued (as meaningless) trivium during 2020 was the video-sharing platform TikTok. Compared to other social media sites like Twitter (with its verified personas) or Instagram (which has become almost completely determined by influencer/follower dynamics, no matter how micro the micro-celebrity), TikTok has a variable relation to the self. Not quite the anonymous squad producer that was

Tumblr, TikTok nevertheless composes with an eye towards clusters and not individuals. While branders—including self-branding entrepreneurs—seek to monetize their interactions and performances, as platformed composition, TikTok operates not primarily through individual users (with fetishized "profiles") but on flows and barrages of mimicry. The power of the filmic camera to alter perception and temporal experience was depicted by Walter Benjamin as ambivalent, leading to either revolutionary audience-actors or fascist leaders and spectators. We can see TikTok in this light, with its filming, editing, and exhibiting powers immersed in peer-to-peer networks yet underpinned by algorithmically engineered capitalist platforms.

While the app constantly rechannels users into algorithmically generated niches, TikTokers also connect through their own desires. Rather than begin as individual users with well-curated profiles, TikTokers show up to a stream already in progress, then enter it through mimicry and invention. They experiment with mimesis, redefining self/other relations through micro-variations. Take, for instance, the duet chain in which a user adds oneself to an initial post, creating a side-by-side resonance, which is then recirculated. TikTok operates via mimetic logics: I first receive your post and then transform it with mine; I *only* post because there is already a chain of imitations; I do not halt the flow to establish a self but imitate and invent in order to generate an already-emerging common. TikTokers loosen their bodily habits to modify themselves through peers rather than through a foundational self-mediation through dominant norms.[64]

TikTokers share sentiments on sociopolitical issues, challenge gender norms, generate coping mechanisms, and defuse micro-aggressions. They yield affects that counter trollish irony with *cringe connectivity* which, according to Joshua Citarella, "is the antidote for late-capitalist nihilism."[65] While trollish microfascist affects like bullying and misogyny creep in, an anti-microfascist milieu awaits them. Perhaps most notably, the mimetic composition is done via replication and transmission of *gestures* rather than words, especially dance, which is mimicry's "oldest function" according to Benjamin.[66] Here we see an experimental milieu in embodiment and transmission—a way of cultivating a mimesis that doesn't replicate the disembodied numb subjects looking for troll or meme wars.

TikTok also gives clues as to how digital mimesis finds its most obvious expression in memes. We have discussed how the Great Meme War and other alt-right operations used memes for fascist composition. Meme war has become central to "digital fascism."[67] The 2017 Punching Richard Spencer meme was a burst of antifascist revolt-energy captured in a widely circulated and remixed video. It recorded a moment of deplatforming (Spencer was being interviewed by a media outlet, after all) and spurred a common compositional power connecting antifascist tendencies, ever so briefly but memorably.

Adrian Wohlleben argues for a more central place in political struggle for "memes-with-force" or "real-life conflicts organized memetically through contagious gestures."[68] Memes can coordinate and channel anger into collective action. Wohlleben distinguishes organizational belonging from a more compositional mimetic process, where "we join ourselves to gestures only by repeating them, introducing variations into them."[69] Memetic movements draw on seemingly apolitical or pre-political spheres (cultural production) to form "leading edges" through gestures. Wohlleben writes along with Paul Torino on gestural memetics in the moment of confrontation and street action.[70] We need to also reconnect such logistical memetics with compositional mimetics. Together, they produce a type of hypersociality, the everyday continuation of a social body in movement and rest.[71]

The examples above demonstrate that micro-antifascism develops as the minor and trivial elements of digital constituent power to decenter, displace, and ward off the ongoing invasions by microfascist culture. Another digital culture is possible, composing alongside and around the microfascist manosphere that has attempted to determine online interactions. Micro-antifascist organization of mimesis appears in the trivium of popular culture to compose a micro antifascist body. Sometimes explicit, at other times not (yet).

Social reproduction and the movement of the concrete

As this book has argued, part of microfascism's long lineage rests in an autogenetic sovereignty implemented via flight and return through *abstraction*. The making of antifascist worlds and living a micro-antifascist life means (re)turning to the concrete, but with a twist. Like mimesis, the concrete is not a realm of flat particularity—it is *composed* in the sphere of social reproduction.

In a 2011 interview with Max Haiven, Silvia Federici defines reproduction not in biological terms but refers to "how communities are built and rebuilt, and how resistance and struggle can be sustained and expanded."[72]

Elise Thorburn defines social reproduction spatially as "the daily and inter-generational processes of reproducing human beings which takes place in the home but also in the school, the hospital, the prison, and . . . online."[73] Social reproduction is about survival (e.g., battling against feminicide) as well as freedom (around bodies, rights, capacities, sexual desire). Social reproduction has been at the heart of decades-long intellectual disputes within Marxism, specifically around gendered labor and value. Now, social reproduction has made its way into the center of struggles and analyses.[74] While social reproduction activism occasionally defines itself explicitly as resisting fascism, the implicit resonance with micro-antifascist thought and praxis is clear.

Leopoldina Fortunati refers to a "movement of the concrete" which she describes as "a large social composition . . . constituted by women who bring with them the feminist and post-feminist experience."[75] The movement of the concrete includes "caregivers, women as well as men who are crafters, makers, new and old peasants, ecologists, volunteers, and all those who want to build a new world, immediately, without waiting on the fall of the capitalist system or without focusing only on the way to destroy it."[76]

Fortunati posits three components to this movement. First is the *science of the concrete*, which "has brought extraordinary gains, such as pottery, weaving, agriculture, knowledge of herbs and minerals, medicines, and the domestication of animals," in other words many of the practices associ-ated with women's work before and during capitalism's organization of this science. [77] Such a science produces "life-exalting technologies" which she starkly contrasts with "life-denying technologies" of abstract sciences like engineering and information.[78] Second, the movement involves the *metis*: "a prudence and cunning intelligence, referring to the intellectual capacity to overcome obstacles by finding ways around them."[79] Finally, this movement involves *care work*: the management of "affects, emotions, and passions" as a foundational emotional communication that allows the social body to persevere.[80]

What we're witnessing, Fortunati argues, is the centralizing of social reproduction but "not as we know it."[81] In her sense, social reproduction is "an immense laboratory of social and political experimentations, hazards, dreams, initiatives, and visions."[82] Recently the movement of the concrete has moved into antagonistic political expressions in Latin American femi-nism. Gago and Aguilar articulate the multilayered project:

First is how we use our energies to work towards revitalizing of a widespread, radical, non-state-centric politics, without ignoring issues that require legislative action. Second is the renewal of forms of togetherness and collective association that overpower established patriarchal, colonial, and capitalist structures . . . Third is the practical capacity to undo the control exercised over our minds and bodies, opening up fountains of human creativity that have historically been buried by imposed beliefs and rancid institutions.[83]

Social reproduction tests commonly accepted notions of movement. Instead of solely relying on visible mass or public actions this social reproduction movement is involved in "a counter-production, a counter-consumption, and a counter-reproduction, beginning now, during the empire of the capitalist system, not after."[84] The power of the movement of the concrete sees important development in the feminist strike, a collective operation that conjoins economic, colonial, and gender refusals in the creation of a Feminist International.

The strike refers less to the visible actions and more to an accelerated composition, developing the social body that underpins the repeated yet punctuated expression of revolts. Desires are woven together, and solidarities are formed in the feminist strike, "a coordination of a force that transmits ways of understanding, that spreads through images, that accumulates practices and organizes a common sensibility."[85]

Gendered antifascism blurs the separation of public/private spheres, but moreover it rebuilds the world through an analysis of, and challenge to, patriarchy's pervasiveness. Gago and Aguilar tie together antimisogyny and antinecrotics at the everyday level when they speak of the feminist "struggles against all *machista* violence . . . which constitute a continuum of daily violence that, painfully, carry feminicide as its most drastic iteration. Which is to say, death."[86] In a word, social reproduction's antagonism challenges patriarchal topography on its terrain of eliminationism—*ubiquity*.

J.K. Gibson-Graham argues that the historical composition of feminism operated through "ubiquity rather than unity."[87] In other words, "emotionally and semiotically, not primarily organizationally."[88] Eschewing an external organizational mechanism (as in the traditional leftist party or union), feminist politics and imaginaries took hold via an "ontological substrate: a vast set of disarticulated 'places'—households, communities, ecosystems, workplaces, civic organizations, bodies, public arenas, urban spaces, diasporas, regions, government agencies, occupations–related analogically rather than organizationally and connected through webs of signification."[89] This ontological substrate is also the space of micro-antifascism.

Social reproduction in the antagonistic/compositional mode makes communication and media central.[90] Stories, performances, and gestures found in campaigns like #MeToo and *#cuéntalo*, for instance, mediated the sharing of experiences to make "a collective memory of patriarchal violence." Campaign slogans like "*Ni una menos*" [Not one less (woman)] and "*Vivas nos queremos*" [We want ourselves alive] connect past to present to preempt a palingenetic elimination and to make a living future. These are inheritances of resistance through stories and gestures, the infinite micrological maneuvers that have refused patriarchal ordering, autogenetic sovereign violence, and necrophilic control.

Social reproduction entails a type of *self-defense* and self-possession; not of sovereign individuals but "bodies and territories, or body-territories, as spaces that generate life, memory, relations, and the struggle for their self-determination."[91] These are ultimately combinatory and coordinated struggles "in defense of life." Life here is more than *bios*, a definition that allows us to temper any tendency to reduce women to the maternal or bio-reproductive type. A micro-antifascism involves "defending forms of life, as concrete collective assemblages, that demand the means to (re) produce themselves."[92]

Xenofeminism gives us vital tools here, as they call for a notion of life as technologically and socially produced. Rather than appeal to a flat plane of pure materiality, the xenofeminist intervention asks what "DIY technologies of seventies self-help have to teach us about bodily autonomy and reproductive sovereignty?"[93] Bodies are not homogenous nor are they feminist because of a special relationship to biological reproduction. Any social reproduction must recognize that "bodies have different susceptibilities and capacities" while affirming the malleability of those features. In accordance with this, nature is not to be approached as "an essentializing underpinning for embodiment or ecology, but as a technologized space of conflict that fundamentally shapes lived experiences."[94]

Such forms of life, unlike the abstract forms of the autogenetic sovereign, are rooted in desire as capacity, or what Gago calls *feminist potencia*: This refers to how bodies range in their capacities, as individual and collective. The body is not a flat universal, "it is reinvented by women's struggles, feminist struggles, and the struggles of sexual dissidences that time and time again *update* that notion of potencia."[95]

Social reproduction has persisted in warding off fascism for centuries, not just by life defined as survival (against death) but as quality and life worth living (potencia). Now social reproduction refers to the expansion of desire-capacity that has been patriarchally organized and subordinated. Renewing everyday life as feminist potencia regenerates the conditions in which a micro-antifascist social movement arises.

The coronavirus pandemic event erupting in 2020 put social reproduction in relief. Patriarchal capitalist recomposition venerated the "care worker" while simultaneously wearing them out. Meanwhile, grassroots mutual aid efforts made social reproduction central to community survival. Pandemic solidarity was both an emergency measure and a foundation for care networks as neoliberalism continued to ravage formal institutions.[96] Social reproduction in the COVID-19 era means more than surviving the devastating effects of a virus: it "is committed not only to overcoming the death cult of capitalism, but to a socialist horizon of life-making . . . beyond our need to merely live through this pandemic or another day of drudgery."[97] Crisis ripens the conditions for both microfascism to reappear as well as anti-microfascism to compose its collective and reproducible body. Any post-traumatic symptoms of microfascism will need healing, a *therapeutic and aesthetic action*.[98] Social reproduction as care recomposes or repairs the invaded and decomposed body.

Social reproduction is a remedy reality, forged as militant care. To their microfascist restorations it offers another "return:" micro-antifascist reparations. Thus, in addition to *fighting* fascism (whose exclusivity could end up being yet another "brother war"), micro-antifascism makes a revivified world through the chain: repair-reparations-reproduction.

Any antifascism needs to both acknowledge and surpass the logistics of the streets and the war band insurrection for its compositional basis. In addition to any grammar of gestures that memetically spreads in the heat of the moment, a compositional movement needs social reproduction that forms the body capable of antifascism. Logistics need *cunningcraft*.

Magic, the witch, and cunningcraft

Cunningcraft is a version of Fortunati's metis in the movement of the concrete. It can be traced to a figure reappearing in this book—the witch. Under the sign of the witch, we have seen the interventions of severe and prolonged violence, the massive decomposition of women's knowledges and skills, the expropriation of powers and wisdom, the destruction of bodies, the reduction of practices into trivialized spheres. This palingenetic eliminationism happens because the witch is "engaged in doing things that are challenging . . . they are presenting ideas and orders that threaten to open up the dominant logic, shift the terrain of what is regarded as mattering."[99] It should surprise no one that the witch has returned in many contexts, especially with the Christian Church's recurring foundational action of detecting witches. In other words, *The Witches Are Coming*—as Lindy West's book announces—and these are figures who aren't always designated as such.

If we return to the trivialized world of popular culture, we see that the popularity of witches has grown. From television series to coven squads to street protests, recent revivals of magic occult actions proliferate, such as the Witch bloc, the Witches of Bushwick, and the frequent networked hexing of Donald Trump while he was US president. In response to being accused of witchery, Michigan Governor Gretchen Whitmer tweeted a picture of herself with West's book. Black girl magic has come to the foreground in digital compositional spheres, a force to counter misogynoir and to shape practices of self-definition.[100] "We are the granddaughters of the witches you could not burn," is plastered in chants and on signs, reviving "herbalists, midwives, doctors, and healers who had their knowledges and their lives expropriated."[101]

Witches activate the ambivalence in autogenetic sovereignty by recirculating what was excluded. Like the autogenetic sovereign, witches also flee, but differently. Imani Perry speaks of how Alice Walker's "witches, Saints, and grandmothers were unbound from their vestibularity. They could see beyond it, fly above it, and scatter themselves."[102] Their transcendence involves herb-induced rites and night-flight reveries to otherworlds. These flights constitute a different departure and return. Via the broomstick and flying ointment they leave their confines as resistance to housewifization in order to survive, reconnect with support networks, and compose their collective powers.

The witch's history is a history of *cunningcraft*. Cunningcraft here refers to folk knowledges, skills, and powers (from the German *kraft*) that comprise the magical practices of healing and survival tactics. It is this cunningcraft that Maria Mies notes was the target of dispossession in the witch hunts and that becomes anathema in contemporary Ecclesiastical counterfeminisms.[103] Coded as feminine, cunningcraft respects the immanence of life's processes and harnesses them through circulation. It does not practice out of fear and it does not flee due to potential dissolution of a self's boundaries.

In the late 1960s in the US and elsewhere, cunningcraft was central to the composition of feminist intellectuality via peer transmission of analysis and know-how. Collective cunningcraft generated theoretical and practical tools to understand gender and power (patriarchy, but also intersections with racism, imperialism, capitalism, heteronormativity). It gave names to experiences like domestic violence, battery of wives, and sexual harassment. We saw the multiplication of feminist educational institutions (workshops, study groups, conferences), collaborative writing and publishing projects (journals, course packets, books), media production, biopolitical information transmission, and underground support networks.[104]

This metis, the movement of the concrete in cunningcraft form, is one basis for the permanence of collective feminist potencia materialized. While microfascist machines appear and reappear, their devastation is historical, provisional, and unsustainable. The ongoing production of the witch-subject attests to this ancient and modern resistance.

For instance, Heather Booth (founder of the Jane Collective, a major feminist health support network) helped form W.I.T.C.H., most often an acronym for "Women's International Terrorist Conspiracy from Hell." Launched on Halloween 1968 as a creative militant offshoot of the Chicago Women's Liberation movement, W.I.T.C.H. was a media and street performance collective, intervening into protests with their own brand of power and playfulness drawn from the history and stereotype of women's magic.

W.I.T.C.H. groups sprang up throughout the United States. University of California-Berkeley teachers formed Red W.I.T.C.H., a socialist spin-off. W.I.T.C.H. operated on the coven model long associated with witches: loosely connected autonomous collectives who passed along knowledge and skills through networked transmission. The acronym was able to be repurposed for the specific coven or action: some called it "Women Inspired to Tell their Collective History" while others saw in it a specific seasonal meaning:

"Women Interested in Toppling Consumer Holidays." As Jo Freeman later put it, W.I.T.C.H. was more of an "idea-in-action than an organization" or what we might call a cunningcraft-based composition.[105] These forms of analogical connection (brigades, patchworks, covens), along with the information transmission and media production, form one legacy of 1968's feminist intellectuality. The W.I.T.C.H. coven model from the late 1960s is now digitally networked, complete with celebrity figures (e.g., Lana Del Rey), popular culture expressions, and technologized covens. A continuity of survival through contestation of the legacy of witch hunts, always composing, always refining.

A paradigm of cunningcraft that is not solely tied to witchery is the trivialized sphere of crafting and craft culture or what I have called *fabriculture*.[106] Revitalized crafting burst onto the cultural scene in the early twenty-first century. It included the 'domestic arts': knitting, crocheting, scrapbooking, quilting, embroidery, sewing, doll-making. Its popularity inhabited the spheres of marketplace commodification (e.g., Martha Stewart, the DIY cable channel), peer-to-peer exchanges (Etsy, Knitty, Craftster), documentaries (*Woman's Work*), and anticapitalist and anti-authoritarian craftivist projects (Cast Off, Craftivism, Anarchist Knitting Circle, MicroRevolt, Anarchist Knitting Mob, Revolutionary Knitting Circle). This revival is a form of feminist technoculture, as it can be found in a variety of online and offline spaces, from microblogs to back rooms of independent shops, from street protests to interventions into digital circuitry.

Craftwork withstood patriarchal capitalism's founding violence, one that eventually subsumed some of craft into the factory while marginalizing others into domestic affinity circles. Fabriculture is a form of resurgence, or a reversion, of something that went dormant or took on other forms under capitalism. But this is no romanticized return to the folk. Craftwork's resurgence is of something already present but scattered, having been relegated to the cracks and margins. It's a matter of piecing it back together and quilting it compositionally.

Tied to social reproduction as the movement of the concrete through history, cunningcraft indexes the longue durée of accumulation and self-valorization that accompanies and wards off microfascism's ubiquitous subjective project. The persistence of cunningcraft has posed an interruption and a threat to autogenetic sovereignty by steadfastly developing mimesis in its ordinary world-making.

The persistence of craft before, through, and despite capitalism tells us that cunningcraft as power, capacity, and social value is never eliminated or fully captured. This realm of a material mimesis preserves knowledge, transmits skills and wisdom, develops affinity circles, and extends craft into new spheres. Amidst capitalism's ruins, this recomposition sees a return of those technics and knowledges that demonstrate an exemplary collective continuity central to any antifascist composed body. Micro-antifascism poses a different type of renewal: to the restoration of mythic violence and patriarchal sovereignty these reversions and revisions multiply to repair and recompose.

Turning to the witch needs to avoid romanticization of folkloric women while still tracing the ever-present resistance to microfascism's intersection of gender, war, and death in the autogenetic sovereign. In a similar vein as histories of antifascism document actions and actors to create a continuity and reactivate archived collective memories, so this invocation of witchery and cunningcraft works to remember without romanticization.

Some closing considerations: On the one hand the return of the witches has a *spiritual* component, as witches were communicating with "supernatural beings, occult forces with a marked talent for ending the patriarchal world."[107] But even this is not some abstraction (as in the Divine Creator or head of an order). Jane Caputi, working on the history of myth in the age of gynecide, notes that feminist mythmaking is a worldview that "imagines and passionately invokes the nonviolent end of the world, the demise of patriarchal cosmogony, and an ongoing encounter with the Powers of Chaos."[108] Gago updates this tradition, saying feminism:

> is a political spirituality precisely because it does not separate the body from the spirit, nor flesh from fantasies, nor skin from ideas. There is a mystical dimension to feminism (as a multifaceted movement). It works from affects and passions. It opens that thorny field of desire, of relationships of love, of erotic swarms, of ritual and celebration, of longings beyond their sanctioned borders.[109]

As a guardrail of a moralizing romantic stance, Gago invokes this spiritual dimension "without requiring that we be turned into pure, heroic, or even good subjects."[110] From another angle, xenofeminism tempers the romanticism of folk spirituality by combining the long history of women's cunningcraft with the most advanced technical developments, specifically around reproductive technologies. They point to "cyborg witches" like the GynePunk collectives to upgrade "a figure seen by second-wave feminists as an exemplar of repressed knowledges and appropriated expertise."[111] These are hybrid updates of the "long 1968" of technological witchery that itself was a revival of longer standing women's magic.

As Imani Perry puts it, witches signify "something beyond the dominant structure and order—something vital, something intellectual and sensual at once; something emotional and affective."[112] This is not to say abstraction, language, and guidance aren't involved in cunningcraft. But its material abstractions are guided by social reproduction rather than the replication of autogenetic self-preservation. Any abstraction is tied to "[c]reative living work that is communal and soulful at the same time" and whose objective "restores the fullness of the senses and sensibilities."[113] Material abstractions of cunningcraft are predicated not on a "consciousness" that needs continual separation, but on commoning, circulating, and composing.

In a particularly acute gesture, this hybridization of body and technology alters the ideas of *sovereignty*. Women's bodies "were historically declared non-sovereign, sentenced as incapable of deciding for themselves—that is, designated as bodies under guardianship or tutelage."[114] The goal of such witchery, as Hester puts it, is "emancipatory, self-directed bodily transformation."[115] In other words, cunningcraft does not belong to a gender, it *applies to* gender in the form of play, proliferation, multiplicity, and fluidity. In sum, we see in the witch a recomposition of sovereignty, packs, flight, renewal: all those components of microfascism traced in this book find their feminine and feminist doublings. But these are not reactions or imitations—they are the primary sources of mimesis that were then simulated by autogenetic sovereignty and are now being revived.

The witch operates in the realm of material mimesis that masculine mimesis (what Adorno and others call magic) tried to simulate and thereby eliminate. Masculine mimesis is based on a microfascist social investment of desire, namely "a fear of what witches knew about different possibilities of social ordering, specifically ones in which the feminine would not necessarily be subject to patriarchal authority."[116] No wonder witches are so viciously targeted—they expose the fragility of those microfascist simulations and autogenetic sovereign orders.

The return of the witch today is the return of this cunningcraft, the metis composing a movement of the concrete, a realm where composition can ward off masculine magics, whether in form of science or religion or the state. Witches combine powers to ward off both the state and the nascent state (aka war bands). As a mode of coping or what Gago calls "neoliberalism from below," cunningcraft machines spin pragmatic and strategic yarns. They are making do via making worlds. Or at another level, a "doing-make" through the densification of solidarity under cover of coping and shelter. In their refusal and reproduction, witches, named and unnamed, make worlds and antifascist forms of life.

From cancel culture to abolition: what is to be (un)done?

Laying out micro-antifascism as a series of doubles, shadows, and pharmakons puts us in stark view of the situation faced today: we are in a moment marked by simultaneous and opposed *abolition-machines.*

On one side, the microfascist line of flight and freedom which turns into a line of abolition, as elaborated in Chapter 4. Microfascism's abolition operates primarily as a renewal of eliminations, or abolition as mythical foundational violence. When they defend the institutions that arise from this eliminationist violence, microfascists reanimate these origins (enslavement, feminicide, subjugation, reductions, social death).

On the other, an antifascist abolition, one aimed at dismantling the clustering of gender, war, and death at the subjective core of autogenetic sovereignty. Platforming and defending antifascist forms of life cultivates some productions of subjectivity, while abolishing others. Building the antifascist body is a daily matter that wards off—to the extent that it can— autogenetic sovereign invasions. Micro-antifascism displaces autogenetic sovereignty with the *social* and palingenesis with *reproduction.*

Anti-microfascism echoes how Natasha Lennard sees antifascism as "one aspect of a broader abolitionist project, which would see all racist policing, prisons and oppressive hierarchies abolished."[117] Adrian Wohlleben calls it *demolitionism*, which resonates with decomposing autogenetic sovereignty when it seeks "to make it logistically and socially impossible for the police and courts *to assert their claim to rule*; in short, to render the situation ungovernable."[118] Prison and police abolition movements seek to dismantle the repressive state apparatus around race- and class-based hierarchies, and we can enrich that with decompositional abolition of gender hierarchies and patriarchal pacted orders.

When it comes to the abolition of autogenetic sovereignty, what Marcello Tarì calls a "destituent strike" would impel "one's own self to dissolve the ego along with the enemy reality during the process of a revolutionary becoming. This self-destitution of the militant simultaneously consists of allowing for the deposition of one's own social identity."[119] When destitution is a project of feminist struggle it takes on the most intimate relations, including the call for the abolition of the nuclear family.[120] Decomposition, destitution, and demolition: these apply to systems and, when starting with a focus on microfascism, they work to make and break relationships, forms of life, and solidarities.

Feminist anti-microfascist decomposition and destitution includes a version of gender abolition, not in the sense of destroying sociogenic efforts to narrate the self around gender, but as constructing a future where gender is not the foundation for power relations. Xenofeminism offers one example of being gender abolitionist, refusing "any social order anchored in identities as a basis of oppression, and in the sense that we embrace sexuate diversity beyond any binary."[121] This abolition through *proliferation* recognizes "innumerable genders [as] a first step in the refusal to accept any gender as a basis of stable signification."[122] Alongside preventive decomposition, then, antifascist insurgencies also invent forms of life.

Micro-antifascist abolitionist machines are thus not simply negationists. As Shane Burley puts it, the "center of antifascism has always been resilient communities, those that are resistant to fascist incursion because of the strength of multiculturalism and their sturdy social networks. Victory requires mutual dependence and a collective vision of the future grounded by unity."[123] This unity finds itself in compositional mimesis rather than abstraction, one that also multiplies its mutations.

Abolition, in addition to decomposing sovereign power to prevent a gender oppressive society, thus multiplies and invents. It cultivates the feminist potencia "to vindicate the indeterminacy of what one can do, of what we can do" to develop "a malleable ontology of life."[124] Micro-antifascism imagines and implements ways of being that hinder and displace the necrotic fantasies. The social desire of fear is countered through sensibilities rooted in mimesis, care, and militant mutability.

Living an antifascist life is an ongoing project. Natasha Lennard prompts us to rethink its status as a noun or adjective; instead, we should consider "anti-fascist as a gerund verb: a constant effort of anti-fascisting against the fascisms that even we ourselves uphold."[125] Microfascism confronts us as proximate yet hostile. The autogenetic sovereign lurks with Ur-Fascism and needs vigilance. We've had socialist and anarchist alternatives that kept the patriarchal pacts in its arsenal. We cannot simply be antifascist; we must also practice and make anti-microfascist habits, generate forms of life that depose "fascizing microcrystallizations."[126]

Abolishing a carceral system or capitalism in other words is not enough to root out microfascism. Abolition of microfascist subjectivity involves a dismantling of the tendencies towards autogenesis. When micro-antifascist abolition forms a machine, it does not just target this institution or that "system" but the very foundations of social ordering, of the mythic violence that establishes the state, of autogenetic sovereignty at the heart of modern Western subjectivity.

The goal: to abolish sovereignty before sovereign abolition takes necropolitics to its extreme conclusion—a global downsurgency. This is a micro-antifascism that intervenes into subjectivity not as a psychological condition or carceral feature of psy-complexes and criminal behavior, but as sociogenetic production of self/other.

Micro-antifascist abolition wards off those subjective elements (blockages, hierarchies, flights, abstractions, lines, violence) that result from fear-based social desires, the foundational *abstract* fear of "losing" oneself (autonomy, capacity, consciousness).[127] As a social production of desire, micro-antifascist subjectivity displaces the fear of excess mimesis that results in a sealed fortress that is self-networked into black holes. Micro-antifascist machines seek to abolish both the state and its war band patriarchal pacts, abolish flight as autogenetic sovereignty, and the resulting subject based on despotic differentiation.

Abolitionist violence tied to micro-antifascism destitutes hostile orders, invaders, and overcoders. It disposes with the ongoing emergence of Männerbund. Micro-antifascism can break the cycle of palingenetic eliminationism, the return of microfascism's production of autogenetic sovereign subject. While destituent power as a concept often refers to a reclaimed transcendence—as with Walter Benjamin's divine-violence—we could also speak of the magical kind, the one that encourages mimetic cunningcraft and mutational multiplicity as a mode of community defense.

Micro-antifascist abolition defends the preservation of life in hostility to the preservation of lethal abstractions characterizing and patriarchal reality-ordering. This antifascism fashions a collective subject who sorts out *what to abolish* and *what to preserve*, a bifurcation departing from the necropolitical sovereign who determines *what is to die* and *what is to live*.

Two abolitionist projects, then: those that hasten the dismantling of autogenetic sovereignty-based institutions versus those that defend them. Abolition that is life-affirming (even in their calls: #BlackLivesMatter, We Love Ourselves Alive) versus abolition that generates fear-based nihilism, homi-suicidal elements, and necrophilic wars. One makes lifeworlds and the other generates life-destroying reality. These abolitions are competing and antagonistic restorations. While microfascists dream of a restorationist violence in the war on women, the micro-antifascist reversion invokes restorative justice. Reparations and recuperations destitute autogenetic sovereignty's violences. Micro-antifascism is never finished; it's an ongoing process of rooting out poisons—not in the name of purity but as preservation of openness to mutability and experimentation.

This metamorphosis machine kills microfascists

Microfascism's palingenesis is fragile, crumbling, inoperable. There are historical moments when microfascism and autogenetic sovereignty are in crisis (in other words, unable to restore easily). The interregnum names such a moment as a passage, in this case, a moment when fascism appears on the scene to save an order in decline. Microfascism's abstractions have been challenged by movements and insurgencies, becoming increasingly fragile and exposed as having been "bound up with the cunning and wickedness of those who have won a temporary victory."[128] The looming future entails a downsurgency: the decreasing capacity to effectively make worlds and shape reality according to a set of governing abstractions. Micro-antifascism is thus an *uprising that meets a downsinking.*

What to do in this downsinking? First, defend the experiments in micro-antifascism from morbid phenomena that seek to usurp subjectivation, simulate mimesis, and direct the abolition to guide the interregnum to full-blown fascism. No-platforming forms a popular security against their downsurgent vortex.

Micro-antifascism means reviving metamorphosis machines rooted in mimesis and materiality without being taken by the Männerbund, while still defending life. Collective continuance in the social body wards off individualism as a dangerous black hole.[129] A different genre of the human can be invented while another story about palingenesis and the end of the world can be told. At times this mimetic multitude means multiplatform mutations, care-based commingling, and support networks among the ruins: "there are other ways of living in this world, even of dying."[130] Against the fascist lines of abolition, we revive a destituent and compositional power; an ontological unraveling or, rather, *another raveling*.

We will never stop fascism unless we dismantle patriarchy's penchant for gendered violence and eliminationism. Stop the witch hunts in myth and seemingly trivial media culture.[131] Don't be enamored with your war band but find a squad. Abolish the abstractions. Shatter the divine fantasies. Interrupt the initiations. Defend and cultivate vulnerability as the way of potencia. Feminist destitution is certainly necessary and it might be sufficient. We will never know until we do so.

Over time, thanks to immense composition in the margins and the trivial, another interregnum passage forms. It bifurcates through other *autos*, *geneses*, relations to past, and making of futures. All that is life-affirming can wage war against the death-machines that would lay waste to reality as their final act of sovereign shaping. Together, this multitude, also archaic and contemporary, makes a world rooted in vigilance against the return of microfascism; an embodied sensibility that could be worthy of the term micro-antifascism.

Notes

Introduction: Why the Micro Matters for Fascist Culture

1. Elisha Fieldstadt, "James Alex Fields, driver in deadly car attack at Charlottesville rally, sentenced to life in prison," NBC News, June 28, 2019, https://www.nbcnews.com/news/us-news/james-alex-fields-driver-deadly-car-attack-charlottesville-rally-sentenced-n1024436.
2. Andreas Huyssen, "Behemoth Rises Again," *n+1*, July 29, 2019, https://nplusonemag.com/online-only/online-only/behemoth-rises-again.
3. Alberto Toscano, "The Long Shadow of Racial Fascism," *Boston Review*, October 28, 2020, https://bostonreview.net/race-politics/alberto-toscano-long-shadow-racial-fascism.
4. Pierre-André Taguieff, "Discussion or Inquisition: The Case of Alain de Benoist," *Telos*, 98–99 (1993/1994): 54. [Quoted in Roger Griffin, "Fascism's New Faces (and New Facelessness) in the 'Post-Fascist' Epoch," in *A Fascist Century: Essays by Roger Griffin*, ed. Matthew Feldman (Basingstoke and New York: Palgrave Macmillan, 2008), 190.
5. Shane Burley, *Fascism Today: What It Is and How to End It* (Oakland: AK Press, 2017); Alexander Reid Ross, *Against the Fascist Creep* (Chico, Oakland, Edinburgh, Baltimore: AK Press, 2017); Mark Bray, *Antifa: The Anti-Fascist Handbook* (Brooklyn and London: Melville House, 2017); Spencer Sunshine, "Three Pillars of the Alt-Right: White Nationalism, Antisemitism, and Misogyny," *Political Research Associates*, December 4, 2017, https://www.politicalresearch.org/2017/12/04/three-pillars-of-the-alt-right-white-nationalism-antisemitism-and-misogyny; Matthew N . Lyons, "CTRL-ALT-DELETE: The origins and ideology of the Alternative Right," *Political Research Associates*, January 20, 2017, https://www.politicalresearch.org/2017/01/20/ctrl-alt-delete-report-on-the-alternative-right.
6. Robert O. Paxton, *The Anatomy of Fascism* (New York: Vintage Books, 2007).
7. Angela Nagle, *Kill All Normies: Online Culture Wars from 4chan and Tumblr to Trump and the Alt-Right* (Winchester, UK and Washington: Zer0 Books, 2017); Dale Beran, "The Boogaloo Tipping Point: What Happens When a Meme Becomes a Terrorist Movement?" *The Atlantic*, July 13, 2020, https://www.theatlantic.com/technology/archive/2020/07/american-boogaloo-meme-or-terrorist-movement/613843.
8. Amanda Marcotte, *Troll Nation: How the American Right Devolved into a Clubhouse of Haters* (New York: Skyhorse Publishing, 2018); Sophie Lewis, *Full Surrogacy Now: Feminism Against Family* (London and New York: Verso, 2019); George Hawley, *Making Sense of the Alt-Right* (New York: Columbia University Press, 2017); David Neiwert, *Alt-America: The Rise of the Radical Right in the Age of Trump* (London and New York: Verso, 2017).
9. Burley, *Fascism Today*, 18.
10. In assessing the alt-right, cultural critic Andreas Huyssen sees its core "neither in the primacy of politics (as in Nazism), nor the primacy of economics (as in traditional Marxism) . . . but in *the primacy of culture*." [Huyssen, "Behemoth Rises Again."]
11. Lutz Koepnick, *Walter Benjamin and the Aesthetics of Power* (Lincoln: University of Nebraska Press, 1999).
12. Koepnick, *Walter Benjamin and the Aesthetics of Power.*
13. Enzo Traverso, *The New Faces of Fascism: Populism and the Far Right* (London and New York: Verso, 2019).
14. Simonetta Falasca-Zamponi, *Fascist Spectacle: The Aesthetics of Power in Mussolini's Italy* (Berkeley, Los Angeles, and Oxford, UK: University of California Press, 1997).
15. Zeev Sternhell, Mario Sznajder, and Maia Ashéri (eds.), *The Birth of Fascist*

Ideology: From Cultural Rebellion to Political Revolution, trans. David Maisel (Princeton: Princeton University Press, 1995), 29; James Hay, *Popular Film Culture in Fascist Italy: The Passing of the Rex* (Bloomington: Indiana University Press, 1987).

16. Sternhell, Sznajder, and Ashéri, *The Birth of Fascist Ideology*, 29.

17. Koepnick, *Walter Benjamin and the Aesthetics of Power*.

18. Christoffer Kølvraa and Bernhard Forchtner, "Cultural Imaginaries of the Extreme Right: An Introduction," *Patterns of Prejudice* 53, no. 3, June 4, 2019: 227–235.

19. Ross, *Against the Fascist Creep*, 168.

20. Griffin argues that "fascism is not to be defined primarily in terms of style (e.g., spectacular politics, uniformed paramilitary forces, the pervasive use of symbols such as the fasces and swastika), or organizational structure (e.g., charismatic leader, single party, the corporatization of economic or cultural production, mass youth, and leisure movements), but in terms of ideology." For him, ideology is an internally produced worldview, made up of "its proponents' own professed diagnosis of society's structural crisis and the remedies proposed to solve it." [Roger Griffin, *A Fascist Century*, 185.]

21. Griffin, *A Fascist Century*, 21.

22. Griffin, *A Fascist Century*, 9.

23. Griffin, *A Fascist Century*, 4.

24. Griffin, *A Fascist Century*, 185.

25. Griffin, *A Fascist Century*, 186.

26. This perspective is similar to Herbert Marcuse's insights into fascism, which have been taken up by Angela Davis and other race-based abolitionist projects. [In Toscano, "The Long Shadow of Racial Fascism."]

27. Peter Gelderloos, *Worshiping Power: An Anarchist View of Early State Formation* (Chico, Oakland, Edinburgh, Baltimore: AK Press, 2016); Guillaume Sibertin-Blanc, *State and Politics: Deleuze and Guattari on Marx*, trans. Ames Hodges (South Pasadena: Semiotext(e), 2016).

28. Julius Evola, *Men Among the Ruins: Postwar Reflections of a Radical Traditionalist*, trans. Guido Stucco (Rochester, VT: Inner Traditions, 2002).

29. David Neiwert, *Alt-America: The Rise of the Radical Right in the Age of Trump* (London and New York: Verso, 2017), 11.

30. Neiwert, *Alt-America*, 11.

31. Daniel Jonah Goldhagen, *Hitler's Willing Executioners: Ordinary Germans and the Holocaust* (New York: Vintage Books, 1997).

32. James Martel, "Histories of Violence: Why We Should All Read Walter Benjamin Today," interview by Brad Evans, *Los Angeles Review of Books*, February 3, 2020, https://lareviewofbooks.org/article/histories-of-violence-why-we-should-all-read-walter-benjamin.

33. Lauren Berlant, "Slow Death (Sovereignty, Obesity, Lateral Agency)," *Critical Inquiry*, Vol. 33, No. 4 (Summer 2007): 759.

34. Berlant, "Slow Death," 762..

35. Berlant, "Slow Death," 761 (footnote 20).

36. Jasbir K. Puar, *The Right to Maim: Debility, Capacity, Disability* (Durham and London: Duke University Press, 2017).

37. In this light, state *indifference* to Black life was as eliminationist as any direct violent action or ethnic hatred.

38. Achille Mbembé, "Necropolitics," trans. Libby Meintjes, *Public Culture*, Vol. 15, No. 1 (Winter 2003): 11–40.

39. Deleuze and Guattari, *A Thousand Plateaus*, 214.

40. Ross, *Against the Fascist Creep*.

41. Raymond Williams, *Marxism and Literature* (Oxford and New York: Oxford University Press, 1977).

42. Félix Guattari, "Everybody Wants to Be a Fascist," in *Chaosophy*, trans. David L. Sweet, Jarred Becker, and Taylor Adkins, (New York: Semiotext(e), 2009), 245.

43. Michael Foucault, "Preface," in Gilles Deleuze and Félix Guattari, *Anti-Oedipus: Capitalism and Schizophrenia*, trans. Robert Hurley, Mark Seem, and Helen R. Lane (Minneapolis: University of Minnesota Press, 1977), xi–xv.

44. Gary Genosko, "Black Holes of Politics: Resonances of Microfascism," *La Deleuziana* 5 (2017), 59.

45. Genosko, "Black Holes of Politics," 59.

46. Guattari, *Chaosophy*, 244.

47. Deleuze and Guattari, *A Thousand Plateaus*, 215.

48. Deleuze and Guattari, *A Thousand Plateaus*, 214.

49. Félix Guattari, "Socially Significant Drugs," in Anna Alexander and Mark S. Roberts (eds.), *High Culture: Reflections on Addiction and Modernity* (Albany: SUNY Press, 2003), 199–208; Gary Genosko, "Micro-Fascism in the Age of Trump," in *Spectres of Fascism: Historical, Theoretical and International Perspectives*, ed. Samir Gandesha (London: Pluto Press, 2020), 167.

50. Genosko, "Black Holes of Politics," 64.

51. Guattari, *Chaosophy*, 245.

52. Rosalind Gill, "Sexism Reloaded, or, It's Time to Get Angry Again!," *Feminist Media Studies* 11, no. 1 (2011): 66.

53. William E. Connolly, *Aspirational Fascism: The Struggle for Multifaceted Democracy under Trumpism* (Minneapolis: University of Minnesota Press, 2017), 46.

54. Michael Hardt and Antonio Negri, *Assembly* (New York: Oxford University Press, 2017), xiv.

55. Mark Coté, "What Is a Media Dispositif? Compositions with Bifo," *Journal of Communication Inquiry*, Vol. 35, No. 4 (2011): 378–386; Aurelia Armstrong, "Some Reflections on Deleuze's Spinoza: Composition and Agency," in *Deleuze and Philosophy: The Difference Engineer*, ed. Keith Ansell Pearson (London and New York: Routledge, 1997), 44–57; Franco "Bifo" Berardi, "Reassessing Recomposition: 40 Years after the Publication of Anti-Oedipus," *Subjectivity* 5, no. 1 (2012): 111–119; Nick Dyer-Witheford, *Cyber-Marx: Cycles and Circuits of Struggle in High-Technology Capitalism* (Urbana and Chicago: University of Illinois Press, 1999); Stevphen Shukaitis, *Imaginal Machines: Autonomy & Self-Organization in the Revolutions of Everyday Life* (London, New York, Port Watson: Minor Compositions, 2009); Steve Wright, *Storming Heaven: Class Composition and Struggle in Italian Autonomist Marxism* (London: Pluto Press, 2002).

56. Bratich, "The Digital Touch."

57. Cultural studies (especially the Gramscian-influenced strain embodied in Stuart Hall's work) is borne out of a strategy that in some ways mirrors—but predates—the alt-right's "metapolitical" strategy: the winning of hearts and minds in the battlefield called culture.

58. Falasca-Zamponi, *Fascist Spectacle.*

59. Susan Sontag, "Fascinating Fascism," *The New York Review of Books*, February 6, 1975. https://www.nybooks.com/articles/1975/02/06/fascinating-fascism/

60. Maik Fielitz and Holger Marcks, "Digital Fascism: Challenges for the Open Society in Times of Social Media," *UC Berkeley: Center for Right-Wing Studies*, July 16, 2019, https://escholarship.org/uc/item/87w5c5gp.

61. Fielitz and Marcks, "Digital Fascism," 2.

62. Natasha Lennard, *Being Numerous: Essays on Non-Fascist Life* (London and New York: Verso, 2021), 55.

63. Lennard, *Being Numerous*, 55.

64. Lennard, *Being Numerous*, 62.

65. Lennard, *Being Numerous*, 66.

66. Guattari, *Chaosophy*, 195.

67. Brad Evans and Julian Reid (eds.), *Deleuze & Fascism: Security: War: Aesthetics* (London and New York: Routledge, 2013), 1.

68. Andrew Johnson, "Ur-Fascism and Neo-Fascism," *The Journal of International Relations, Peace Studies, and Development*, Vol. 5, No. 1 (2019): 2.

69. Umberto Eco, "Ur-Fascism," *The New York Review of Books*, Vol. 42, No. 11 (1995): 12–15. https://www.nybooks.com/articles/1995/06/22/ur-fascism/.

70. Johnson, "Ur-Fascism and Neo-Fascism," 2.

71. Johnson, "Ur-Fascism and Neo-Fascism," 3.

72. Guattari, *Chaosophy*, 162.

73. Guattari, *Chaosophy*, 162.

74. Guattari, *Chaosophy*, 162.

75. Guattari, *Chaosophy*, 163

76. Martel, "Histories of Violence."

77. Michel Foucault, *"Society Must Be Defended": Lectures at the Collége de France, 1975–1976*, trans. David Macey (London: Picador, 2003), 55.

78. Martel, "Histories of Violence."

79. Martel, "Histories of Violence."

80. David Roediger, *The Wages of Whiteness: Race and the Making of the American Working Class* (London and New York: Verso Books, 1991).

81. Jessie Daniels, *Cyber Racism: White Supremacy Online and the New Attack on Civil Rights* (Lanham, Boulder, New York, Toronto, Plymouth, UK: Rowman & Littlefield Publishers, Inc., 2009), 7.

82. Daniels, *Cyber Racism*, 24.

83. Silvia Federici pinpoints this eruption: "By the sixteenth century, however, women's social position had begun to deteriorate, satire giving way to what without exaggeration can be described as a war on women, especially of the lower classes, reflected in the increasing number of attacks on women as 'scolds' and domineering wives and of witchcraft accusations." [Silvia Federici, *Witches, Witch-hunting, and Women* (Oakland: PM Press, 2018), 38.]

84. Verónica Gago, Marta Malo, and Liz Mason-Deese, "Introduction: The New Feminist Internationale," *South Atlantic Quarterly*, Vol. 119, No. 3 (2020): 620–628.

85. Gago, Malo, and Mason-Deese, "Introduction: The New Feminist Internationale," 627.

86. Lucía Cavallero and Verónica Gago, "Feminism, the Pandemic, and What Comes Next," trans. Liz Mason-Deese, *Critical Times: Interventions in Global Critical Theory*, April 12, 2020, https://ctjournal.org/2020/04/21/feminism-the-pandemic-and-what-comes-next/.

87. The necropolitical solution to the crisis of neoliberalism has only become more exacerbated in the COVID-19 era, when there are "different forms of quarantine, differentiated by gender, class, and race." [Cavallero and Gago, "Feminism, the Pandemic, and What Comes Next."]

88. I have argued elsewhere that craft culture poses a stark challenge to analyses that subordinate gender to capitalism in any mechanical manner—even revising our notions of the cycle of struggle and temporality itself. [Jack Bratich, "The Digital Touch: Craft-Work as Immaterial Labour and Ontological Accumulation," *Ephemera: Theory & Politics in Organization*, Vol. 10, No. 3–4 (2010): 303–310.]

89. The excellent projects that analyze reactionary revivals as racist and colonialist projects most often prioritize state forms (e.g., carceral systems, including prisons and police) or, in the cultural realm, the organizing efforts of ethno- or white nationalists.

90. Antonio Gramsci, *Prison Notebooks*, Volume II, ed. and trans. Joseph A. Buttigieg (New York: Columbia University Press, 1996), 32–33.

1. These were generally titled "Bang X" (where X would be replaced by whatever nation the king annexed).

2. Donna Zuckerberg, *Not All Dead White Men: Classics and Misogyny in the Digital Age* (Cambridge, MA and London: Harvard University Press, 2018), 238.

3. Sarah Banet-Weiser, *Empowered: Popular Feminism and Popular Misogyny* (Durham: Duke University Press), 2018, 120.

4. Zuckerberg, *Not All Dead White Men*, 46.

5. Zuckerberg, *Not All Dead White Men*, 46–47.

6. Not even Western monarchical power was enough for this sovereign. In 2019, he converted to the Armenian Orthodox Church, where his gender politics could find expression in control over women's reproduction as well as desire. In May 2021, he found an even more appealing supernatural structure for his misogyny in the Russian Orthodox Church. Who needs the divine right of kings when you can become a divine channeler?

7. Banet-Weiser, *Empowered*, 126. See also Sarah Banet-Weiser, "'Ruined' Lives: Mediated White Male Victimhood," *European Journal of Cultural Studies* 24, no. 1 (February 2021): 60–80.

8. Gilles Deleuze, *Spinoza: Practical Philosophy* (San Francisco: City Lights, 1988), 25.

9. Judith Butler, "Contingent Foundations: Feminism and the Question of Postmodernism," in Judith Butler and Joan Scott (eds.), *Feminists Theorize the Political* (New York: Routledge, 1992), 9.

10. Susan Buck-Morss, "Aesthetics and Anaesthetics: Walter Benjamin's Artwork Essay Reconsidered," *October* 62 (Autumn 1992): 7–8.

11. Buck-Morss, "Aesthetics and Anaesthetics," 7 (footnote 19).

12. Buck-Morss, "Aesthetics and Anaesthetics," 7 (footnote 19).

13. Jack Holland, *A Brief History of Misogyny: The World's Oldest Prejudice* (London: Little, Brown & Company, 2006), 518.

14. Mircea Eliade's work on shamanism highlights (in an affirmative and ideological manner) some specific mimicking operations. Shamanic magic introduces the Divine into the mimetic faculty. In their rites of passage, men imitate Divine Creators (those who generated the cosmos), introducing birth into the universe at the moment the men are reborn as men. Shamanic magic thus mimics an abstraction. It bypasses women by replicating birth (the symbology of wombs, often doubling as tombs) as well as transforming material bodies (ritualistic substitution of organs with spiritual fluid). [Mircea Eliade, *Myths, Dreams and Mysteries*, trans. Philip Mairet (New York: Harper & Row, 1967).]

15. Judith Butler, *Bodies that Matter: On the Discursive Limits of Sex* (Oxford, UK and New York: Routledge, 2011), 16–17.

16. Holland, *A Brief History of Misogyny*, 518.

17. Holland, *A Brief History of Misogyny*, 172.

18. Holland, *A Brief History of Misogyny*, 506.

19. Butler, *Bodies that Matter*, 16–17; Judith Butler, "Contingent Foundations," 9.

20. Holland, *A Brief History of Misogyny*, 520.

21. This circuit is reminiscent of Julius Evola's schema for "Man," a differentiation from all that is coded as feminine in order to give birth to an order. This rite of passage becomes the mystical foundation for the state, not just the individual. The state then authorizes itself, through a repression of its dependency, to subjugate women. What Evola declares as traditional, absolute, and necessary reappears now with critique.

22. Guattari, *Chaosophy*, 154; 171.

23. John Protevi, "'A Problem of Pure Matter': Deleuze and Guattari's Treatment of Fascist Nihilism in *A Thousand Plateaus*," in Keith Ansell Pearson and Diane

Morgan (eds.), *Nihilism Now! Monsters of Energy* (Hampshire and London: Palgrave Macmillan 2000), 177.

24. For an overview of mimesis in social thought, see: Christian Borch (ed.), *Imitation, Contagion, Suggestion: On Mimesis and Society* (Oxon and New York: Routledge, 2019); Michael Taussig, *Mimesis and Alterity: A Particular History of the Sense*s (New York and London: Routledge, 1993).

25. Cited in Taussig, *Mimesis and Alterity*, 38.

26. Taussig, *Mimesis and Alterity*, 39.

27. It's important to note here that mimesis' realm of connection involves imitation with invention. Mimicry is not repetition of the same, but a transmission of transformations. Using language from later in the book, we could say mimesis is the realm where metamorphosis machines proliferate. The work of Gabriel Tarde is relevant here, see: Gabriel Tarde, *The Laws of Imitation*, trans. Elsie Clews Parsons (Gloucester, MA: Peter Smith, 1962; Anna Gibbs, "Panic! Affect Contagion, Mimesis and Suggestion in the Social Field," *Cultural Studies Review* 14, no. 2 (2008): 130–145.

28. Theodor Adorno and Max Horkheimer, *Dialectic of Enlightenment: Philosophical Fragments* (London: Verso, 1986[/1944]), 256. Quoted in Owen Hulatt, "Reason, Mimesis, and Self-Preservation in Adorno," *Journal of the History of Philosophy* 54, no. 1 (2016): 135–151, 138.

29. Adorno and Horkheimer, *Dialectic of Enlightenment,* 189. Quoted in Hulatt, "Reason, Mimesis, and Self-Preservation in Adorno," 140.

30. Hulatt, "Reason, Mimesis, and Self-Preservation," 141. See also Vicki Bell, "Mimesis as Cultural Survival: Judith Butler and Anti-Semitism," *Theory, Culture & Society* 16, no. 2 (1999): 133–161.

31. Ewa Plonowska Ziarek, "Mimesis in Black and White: Feminist Aesthetics, Negativity, and Semblance," in John J. Joughin and Simon Malpas (eds.), *The New Aestheticism* (Manchester and New York: Manchester University Press, 2003), 55.

32. Theweleit, *Male Fantasies, Volume 1*, xiv.

33. Mary Daly, *Gyn/Ecology: The Metaethics of Radical Feminism* (Boston: Beacon Press, 2016). 11.

34. Holland, *A Brief History of Misogyny*, 508.

35. Puar, *The Right to Maim*, 267; Berlant, "Slow Death."

36. Celia Amorós, "Thinking Patriarchy," in *Feminist Philosophy in Latin America and Spain*, ed. María Luisa Femenías and Amy A. Oliver (Amsterdam and New York: Editions Rodopi, 2007), 123.

37. Susan Bordo, *The Flight to Objectivity: Essays on Cartesianism and Culture* (Albany: State University of New York Press, 1987), 97.

38. Bordo, *The Flight to Objectivity*, 109.

39. Bordo, *The Flight to Objectivity*, 109.

40. Bordo, *The Flight to Objectivity*, 109. Bordo cites Merchant on Bacon's infamous words.

41. Bordo, *The Flight to Objectivity*, 109. Bordo cites Merchant again.

42. Bordo, *The Flight to Objectivity*, 109.

43. Bordo, *The Flight to Objectivity*, 128. Bordo cites Ehrenreich and English here.

44. Bordo, *The Flight to Objectivity*, 112. In a way that prefigures one feature of what we'll examine later as *social necrophilia* (technological substitution), Bordo cites Adrienne Rich on how the "hands of iron" of masculinized reproduction replace the "hands of flesh" of women (128).

45. Holland, *A Brief History of Misogyny*, 52.

46. Holland, *A Brief History of Misogyny*, 52.

47. Banet-Weiser, *Empowered*; Banet-Weiser, "'Ruined' Lives."

48. Theweleit, *Male Fantasies, Volume 1*, 221.

49. Buck-Morss, "Aesthetics and Anaesthetics," 6.

50. Theweleit, *Male Fantasies, Volume 1*, 216.

51. Buck-Morss, "Aesthetics and Anaesthetics," 9.

52. Eco, "Ur-Fascism."

53. Gillian Branstetter, "The Alt-Right Is A Doomsday Cult," *Medium*, February 10, 2017, https://gillbranstetter.medium.com/the-alt-right-is-a-doomsday-cult-b40edd66062a.

54. Julius Evola, *Ride the Tiger: A Survival Manual for the Aristocrats of the Soul*, trans. Joscelyn Godwin and Constance Fontana (Rochester, VT: Inner Traditions, 2018), 41.

55. Evola, *Ride the Tiger*, 41.

56. Man is not used in the ideological sense that stands in for *human*, but is unabashedly gendered by Evola.

57. Evola, *Ride the Tiger*, 42.

58. Evola, *Ride the Tiger*, 43.

59. Evola, *Ride the Tiger*, 176.

60. Evola, *Ride the Tiger*, 61.

61. Evola, *Ride the Tiger*, 65.

62. Evola, *Ride the Tiger*, 66.

63. Julius Evola, *Men Among the Ruins: Post-War Reflections of a Radical Traditionalist*, trans. Guido Stucco, (Rochester, VT: Inner Traditions, 2002), 109.

64. Evola, *Men Among the Ruins*, 109.

65. Evola, *Men Among the Ruins*, 140.

66. Evola, *Men Among the Ruins*, 109.

67. Evola, *Men Among the Ruins*, 110.

68. Evola, *Men Among the Ruins*, 110.

69. Evola, *Men Among the Ruins*, 110.

70. Evola, *Men Among the Ruins*, 118.

71. Evola, *Men Among the Ruins*, 258.

72. Evola, *Men Among the Ruins*, 124.

73. Evola, *Men Among the Ruins*, 139.

74. Evola, *Men Among the Ruins*, 132.

75. Evola, *Ride the Tiger*, 222.

76. Evola, *Men Among the Ruins*, 222.

77. Evola, *Men Among the Ruins*, 222.

78. Evola, *Men Among the Ruins*, 225.

79. Evola, *Men Among the Ruins*, 131.

80. Evola, *Men Among the Ruins*, 113.

81. Buck-Morss, "Aesthetics and Anaesthetics," 8.

82. Buck-Morss, "Aesthetics and Anaesthetics," 10.

83. Buck-Morss, "Aesthetics and Anaesthetics," 8.

84. Buck-Morss, "Aesthetics and Anaesthetics," 9.

85. Buck-Morss, "Aesthetics and Anaesthetics," 8.

86. Falasca-Zamponi, *Fascist Spectacle*, 12.

87. Buck-Morss, "Aesthetics and Anaesthetics," 18.

88. Franco Berardi has elaborated this numbed yet hyperactivated subject in a range of works, including one on mass shooters. See Franco Berardi, *Heroes: Mass Murder and Suicide* (London and New York: Verso Books, 2015).

89. Éric Alliez and Maurizio Lazzarato, *Wars and Capital*, trans. Ames Hodges (South Pasadena: Semiotext(e), 2018).

90. Lawrence Rainey, "Introduction: F. T. Marinetti and the Development of Futurism," in Lawrence Rainey, Christine Poggi, Laura Wittman (eds.), *Futurism: An Anthology* (New Haven and London: Yale University Press, 2009), 17.

91. Kellyanne Conway (@KellyannePolls), "Get used to it. @POTUS is a man of action and impact," Twitter, January 28, 2017, https://twitter.com/kellyannepolls/status/825358733945475073?lang=en.

92. Joshua Citarella, "Irony Politics & GEN Z" (2019), *New Models*, https://newmodels.io/proprietary/irony-politics-gen-z-2019-citarella.

93. Rebecca Solnit, "Not Caring is a Political Art Form: On Melania Trump and the Politics of Disconnection," *Literary Hub*, June 22, 2018, https://lithub.com/rebecca-solnit-not-caring-is-a-political-art-form/.

94. Rosalind Gill, *Gender and the Media* (Cambridge, UK and Malden, MA: Polity Press, 2007).

95. Susan J. Douglas, *Enlightened Sexism: The Seductive Message That Feminism's Work Is Done* (New York: Times Books/Henry Holt and Company, 2010).

96. Judith Williamson, "Sexism with an alibi," *The Guardian*, May 31, 2003, https://www.theguardian.com/media/2003/may/31/advertising.comment.

97. Alissa Quart, "The Age of Hipster Sexism," *The Cut*, October 30, 2012, https://www.thecut.com/2012/10/age-of-hipster-sexism.html.

98. Karla Mantilla, *Gendertrolling: How Misogyny Went Viral* (Santa Barbara and Denver: Praeger, 2015), 157.

99. This manospheric Internet event challenges men to avoid giving attention and money to women without the return of sexual favors. This includes media consumption. [Miles Klee, "We Stand Against 'No Simp September'" (2020), *MEL Magazine*, https://melmagazine.com/en-us/story/no-simp-september.]

100. Miles Klee, "4chan's 'Doomer' Memes Are A Strange Frontier In Online Extremism" (2020), *MEL Magazine*, https://melmagazine.com/en-us/story/4chan-doomer-gloomer-memes-music-playlists.

101. Zack Beauchamp, "Our Incel Problem," *Vox*, April 23, 2019, vox.com/the-highlight/2019/4/16/18287446/incel-definition-reddit.

102. Guattari, "Socially Significant Drugs," 201.

103. Filippo Del Lucchese, "Democracy, Multitudo and the Third Kind of Knowledge in the Works of Spinoza," *European Journal of Political Theory* 8, no. 3 (2009): 350.

104. Guattari, *Chaosophy*, 171.

105. Genosko, "Black Holes of Politics," 62.

106. Genosko, "Black Holes of Politics," 65.

107. Genosko, "Black Holes of Politics," 65.

108. Berardi, *Heroes*.

109. Robert Evans, "Shitposting, Inspirational Terrorism, and the Christchurch Mosque Massacre," *Bellingcat,* March 15, 2019, https://www.bellingcat.com/news/rest-of-world/2019/03/15/shitposting-inspirational-terrorism-and-the-christchurch-mosque-massacre/.

110. Ryan Broderick, "Christchurch: This Will Keep Happening," *BuzzFeed News*, March 15, 2019, https://www.buzzfeednews.com/article/ryanhatesthis/murder-as-a-meme-white-male-violence-is-being-distributed.

111. William E. Connolly, *Aspirational Fascism: The Struggle for Multifaceted Democracy under Trumpism* (Minneapolis: University of Minnesota Press, 2017), 142.

112. Genosko, "Black Holes of Politics," 64.

113. Walter Benjamin, Illuminations: Essays and Reflections, trans. (New York: Schocken Books, 2007), 242.

114. Butler, "Contingent Foundations," 10.

115. Theweleit, *Male Fantasies, Volume 1*, 221.

2. Gender

1. Joe Hernandez, "A California Father Claims QAnon Conspiracy Led Him To Kill His 2 Children, FBI Says," *NPR.org*, August 13, 2021, https://www.npr.org/2021/08/13/1027133867/children-dead-father-claims-qanon-conspiracy-led-him-to-kill.

2. Hernandez, "A California Father Claims QAnon Conspiracy Led Him To Kill His 2 Children, FBI Says."

3. See https://iharare.com/man-shoots-wife-and-daughter1-after-she-won-2-million-in-lottery/IN.

4. While *femicide* and *feminicide* have been used interchangeably, I'm choosing the term *feminicide* because it speaks to more than the gendered demographic of the dead person—it refers to the killing of women *qua women*, in other words, "based on gendered power structures and the inequalities created by social, political, and cultural institutions." [Alice Driver, *More or Less Dead: Feminicide, Haunting, and the Ethics of Representation in Mexico* (Tucson: University of Arizona Press, 2015), 4.]

5. Julyssa Lopez, "Donald Trump's History of Calling Women 'Dogs' Just Got Longer With New Omarosa Tweet," *Glamour*, August 14, 2018, https://www.glamour.com/story/donald-trump-history-of-calling-women-dogs-omarosa.

6. Carol Gilligan and David A.J. Richards, *Darkness Now Visible: Patriarchy's Resurgence and Feminist Resistance* (Cambridge, UK and New York: Cambridge University Press, 2018), 13. Mary Daly calls it "her profoundly antipatriarchal book." *Mary Daly, The Mary Daly Reader*, 402.

7. Gilligan and Richards, *Darkness Now Visible*, 7

8. Gilligan and Richards, *Darkness Now Visible*, 7.

9. Gilligan and Richards, *Darkness Now Visible*, 14.

10. Daly, *Gyn/Ecology*, 717.

11. Theweleit, *Male Fantasies, Volume 2*, 271–280.

12. Theweleit, *Male Fantasies, Volume 2*, 380.

13. Theweleit, *Male Fantasies, Volume 2*, 162.

14. Theweleit, *Male Fantasies, Volume 1*, 227. See also, antifascist journalist and political analyst Jason Wilson's definition of fascism as "an exacerbation, a more militant extension, of the patriarchal relationships between men and women that have persisted for centuries. It is a worsening of the fantasies, the violence, the misshapen desires that the whole system of gender relationships that have long pertained in European societies and those in the new world that are descended from them. Rather than a thing, which is categorically distinct from other social and political systems, fascism is a process, which can easily recur, and wherein we can see men, and groups of men, who have commenced the journey." [Jason Wilson, "What do incels, fascists and terrorists have in common? Violent misogyny," *The Guardian*, May 4, 2018, https://www.theguardian.com/commentisfree/2018/may/04/what-do-incels-fascists-and-terrorists-have-in-common-violent-misogyny.]

15. White women were not simply idealized while nonwhites were rendered abject and nonhuman. German women, too, were considered an inherent threat that needed taming. Eliminationism takes aim at two different categories of women: the disposable Other and the indispensable internal threat. Both have relative speeds (of slow death) and degrees of visibility.

16. Jennifer Wright, "Why Donald Trump Keeps Calling Women 'Bloody,'" *Bazaar*, June 29, 2017, https://www.harpersbazaar.com/culture/features/a10241058/mika-brzezinski-donald-trump-tweet/.

17. Gilligan and Richards, *Darkness Now Visible*, 6..

18. Gilligan and Richards, *Darkness Now Visible*, 6; 34.

19. Federici, *Witches, Witch-hunting, and Women*, 46.

20. Federici, *Witches, Witch-hunting, and Women*, 28.

21. Alliez and Lazzarato, *Wars and Capital*; Federici, *Witches, Witch-hunting, and Women*, 27.

22. Gayle Rubin, "The Traffic in Women: Notes on the 'Political Economy' of Sex," in Rayna R. Reiter (ed.), *Toward an Anthropology of Women* (New York: Monthly Review Press, 1975), 157–210; 163.

23. Trudy, "Explanation of Misogynoir," *Gradient Lair*, April 28, 2014, https://www.gradientlair.com/post/84107309247/ define-misogynoir-anti-black-misogyny-moya-bailey-coined.

24. Moya Bailey and Trudy, "On Misogynoir: Citation, Erasure, and Plagiarism," *Feminist Media Studies* 18, no. 4 (2018): 762–768.

25. Trudy, "Explanation of Misogynoir."

26. Trudy, "Misogyny, In General vs. Anti-Black Misogyny (Misogynoir), Specifically," *Gradient Lair*, September 11, 2013, https://www.gradientlair.com/post/60973580823/ general-misogyny-versus-misogynoir.

27. Trudy, "Explanation of Misogynoir."

28. Trudy, "Misogyny, In General."

29. The work of the Institute of Research on Male Supremacy is empirically grounded, important, and transformative. The notion they prefer is "Male Supremacy," which tends to refer to a collection of attitudes, beliefs, and behaviors. Such a social-psychological approach has its interventionist merits. For example, a concept like patriarchy opens to ordering principles and histories that are more material and systematic.

30. Rubin, "The Traffic in Women," 176

31. Rubin, "The Traffic in Women," 177.

32. Rubin, "The Traffic in Women," 168. These men's associations rely on and produce a gendered topography: the rites of passage that involve removal of the boy from the home, separating through flight and isolation into the woods, the desert, or other extremes).

33. Amorós, "Thinking Patriarchy," 111.

34. Amorós, "Thinking Patriarchy," 111.

35. Amorós, "Thinking Patriarchy," 119.

36. Amorós, "Thinking Patriarchy," 120.

37. Amorós, "Thinking Patriarchy," 120.

38. Amorós, "Thinking Patriarchy," 120.

39. Amorós, "Thinking Patriarchy," 113. Italics added for emphasis.

40. Amorós, "Thinking Patriarchy," 120.

41. Amorós, "Thinking Patriarchy," 120.

42. Amorós, "Thinking Patriarchy," 123.

43. Amorós, "Thinking Patriarchy," 123.

44. Eliade and others note the physical removal of boys from their mother's care, which is then replicated in the ritual transformations as the world of nature is coded as chaos and as feminine. The mother becomes abstraction.

45. Amorós, "Thinking Patriarchy," 124–125.

46. Andrea Martinelli, "Witch Hunts Are Back—And This Time They're Targeting Female Activists," *HuffPost*, November 1, 2019, https://www.huffpost.com/ entry/witch-hunts-targeting-female-activists_n_5dbc776fe4b0fffdb0f681c8; Charlotte Müller and Sertan Sanderson, "Witch Hunts: A Global Problem in the 21st Century," *DW*, August 10, 2020, https://www.dw.com/en/ witch-hunts-a-global-problem-in-the-21st-century/a-54495289.

47. Martin Pengelly, "Whitmer Won't Go 'Punch for Punch' with Republican who Called Her a Witch," *The Guardian*, April 11, 2021, https://www.theguardian.com/ us-news/2021/apr/11/gretchen-whitmer-michigan-governor-witch-burn-stake.

48. Amorós, "Thinking Patriarchy," 116.

49. Carole Pateman, "Feminist Critiques of the Public/Private Dichotomy," in Stanley I. Benn and Gerald F. Gaus (eds.), *Public and Private in Social Life* (New York: St. Martin's Press, 1983), 281.

50. Maria Mies, *Patriarchy and Accumulation on a World Scale: Women in the International Division of Labour* (London: Zed Books, 2014).

51. Jacqueline Ryan Vickery and Tracy Everbach, "The Persistence of Misogyny: From the Streets, to Our Screens, to the White House," in *Mediating Misogyny: Gender, Technology, and Harassment* (Cham, Switzerland: Palgrave Macmillan, 2018), 13.

52. A few have tied misogyny directly to the alt-right and right-wing resurgence. I mention this not to say that work on gender should have connected to fascism, but rather the reverse. Whenever fascism studies mention the rise of misogyny it is again as a gateway.

53. Gill, *Gender and the Media*: sexism considered as a thoroughgoing ideology or discourse that is constitutive of common sense and of our most taken for granted ways of thinking, feeling, and being in the world.

54. Berlant, "Slow Death," 754.

55. Sarah Banet-Weiser, *Empowered*.

56. Kate Manne, *Down Girl: The Logic of Misogyny* (New York: Oxford University Press, 2017), 71.

57. Debbie Ging and Eugenia Siapera, "Introduction: Special issue on online misogyny," *Feminist Media Studies* 18, no. 4 (2018): 523.

58. Mary Maynard and Jalna Hanmer, "Introduction: Violence and Gender Stratification," in Jalna Hanmer and Mary Maynard (eds.), *Women, Violence and Social Control* (Houndmills, Basingstoke, Hampshire and London: Macmillan Press Ltd., 1987), 5.

59. Manne, *Down Girl*, 68.

60. Holland notes here: "There is only one prejudice that makes similar claims on a consistent basis over the centuries, and that is anti-Semitism." [Holland, *A Brief History of Misogyny*, 538.]

61. Mary Daly notes that this reduction is based on an ongoing and archaic annulment of the goddess Trivia: "The Goddess's name, Trivia, then, should function as a constant reminder of patriarchal religious reduction of real, multidimensional presence to the Nothingness which is created by the fathers in their own image and likeness. Whenever Hags hear the terms trivia, trivial, trivialize, these should function as reminders of the omnipresence of Reversal." [Daly, *Gyn/Ecology*, 259.]

62. Federici, *Witches, Witch-hunting, and Women*.

63. An intersectional approach places gender-based violence in a matrix of race, class, sexuality, ability, geography, age, and religion. See Bailey and Trudy, "On Misogynoir"; Lucy Hackworth, "Limitations of 'Just Gender,'" in *Mediating Misogyny: Gender, Technology, and Harassment*, 51–70.

64. Banet-Weiser, *Empowered*, 6.

65. Toscano, "The Long Shadow of Racial Fascism."

66. Federici, *Witches, Witch-hunting, and Women*, 46.

67. Verónica Gago, *Feminist International: How to Change Everything* (New York and London: Verso Books, 2020, 780.

68. Judith Butler, "Anti-gender Ideology and the New Fascism," paper presented at the New School for Social Research, New York City, February 21, 2019; Gago, *Feminist Strike*, 855.

69. Vickery and Everbach, "The Persistence of Misogyny,"18.

70. Banet-Weiser, *Empowered*.

71. On a material note, we could point to the research that shows how the frequency of catcalls and harassment against women increases in zones containing ads with women featured as fetishized desire-objects. Images here are an affordance and an invitation to act. The images create a scene, a microcosm of the world promised by patriarchy. Media can be a prompt, a license, and an entitlement trigger.

72. Gaye Tuchman, "The Symbolic Annihilation of Women by the Mass Media," in Stanley Cohen and Jock Young (eds.), *The Manufacture of News: Social Problems, Deviance and the Mass Media* (London: Constable, 1981).

73. Tuchman, "The Symbolic Annihilation of Women," 169.

74. Tuchman, "The Symbolic Annihilation of Women," 169–170.
75. See Ana Sofia Elias, Rosalind Gill, and Christina Scharff (eds.), *Aesthetic Labour: Rethinking Beauty Politics in Neoliberalism* (London: Palgrave Macmillan, 2017).
76. Banet-Weiser, *Empowered.*
77. Catherine Rottenberg, *The Rise of Neoliberal Feminism* (Oxford and New York: Oxford University Press, 2018.
78. Gill, *Gender and the Media.*
79. Banet-Weiser, *Empowered.*
80. Banet-Weiser, *Empowered.*
81. Jilly Boyce Kay, *Gender, Media and Voice: Communicative Injustice and Public Speech* (Cham, Switzerland: Palgrave Macmillan, 2020).
82. See: Emma Jane, *Misogyny Online: A Short (and Brutish) History* (Los Angeles, London, New Delhi, Singapore, Washington, DC, Melbourne: Sage Swifts, 2016); Alison Adam, "Cyberstalking and Internet Pornography: Gender and the Gaze," *Ethics and Information Technology* 4, no. 2, (2002): 133–142.
83. Ging and Siapera, "Introduction: Special issue on online misogyny," 516.
84. Ging and Siapera, "Introduction: Special issue on online misogyny," 521.
85. "AirDrop" is a proprietary iOS term for the ability to share—or in this case to push—images via Bluetooth networking directly from one device to another. The AirDrop vulnerability has been a default setting in iOS mobile devices, with many people being unaware that the technology exists. The sudden appearance of lewd and obscene images—accompanied by a notification that someone is sharing them with you—becomes an intimate violation.
86. Natalie Gil, "Women Who've Been Cyberflashed On Why Dick Pics Are No Laughing Matter, *Refinery 29*, February 8, 2019, https://www.refinery29.com/en-gb/2019/01/222278/cyberflashing-dick-pics.
87. Molly Dragiewicz, Jean Burgess, Ariadna Matamoros-Fernández, Michael Salter, Nicolas P. Suzor, Delanie Woodlock and Bridget Harris, "Technology Facilitated Coercive Control: Domestic Violence and the Competing Roles of Digital Media Platforms," *Feminist Media Studies* 18, no. 4 (2018): 609–625; See also Anita Sarkeesian, "Image Based Harassment and Visual Misogyny," *Feminist Frequency*, July 1 2012, https://feministfrequency.com/2012/07/01/image-based-harassment-and-visual-misogyny.
88. Soraya Chemaly and Debjani Roy, members of the Women's Media Center Speech Project, created "The Online Abuse Wheel," listing the following abusive actions: "gender-based slurs and harassment, nonconsensual photography (a.k.a. revenge porn), exploitation, doxxing . . . , defamation, death or rape threats, mob attacks, hate speech, stalking, unsolicited (often violent) pornography, online impersonation, spying and sexual surveillance, slut-shaming, swatting (filing false police reports in order to send unnecessary emergency services to someone's home or business), and grief trolling." [In Vickery and Everbach, "The Persistence of Misogyny," 12.]
89. Vickery and Everbach, "The Persistence of Misogyny," 15.
90. Ging and Siapera, "Introduction: Special issue on online misogyny," 516.
91. Heather Savigny, *Cultural Sexism: The Politics of Feminist Rage in the #MeToo Era* (Bristol: Bristol University Press, 2020).
92. Vickery and Everbach, "The Persistence of Misogyny," 14.
93. It is worth noting that both Jack Posobiec and Mike Cernovich, two prominent alt-right media personalities, got their start and their tactics from everyday online sexism.
94. Jacob Johannsen's forthcoming book applies Klaus Theweleit's insights to the manosphere: Jacob Johannsen, *Fantasy, Online Misogyny and the Manosphere: Male Bodies of Dis/Inhibition* (New York and London: Routledge, 2021).

95. Incels have gone even further back in history to claim killers as their own, including: Marc Lépine of the 1989 École Polytechnique massacre in Montreal; Charles Carl Roberts IV, who sorted girls from boys in an Amish schoolhouse in 2006 and shot eight of ten girls, killing five; Seung-Hui Cho, the Virginia Tech student who, after being rejected by his girlfriend, killed thirty-two fellow students.

96. Cited in Julie Bosman, Kate Taylor, and Tim Arango, "A Common Trait Among Mass Killers: Hatred Toward Women," *The New York Times*, August 10, 2019, https://www. nytimes.com/2019/08/10/us/mass-shootings-misogyny-dayton.html.

97. Mass shootings often have a gendered dimension to them. Among the dozens of mass shootings in the United States from 2009 to 2017, in addition to being almost exclusively carried out by men, the "one common thread that connects many of them— other than access to powerful firearms—is a history of hating women, assaulting wives, girlfriends and female family members, or sharing misogynistic views online." [Bosman, Taylor, and Arango, "A Common Trait among Mass Killers."]

98. That white nationalists have been involved in misogynistic violence is well documented.

99. Decentralized, the actions will inevitably recur, though the particular expressions are unpredictable. Rhetoric predictably leads to unpredictable moment of action.

100. Carol Gilligan and David A. J. Richards, *The Deepening Darkness: Patriarchy, Resistance, and Democracy's Future* (New York: Cambridge University Press, 2008), 212.

101. Laurie Penny, "Peterson's complaint," *Longreads*, July 12, 2018, https://longreads. com/2018/07/12/petersons-complaint/.

3. War

1. Ben Schreckinger, "World War Meme: How A Group of Anonymous Keyboard Commandos Conquered the Internet for Donald Trump—And Plans to Deliver Europe to the Far Right," *Politico*, March/April 2017, https://www.politico.com/ magazine/story/2017/03/memes-4chan-trump-supporters-trolls-internet-214856/.

2. Schreckinger, "World War Meme."

3. Schreckinger, "World War Meme."

4. Burley, *Fascism Today*, 72.

5. Louis Beam, "Leaderless Resistance," *Inter-Klan Newsletter*, 1983; republished in *The Seditionist* 12 (February 1992). For analysis, see: Matthew Lyons, *Insurgent Supremacists: The U.S. Far Right's Challenge to State and Empire* (Oakland: PM Press, 2018), 154–156.

6. Rebecca Lewis, 2018, "Alternative Influence Broadcasting the Reactionary Right on YouTube" (report), *Data & Society*, September 18, 2018, https://datasociety.net/library/ alternative-influence/.

7. Graeme Turner, Ordinary People and the Media: The Demotic Turn (London, Thousand Oaks, New Delhi, Singapore: Sage Publications, Ltd., 2010).

8. Susie Khamis, Lawrence Ang, and Raymond Welling, "Self-branding, 'micro-celebrity' and the rise of Social Media Influencers," *Celebrity Studies* 8, no. 1 (2017): 191–208.

9. Evans, "Shitposting, Inspirational Terrorism, and the Christchurch Mosque Massacre."

10. Kevin Roose, "A Mass Murder of, and for, the Internet," *The New York Times*, March 15, 2019, https://www.nytimes.com/2019/03/15/technology/facebook-youtube-christ-church-shooting.html.

11. Tom Cleary, "John Earnest: 5 Fast Facts You Need to Know," Heavy.com, Apr 29, 2019, https://heavy.com/news/2019/04/john-earnest/.

12. Guattari, *Chaosophy*, 245.

13. Griffin, "From Slime Mould to Rhizome," 30.

14. Griffin, "From Slime Mould to Rhizome," 28.

15. Griffin, "From Slime Mould to Rhizome," 28–29; 41.

16. Griffin, *A Fascist Century*, 199; Roger Griffin, "Interregnum or Endgame? The Radical Right in the 'Post-Fascist' Era," *Journal of Political Ideologies* 5, no. 2 (2000): 171.

17. The platforming of this groupuscule was announced as an act of refusal (against "cancel culture") and of freedom. Some key exceptions to this freedom included coercive opt-in features (users were automatically subscribed to preferred status influencers) and religious dogma (users were banned for "using the Lord's name in vain").

18. Andrew Torba, "The Silent Christian Secession," Gab.com, February 1, 2021, https://news.gab.com/2021/02/01/the-silent-christian-secession/.

19. Jane, *Misogyny Online*, 3.

20. Jack Luna, "The Only Possible Way to Understand White Trump Voters," *Medium*, September 9, 2020, https://everythinghereistrue.medium.com/the-only-way-to-understand-white-trump-voters-6122ed88f4d2.

21. Luna, "The Only Possible Way."

22. Joshua Partlow and Isaac Stanley-Becker, "As clashes between armed groups and leftist protesters turn deadly, police face complaints of tolerating vigilantes," *Washington Post*, August 30, 2020, https://www.washingtonpost.com/politics/as-clashes-between-armed-groups-and-leftist-protesters-turn-deadly-police-face-complaints-of-tolerating-vigilantes/2020/08/30/d2c36c20-e952-11ea-a414-8422fa3e4116_story.html.

23. Genosko, "Black Holes of Politics," 61.

24. Griffin doesn't cite Guattari directly on groupuscules (does so more on rhizomatic networks) though the term is found scattered in Guattari's writings. Guattari tends to use it as a synonym for "splinter groups" (associated with Trotskyism) or perhaps "cells." They don't seem to have the amorphous and distributed character that Griffin ascribes to them.

25. Marco Deseriis, *Improper Names: Collective Pseudonyms from the Luddites to Anonymous* (Minneapolis: University of Minnesota Press, 2015).

26. Griffin, *A Fascist Century*, 199.

27. Mimmo Franzinelli, "Squadrism," in *The Oxford Handbook of Fascism*, ed. R. J. B. Bosworth (Oxford: Oxford University Press, 2009), 91–108; Maddalena Gretel Cammelli, "Fascism as a Style of Life: Community Life and Violence in a Neofascist Movement in Italy," *Focaal—Journal of Global and Historical Anthropology* 79 (2017): 89–101.

28. Cammelli, "Fascism as a Style of Life," 96.

29. Matt Novak, "Why Are Trump Supporters Offering People 'Free Helicopter Rides' Online?" *Gizmodo*, October 12, 2018, https://gizmodo.com/why-are-trump-supporters-offering-people-free-helicopte-1829705238.

30. Griffin, "From Slime Mould to Rhizome," 31.

31. Fielitz and Marcks, "Digital Fascism."

32. Antoine Acker, "How Fascism Went Digital: A Historian's Perspective on Bolsonaro's Victory in Brazil," *Geschichte der Gegenwart* (2018), https://www.zora.uzh.ch/id/eprint/203848/1/Acker_How_Fascism_Went_Digital.pdf.

33. Griffin, "Interregnum or Endgame?," 171.

34. Franzinelli, "Squadrism," 91.

35. Mike Wendling, *Alt-Right: From 4chan to the White House* (London: Pluto Press, 2018), 76.

36. Robin Andersen, "That's Militainment! The Pentagon's Media-Friendly 'Reality' War," *Extra!*, May 1, 2003, https://fair.org/extra/thats-militainment/; Roger Stahl, *Militainment, Inc.: War, Media, and Popular Culture* (New York and Abingdon, Oxon: Routledge, 2010).

37. Alliez and Lazzarato, *Wars and Capital*.

38. Sahana Udupa, "Nationalism in the Digital Age: Fun as a Metapractice of Extreme Speech," *International Journal of Communication* 13 (2019): 3144.

39. Udupa, "Nationalism in the Digital Age," 3151.

40. Udupa, Nationalism in the Digital Age," 3151.

41. Wendling, *Alt-Right*, 76.

42. Neiwert, *Alt-America*, 494.

43. Neiwert, *Alt-America*, 493.

44. Luna, "The Only Possible Way."

45. Beam, "Leaderless Resistance."

46. Zuckerberg, *Not All Dead White Men*, 147.

47. Courtney Marie Burrell, "Otto Höfler's Männerbund Theory and Popular Representations of the North," *NORDEUROPAforum: Zeitschrift für Kulturstudien [Journal for the Study of Culture]*, December 30, 2020: 228–266.

48. Guattari, *Chaosophy*, 162.

49. Cristiano Grottanelli examines the connections between Evola and Eliade, along with Carl Schmitt and other leaders of the cultural front of fascism. Editor Horst calls this group of European thinkers "an intellectual circle or 'Männerbund' with a clear pro-fascist leaning." [Cristiano Grottanelli, "War-Time Connections: Dumézil and Eliade, Eliade and Schmitt, Schmitt and Evola, Drieu La Rochelle and Dumézil." In *The Study of Religion under the Impact of Fascism*, edited by Horst Junginger, 303–314. Leiden and Boston: Brill, 2007].

50. Mircea Eliade, *Rites and Symbols of Initiation: The Mysteries of Birth and Rebirth* (New York, Hagerstown, San Francisco, London: Harper & Row, 1958), x.

51. Amorós, "Thinking Patriarchy," 123.

52. Mircea Eliade, *Myths, Dreams and Mysteries: The Encounter Between Contemporary Faiths and Archaic Realities*, trans. Philip Mairet (New York: Harper & Row, 1967), 197.

53. Amorós, "Thinking Patriarchy," 123.

54. Amorós, "Thinking Patriarchy," 123.

55. Eliade, *Myths, Dreams and Mysteries*, 99–105, 197.

56. Eliade, *Myths, Dreams and Mysteries*, 198.

57. Eliade, *Rites and Symbols of Initiation*, xiii.

58. Eliade, *Myths, Dreams and Mysteries*, 198.

59. Eliade, *Rites and Symbols of Initiation*, xiv.

60. Eliade, *Myths, Dreams and Mysteries*, 196.

61. Eliade, *Myths, Dreams and Mysteries*, 198.

62. Eliade, *Myths, Dreams and Mysteries*, 198.

63. Eliade, *Rites and Symbols of Initiation*, xiii.

64. Amorós, "Thinking Patriarchy," 123.

65. Amorós, "Thinking Patriarchy," 123.

66. Harris notes that ritual rebirth, or birth without women, involved necrotic incantations and performances: "candidates for initiation and brothers often stand in a closer relation to death and the dead than do excluded males, children, and women; often they are the dead, ritually speaking." In a foreshadowing of the necropolitical dynamics between fascist leaders and followers, Harris sees this death-proximity in the militarized form of "self-sacrifice" found in images of soldiers piling on the "fallen body of their leader who, however, escapes alive from the heap of corpses." [Joseph Harris, "Love and Death in the Männerbund: An Essay with Special Reference to the Bjarkamál and the Battle of Maldon," in Joseph Harris, *"Speak Useful Words or Say Nothing": Old Norse Studies*, ed. Susan E. Deskis and Thomas D. Hill (Ithaca: Cornell University Library, 2008).]

67. In a telling passage, Eliade, after contorting his analysis to avoid speaking of gendered power differences in the formation of men's societies, posits that women had their own secret societies (which are basically just domestic circles of training in crafts). And, in a flattening gesture indicative of his patriarchal sovereign loyalties, Eliade speaks of "a lasting tension, and even a conflict, between the secret societies of women and . . . the Männerbund. The men and their gods, during the night, attack the spinsters, destroy their work, break their shuttles and weaving-tackle." Calling such a brutal invasion, as part of the war on women, a "lasting tension" or even "conflict" occludes the ongoing violence at the root of patriarchy. [Eliade, *Myths, Dreams and Mysteries*, 211.]

68. Evola's editor for *Men Among the Ruins* (2002) retains the German term *Männerbünde* in his text (Evola was writing in Italian) because he doesn't think any English translation adequately captures the original phenomena.

69. Harris, "Love and Death in the Männerbund," 290.

70. Harris, "Love and Death in the Männerbund," 291.

71. Harris, "Love and Death in the Männerbund," 291; 301.

72. Harris, "Love and Death in the Männerbund," 304.

73. Evola, *Men Among the Ruins*, 112.

74. Evola, *Men Among the Ruins*, 114; 129.

75. Evola, *Men Among the Ruins*, 195–196.

76. Evola, *Men Among the Ruins*, 197.

77. Evola, *Men Among the Ruins*, 176.

78. Evola, *Men Among the Ruins*, 201.

79. Evola, *Men Among the Ruins*, 202.

80. Evola notes that while occasional extermination of others may occur, it is not done out of "hatred, anger, animosity, and contempt for the enemy" for these are "lowly feelings . . . energized by propaganda, smoky rhetoric, and lies." [Evola, *Men Among the Ruins*, 202.]

81. This recalls Georges Bataille's critical analysis of the psychological structure of fascism. He too sees fascism endeavoring to transform the world through sovereign self-affirmation. This becomes clear when re-evaluating the values of dishonorable actions by pure affirmation: "every affirmed social action necessarily takes the unified psychological form of sovereignty; every lower form, every ignominy, being by definition passive, is transformed into its opposite by the simple fact of a transition to action. Slaughter is ignoble; but . . . becomes noble . . . if the action effectively affirm[s] itself as such." An army's ignoble actions (torture, rape, massacres) can, via the sovereign affirmation, be recoded as honor and duty. [Georges Bataille, "The Psychological Structure of Fascism," *New German Critique*, no. 16 (1979): 64–87; 78.]

82. Evola, *Men Among the Ruins*, 131.

83. Evola, *Men Among the Ruins*, 198.

84. Jack Bratich, "Civil Society Must be Defended: Misinformation, Moral Panics, and Wars of Restoration," *Communication, Culture, and Critique* 13, no. 3 (September 2020): 311–332.

85. In Burrell, "Otto Höfler's Männerbund Theory," 253.

86. Burrell, "Otto Höfler's Männerbund Theory," 253.

87. Sarah Banet-Weiser and Kate Miltner, "#MasculinitySoFragile: Culture, Structure, and Networked Misogyny, *Feminist Media Studies* 16, no. 1 (2015): 171–174.

88. Redpilling takes on its full religious form with QAnon, as it preserves and extends the practice of "being saved." QAnon adherents may be "born again," not just through QAnon but via various types of charismatic Christianity.

89. See https://www.redpillliving.com/we-believe/.

90. Gilligan and Richards, *Darkness Now Visible*, 50.

91. Kathleen Belew, *Bring the War Home: The White Power Movement and Paramilitary America* (Cambridge, MA: Harvard University Press, 2019).

4. Necrotics

1. Chris Hedges, "America's Death March," *MintPress News*, August 10, 2020, https://www.mintpressnews.com/chris-hedges-hypernationalism-crisis-cults-signs-united-states-decline/270236/?fbclid=IwAR3o_z2WbYNGropx8KY5ooVKacWTn-Pn23u8CcWuPllfV-7x8h_-mh2FYsbM.

2. Judith Butler, "Genius or Suicide," *London Review of Books* 41, no. 20 (2019), https://www.lrb.co.uk/the-paper/v41/n20/judith-butler/genius-or-suicide.

3. Chauncey DeVega, "Novelist and Screenwriter Aleksandar Hemon on the 'Magnitude of Catastrophe' Facing America," *Salon*, https://www.salon.com/2020/06/03/novelist-and-screenwriter-aleksandar-hemon-on-the-magnitude-of-catastrophe-facing-america/.

4. Nadia Prupis, "Bannon Heralds 'Deconstruction of Administrative State' and Trump's 'New Political Order,'" *Common Dreams*, February 23, 2017, https://www.commondreams.org/news/2017/02/23/bannon-heralds-deconstruction-administrative-state-and-trumps-new-political-order.

5. *Time* staff. "Here's Donald Trump's Presidential Announcement Speech," *Time*, June 16, 2015. https://time.com/3923128/donald-trump-announcement-speech/.

6. Sarah Wildman, "Trump's speech in Poland sounded like an alt-right manifesto," Vox.com, Jul 6, 2017, https://www.vox.com/world/2017/7/6/15927590/trump-alt-right-poland-defend-west-civilization-g20.

7. Quoted in Neiwert, *Alt-America*, 501.

8. DeVega, "Novelist and Screenwriter Aleksandar Hemon on the 'Magnitude of Catastrophe' Facing America."

9. Bill Chappell, "'STOP GETTING TESTED' For Coronavirus, Ohio Politician Tells Constituents," *NPR*, July 9, 2020, https://www.npr.org/sections/coronavirus-live-updates/2020/07/09/889356233/stop-getting-tested-ohio-politician-tells-constituents

10. Brittney Cooper (@ProfessorCrunk), They are literally willing to die from this cluster-fucked COVID response rather than admit that absolutely anybody other than him would have been a better president. And when whiteness has a death wish, we are all in for a serious problem." Twitter, April 28, 2020. https://twitter.com/ProfessorCrunk/status/1255117671273824257

11. Theweleit, *Male Fantasies, Volume 1*, 221.

12. Kathryn Krawczyk, "Arizona's Republican Party asks followers if they're willing to die to 'Stop the Steal'," *Yahoo.com*, December 8, 2020, https://news.yahoo.com/arizonas-republican-party-asks-followers-145000628.html

13. Guattari, *Chaosophy*, 168–169.

14. Traverso, *The New Faces of Fascism*.

15. Jason Stanley, *How Fascism Works: The Politics of Us and Them* (New York: Random House, 2020).

16. Stanley, *How Fascism Works*, 35.

17. Christian Goeschel, *Suicide in Nazi Germany* (Oxford, UK and New York: Oxford University Press, 2009), 64.

18. Finchelstein, *Fascist Lies*, 73–81.

19. Finchelstein, *Fascist Lies*, 87.

20. Finchelstein, *Fascist Lies*, 89.

21. Finchelstein, *Fascist Lies*, 89.

22. Deleuze and Guattari, *A Thousand Plateaus*, 230. This might strike the reader as odd given the way Deleuze and Guattari's notion of lines of flight have been typically interpreted as essentially oriented to liberation. We have to alter the typical association with lines of flight as freedom or escape from confinement. While lines of flight contain those possibilities, they are accompanied by inherent dangers that must be accounted for and ambivalent tendencies to be experimented with carefully. Lines of flight attached to war machines that run through the state can have devastating consequences, especially when they get channeled into pure war only, in which case destruction becomes its only orientation—lines of abolition.

23. Deleuze and Guattari, *A Thousand Plateaus*, 231.

24. Deleuze and Guattari, *A Thousand Plateaus*, 230.

25. Deleuze and Guattari, *A Thousand Plateaus*, 230.

26. Deleuze and Guattari, *A Thousand Plateaus*, 231

27. Nicholas Michelsen, "Fascist Lines of the Tokkotai," in *Deleuze & Fascism*, 160.

28. Mark Neocleous, *The Monstrous and the Dead: Burke, Marx, Fascism* (Cardiff: University of Wales Press, 2005), 152.

29. Franco 'Bifo' Berardi, *Futurability: The Age of Impotence and the Horizon of Possibility* (London and New York: Verso Books, 2017), 137.

30. Subhabrata Bobby Banerjee, "Live and Let Die: Colonial Sovereignties and the Death Worlds of Necrocapitalism," *Borderlands* 5, no. 1 (2006); Subhabrata Bobby Banerjee, "Necrocapitalism," *Organization Studies* 29, no. 12 (2008): 1541–1563.

31. Thuy Linh Tu and Nikhil Pal Singh, "Morbid Capitalism and its Racial Symptoms," *n+1* 30 (Winter 2018), https://www.nplusonemag.com/issue-30/essays/morbid-capitalism/.

32. Warren Montag, "Necro-Economics: Adam Smith and Death in the Life of the Universal," *Radical Philosophy* 137, no. 7 (2005): 16.

33. Justin McBrien, "Accumulating Extinction: Planetary Catastrophism in the Necrocene," in *Anthropocene or Capitalocene? Nature, History, and the Crisis of Capitalism*, ed. Jason W. Moore (Oakland: PM Press, 2016), 116.

34. McBrien, "Accumulating Extinction," 117.

35. Achille Mbembé, "Necropolitics," trans. Libby Meintjes, *Public Culture* 15, no. 1 (2003): 12.

36. Mbembé, "Necropolitics," 14.

37. The dead-raising has another layer, as the MAGA phrase was already a resurrection of walking dead Ronald Reagan's presidential campaign in 1979.

38. Mbembé, "Necropolitics," 24.

39. Mbembé, "Necropolitics," 25.

40. Mbembé, "Necropolitics," 40. In a similar manner, Russ Castronovo coined the term *necro citizenship* to describe how in the US settler colonial system, subjective life is turned into dead citizen subjects. He also highlights the social death of slavery which forms the basis of US citizenship. [Russ Castronovo, *Necro Citizenship: Death, Eroticism, and the Public Sphere in the Nineteenth-Century United States* (Durham: Duke University Press, 2001).]

41. Mbembé, "Necropolitics," 17.

42. Mbembé, "Necropolitics," 36.

43. Mbembé, "Necropolitics," 35.

44. Melissa W. Wright, "Necropolitics, Narcopolitics, and Femicide: Gendered Violence on the Mexico-US Border," *Signs: Journal of Women in Culture and Society* 36, no. 3 (2011): 709.

45. Wright, "Necropolitics, Narcopolitics, and Femicide," 710.

46. Wright, "Necropolitics, Narcopolitics, and Femicide," 710.

47. Wright, "Necropolitics, Narcopolitics, and Femicide," 726.

48. Shatema Threadcraft, "North American Necropolitics and Gender: On #BlackLivesMatter and Black Femicide," *South Atlantic Quarterly* 116, no. 3 (2017): 553–579.

49. Most mass shootings were instances of domestic and intimate partner violence: 57 percent of mass shootings between January 2009 and June 2014 involved a perpetrator killing female intimates and their children; 70 percent of mass shooting incidents occurred at home; and 42 percent involved a current or former intimate partner. [Cited in Threadcraft, "North American Necropolitics and Gender," 576.]

50. Diana E. H. Russell, "The Origin and Importance of the Term Femicide," December 2011, https://www.dianarussell.com/origin_of_femicide.html.

51. Russell, "Femicide."

52. Erich Fromm, *The Anatomy of Human Destructiveness* (New York: Holt, Rinehart and Winston, 1973), 332.

53. Fromm, *The Anatomy of Human Destructiveness*, 28.

54. Erich Fromm, *War Within Man: A Psychological Enquiry into the Roots of Destructiveness*. Philadelphia: Peace Literature Service of the American Friends Service Committee, 1963.Cited in Joan Braune, "Erich Fromm and Thomas Merton: Biophilia, Necrophilia, and Messianism," *Fromm Forum* 15 (2011): 5.

55. Charles Thorpe, *Necroculture* (New York: Palgrave Macmillan, 2016), 2.

56. The fascist "union" is only a restoration of the womb *as tomb* (as he calls it) because of a prior founding violence against it. The tomb is the instrumentalized and reduced feminine figure that allows patriarchal pacts to cohere.

57. Daly, *Gyn/Ecology*, 975 (footnote 36).

58. Daly, *Gyn/Ecology*, 218.

59. Daly, *Gyn/Ecology*, 223.

60. Daly, a contested figure in feminist studies as well as praxis, defined her intemperance as a matter of urgency: "This is an extremist book, written in a situation of extremity, written on the edge." [Daly, *Gyn/Ecology*, 136.]

61. Daly, The Mary Daly Reader, 732.

62. *Daly,* The Mary Daly Reader, 732.

63. Daly, *Gyn/Ecology*, 221.

64. As Jack Holland notes, "in the Pandora story, her loss of virginity—the uncorking of the jar—lets death into the world," as "their beauty causes desire, starting the cycle of life and death." [Holland, *A Brief History of Misogyny*, 320.]

65. Andrea Dworkin, *Woman Hating* (New York: Penguin, 1974), 138.

66. Holland, *A Brief History of Misogyny*, 33. Holland refers here to Virgin Mary as "Mother of God" as example.

67. Robert Evans, "Ignore The Poway Synagogue Shooter's Manifesto: Pay Attention To 8chan's /pol/ Board," *Bellingcat*, https://www.bellingcat.com/news/americas/2019/04/28/ignore-the-poway-synagogue-shooters-manifesto-pay-attention-to-8chans-pol-board/.

68. Griffin, *A Fascist Century*, 12.

69. Schnapp quoted in Griffin, *A Fascist Century*, 12.

70. Griffin, *A Fascist Century*, 14.

71. Ned Crankshaw, Joseph E. Brent, and Maria Campbell Brent, "The Lost Cause and Reunion in the Confederate Cemeteries of the North," *Landscape Journal* 35, no. 1 (2016): 1–21.

72. Quoted in Crankshaw, Brent, and Brent, "The Lost Cause and Reunion," 5.

73. Jason Cochran, "Those Confederate Statues Were Put There as Propaganda: Meet the Women Who Got Away With It," *Medium*, June 24, 2020, https://medium.com/@ReadJasonCochran/those-confederate-statues-were-put-there-as-propaganda-meet-the-women-who-got-away-with-it-c431d286ab37.

74. Michael Taussig, *The Magic of the State* (New York and London: Routledge, 1997), 165.

75. As historians remind us, most of the confederate statues were erected during the Jim Crow era. Statues were placed in town squares and other public gathering areas, erected to patrol boundaries beyond which Black populations were forbidden to explore.

76. Jacob Siegel, "Teens Bring 4chan Politics to Boston," *The Daily Beast*, May 15, 2017, https://www.thedailybeast.com/teens-bbring-4chan-politics-to-boston.

77. CrimethInc., "Why The Alt-Right Are So Weak: And Why They're Becoming So Dangerous," *It's Going Down*, April 17, 2017, https://itsgoingdown.org/alt-right-weak-theyre-becoming-dangerous/.

78. Taussig, *The Magic of the State*, 114.

79. Meghan O'Donnell, "Dangerous Undercurrent: Death, Sacrifice and Ruin in Third Reich Germany," *International Journal of Humanities and Social Sciences* 2, no. 9 (2012): 231–239.

80. O'Donnell, "Dangerous Undercurrent," 233. O'Donnell also remarks that in Wagner's *Tristan und Isolde* the final aria is called "*Liebestod*" [Death love].

81. O'Donnell, "Dangerous Undercurrent," 233.

82. Frederic Spotts, *Hitler and the Power of Aesthetics* (New York: Overlook Press, 2003), 70–71.

83. O'Donnell, "Dangerous Undercurrent," 238.

84. Doha Madani, "Dan Patrick on coronavirus: 'More important things than living,'" *NBC News*, April 21, 2020, https://www.nbcnews.com/news/us-news/texas-lt-gov-dan-patrick-reopening-economy-more-important-things-n1188911.

85. Castronovo, *Necro Citizenship*.

86. Cavallero and Gago, "Feminism, the Pandemic, and What Comes Next."

87. Cavallero and Gago, "Feminism, the Pandemic, and What Comes Next."

88. M.I. Asma (J. Moufawad-Paul, Devin Zane Shaw, Mateo Andante, Johannah May Black, Alyson Escalante, D. W. Fairlane), *On Necrocapitalism: A Plague Journal* (Montreal: Kersplebedeb, 2021).

89. Theweleit, *Male Fantasies, Volume 1*, 215.

90. Theweleit, *Male Fantasies, Volume 1*, 215.

91. Theweleit, *Male Fantasies, Volume 1*, 217.

92. Theweleit, *Male Fantasies, Volume 1*, 218.

93. Theweleit, *Male Fantasies, Volume 1*, 218.

94. Theweleit, *Male Fantasies, Volume 1*, 218.

95. Wendy Brown, *In the Ruins of Neoliberalism: The Rise of Antidemocratic Politics in the West* (New York: Columbia University Press, 2019), 168.

96. Brown, *Ruins of Neoliberalism*, 180.

5. Platforming Micro-Antifascism

1. Guattari, *Chaosophy*, 164.

2. Bray, *Antifa*, xvi.

3. Bray, *Antifa*, xv.

4. Bray, *Antifa*, xv.

5. Bray, *Antifa*, 206.

6. Lee Petronella, *Anti-Fascism Against Machismo: Gender, Politics, and the Struggle Against Fascism* (Hamilton: The Tower InPrint, 2019), https://north-shore.info/wp-content/uploads/2019/10/Antifa-machismo-Body-v3.0-imp.pdf.

7. Herausgeber innenkollektiv, *Fantifa: Feministische Perspektiven Antifaschistischer Politiken* (Münster, DE: Edition Assemblage, 2013); Hope Worsdale, "Anti-Fascism is a Feminist Issue," *Red Pepper*, December 7, 2018, https://www.redpepper.org.uk/anti-fascism-is-feminist-issue/; Lee, *Anti-Fascism Against Machismo*.

8. Less visible but still oriented around public displays are struggles over immigration (with a spatiality of abductions, border bans, and walls). White supremacism is also often routine and mundane, as explained by writers on white privilege in everyday interactions. Lennard, *Being Numerous*, 64.

9. Lennard, *Being Numerous*, 64.

10. Rianka Singh and Sarah Banet-Weiser, "Sky High: Platforms and the Feminist Politics of Visibility," in *Re-Understanding Media: Feminist Extensions of Marshall McLuhan*, ed. Sarah Sharma and Rianka Singh (Durham: Duke University Press, 2022).

11. Guattari, *Chaosophy*, 162.

12. Guattari, *Chaosophy*, 195.

13. Martel, "Histories of Violence."

14. Foucault, *Society Must Be Defended*, 55.

15. Daly, *Gyn/Ecology*, 170.

16. Gago, *Feminist International*, 788.

17. Gago, *Feminist International*, 779.

18. Laurie Penny, *Sexual Revolution: Modern Fascism and the Feminist Fightback* (New York: Bloomsbury Publishing, 2022).

19. Ging and Siapera, "Introduction: Special issue on online misogyny," 521.

20. Limor Shifman and Dafna Lemish, "Between Feminism and Fun(ny)mism," *Information, Communication and Society* 13, no. 6 (2010): 870–891.

21. Sam Hart, Toby Shorin, and Laura Lotti, "Squad Wealth," *Other Internet*, August 19, 2020, https://otherinter.net/squad-wealth/.
22. Hart, Shorin, and Lotti, "Squad Wealth."
23. Warrior girl squads and militant covens undercut any attempt to organize the world through a binary linking men to war and women to peace.
24. Burley, *Fascism Today*, 374.
25. Virginia Woolf, *A Room of One's Own* and *Three Guineas*, ed. Anna Snaith (Oxford: Oxford University Press, 2008), 853.
26. Reynaldo Anderson and Tiffany E. Barber, "The Black Angel of History and the Age of Necrocapitalism," *Terremoto* 18, June 12, 2020, https://terremoto.mx/issue/issue-18-of-passageways-and-portals/.
27. Anderson and Barber, "The Black Angel of History."
28. Indigenous Action, "Rethinking the Apocalypse: An Indigenous Anti-Futurist Manifesto," *Indigenous Action*, March 19, 2020, https://www.indigenousaction.org/rethinking-the-apocalypse-an-indigenous-anti-futurist-manifesto/.
29. Indigenous Action, "Rethinking the Apocalypse."
30. Marcello Tarì, *There Is No Unhappy Revolution: The Communism of Destitution* (Brooklyn: Common Notions, 2021), 3.
31. Black Youth Project 100, https://www.byp100.org/.
32. She Safe, We Safe, https://www.shesafewesafe.org.
33. Anderson and Barber, "The Black Angel of History."
34. Anderson and Barber, "The Black Angel of History."
35. See, for instance: Judith Butler, Zeynep Gambetti, and Leticia Sabsay (eds.), *Vulnerability in Resistance* (Durham and London: Duke University Press, 2016); Sarah Banet-Weiser, "*Radical vulnerability: feminism, victimhood and agency,*" in *Re-writing Women as Victims: From Theory to Practice*, ed. María José Gámez Fuentes, Sonia Núñez Puente, and Emma Gómez Nicolau (New York and London: Routledge, 2019), 167–181.
36. Frédéric Lordon, *Willing Slaves of Capital: Spinoza and Marx on Desire* (New York: Verso, 2014), 109.
37. Laura U. Marks, "Which Came First, Fascism or Misogyny? Reading Klaus Theweleit's Male Fantasies," in *Spectres of Fascism: Historical, Theoretical and International Perspectives,* ed. Samir Gandesha (London: Pluto Press, 2020), 116.
38. Marks, "Which Came First, Fascism or Misogyny?," 118.
39. Marks, "Which Came First, Fascism or Misogyny?," 118.
40. Marks, "Which Came First, Fascism or Misogyny?," 118.
41. Marks, "Which Came First, Fascism or Misogyny?," 116.
42. Sylvia Wynter and Katherine McKittrick, "Unparalleled Catastrophe for Our Species? Or, to Give Humanness a Different Future: Conversations," in *Sylvia Wynter: On Being Human as Praxis*, ed. Katherine McKittrick (Durham and London: Duke University Press, 2015), 37.
43. Wynter and McKittrick, "Unparalleled Catastrophe for Our Species?," 27.
44. Patricia Hill Collins, *Black Feminist Thought: Knowledge, Consciousness, and the Politics of Empowerment* (New York and London: Routledge, 2002), 300.
45. Elizabeth Freeman, *Beside You in Time: Sense Methods and Queer Sociabilities in the American Nineteenth Century* (Durham and London: Duke University Press, 2019), 14.
46. Freeman, *Beside You in Time*, 14.
47. Sam Maggs, *Girl Squads: 20 Female Friendships That Changed History* (Philadelphia: Quirk Books, 2018).
48. Kerri Jarema, "11 New Books with Kickass Girl Squads to Inspire You to Close Out 2018 with a Bang," *Bustle*, November 14, 2018, https://www.bustle.com/p/11-new-books-with-kickass-girl-squads-to-help-you-finish-out-the-year-strong-13115632.

49. Kayleen Schaefer, *Text Me When You Get Home: The Evolution and Triumph of Modern Female Friendship* (New York: Dutton, 2018).

50. Alison Winch, "Brand Intimacy, Female Friendship and Digital surveillance networks." *New Formations: A Journal of Culture/Theory/Politics* 84–85 (2015): 229.

51. Cassie Thornton. *The Hologram: Feminist, Peer-to-Peer Health for a Post-Pandemic Future* (London: Pluto Press, 2020).

52. Catherine Rottenberg, Jo Litter, Andreas Chatzidakis, and Jamie Hakim, *The Care Manifesto: The Politics of Interdependence* (London and New York: Verso Books, 2020), 116.

53. Helen Hester, *Xenofeminism* (Cambridge, UK and Medford, MA: Polity Press, 2018), 4.

54. Hester, *Xenofeminism*, 63.

55. Hester, *Xenofeminism*, 57.

56. Koepnick, *Walter Benjamin and the Aesthetics of Power*, 193.

57. Bell, "Mimesis as Cultural Survival: Judith Butler and Anti-Semitism;" Rosi Braidotti, "Of Bugs and Women: Irigaray and Deleuze on the Becoming-Woman," in *Engaging with Irigaray: Feminist Philosophy and Modern European Thought*, ed. Carolyn Burke, Naomi Schor, and Margaret Whitford (New York: Columbia University Press, 1994), 111–137.

58. See Nidesh Lawtoo's writings as well as his *Homo Mimeticus* project (http://www.homo-mimeticus.eu/home/).

59. Katherine Hayles, "Survival as Mimesis: Microbiomimesis and the Production of Posthuman Bodies," keynote address for the Posthuman Mimesis conference, *Homo Mimeticus* (HOM), Institute of Philosophy at KU Leuven, May 21, 2021, https://www.youtube.com/watch?v=DP-OnWEjGus&t=21s.

60. In the US but also elsewhere, youth culture had for some years been developing amidst economic and compositional depression punctuated by antagonism in schools (walkouts against gun violence, police abuse, gendered control of school fashion). With COVID-based lockdowns, young people were isolated in their homes for months and then found each other via media culture.

61. André Brock, Jr., *Distributed Blackness: African American Cybercultures* (New York: New York University Press, 2020).

62. Sarah Florini, *Beyond Hashtags: Racial Politics and Black Digital Networks* (New York: New York University Press, 2019).

63. Catherine Knight Steele, *Digital Black Feminism* (New York: New York University Press, 2021); Sarah J. Jackson, Moya Bailey, Brooke Foucault Welles, *#HashtagActivism: Networks of Race and Gender Justice* (Cambridge, MA and London: The MIT Press, 2020); Meredith D. Clark, "DRAG THEM: A Brief Etymology of So-Called 'Cancel Culture,'" *Communication and the Public* 5, no. 3–4 (September 2020): 88–92.

64. Mimesis, as demonstrated by various digitally enhanced subcultures, is not just relegated to humans. See, for example, the hybrid identity production known as "otherkin."

65. Joshua Citarella, "Irony Politics & GEN Z," *New Models*, April 2019, https://newmodels.io/proprietary/irony-politics gen-z-2019-citarella.

66. Stassa Edwards, "Dancing through Our Bad Year," *Jezebel*, April 22, 2020, https://jezebel.com/dancing-through-our-bad-year-1842274184.

67. Fielitz and Marcks, "Digital Fascism"; Lisa Bogerts and Maik Fielitz, "'Do You Want Meme War?': Understanding the Visual Memes of the German Far Right," in *Post-Digital Cultures of the Far Right: Online Actions and Offline Consequences in Europe and the US*, ed. Maik Fielitz and Nick Thurston (Bielefeld, DE: transcript Verlag, 2019), 147–153.

68. Adrian Wohlleben, "Memes without End," *Ill Will*, May 16, 2021, https://illwill.com/memes-without-end. See also Paul Torino and Adrian Wohlleben, "Memes with Force: Lessons from the Yellow Vests," *Mute*, February 26, 2019, https://www.metamute.org/editorial/articles/memes-force—lessons-yellow-vests.

69. Wohlleben, "Memes without End."

70. Torino and Wohlleben, "Memes with Force."

71. Freeman, *Beside You in Time.*

72. Max Haiven, "Occupy and the Struggle over Reproduction: An Interview with Silvia Federici," November 27, 2011, https://libcom.org/library/feminism-finance-future-occupy-interview-silvia-federici.

73. Elise Thorburn, "Networked Social Reproduction: Crises in the Integrated Circuit," *tripleC: Communication, Capitalism & Critique* 14, no. 2 (2016): 2.

74. Mariarosa Dalla Costa and Selma James, *The Power of Women and the Subversion of the Community* (Bristol: Falling Wall Press, 1975); Silvia Federici, *Caliban and the Witch* (Brooklyn: Autonomedia, 2004); Leopoldina Fortunati, *The Arcane of Reproduction: Housework, Prostitution, Labor and Capital*, trans. Hilary Creek (Brooklyn: Autonomedia, 1996).

75. Leopoldina Fortunati, "Social Reproduction, But Not As We Know It," *Viewpoint Magazine* 5, October 31, 2015, https://viewpointmag.com/2015/10/31/social-reproduction-but-not-as-we-know-it/.

76. Fortunati, "Social Reproduction."

77. Fortunati, "Social Reproduction."

78. Fortunati draws on Lewis Mumford here; in Fortunati, "Social Reproduction."

79. Fortunati, "Social Reproduction."

80. Fortunati, "Social Reproduction."

81. Fortunati, "Social Reproduction."

82. Fortunati, "Social Reproduction."

83. Verónica Gago and Raquel Gutiérrez Aguilar, "Women Rising in Defense of Life: Tracing the Revolutionary Flows of Latin American Women's Many Uprisings," *NACLA Report on the Americas* 50, no. 4 (2018): 365.

84. Fortunati, "Social Reproduction."

85. Gago, Malo, and Mason-Deese, "Introduction: The New Feminist Internationale," 623.

86. Gago and Aguilar, "Women Rising in Defense of Life," 367.

87. J.K. Gibson-Graham, *A Postcapitalist Politics* (Minneapolis: University of Minnesota Press, 2006), xxiv.

88. Gibson-Graham, *A Postcapitalist Politics*, xxiii.

89. Gibson-Graham, *A Postcapitalist Politics*, xxiv.

90. Fortunati, "Social Reproduction"; See also Thorburn, "Networked Social Reproduction."

91. Gago, Malo, and Mason-Deese, "Introduction: The New Feminist Internationale," 626.

92. Gago, Malo, and Mason-Deese, "Introduction: The New Feminist Internationale," 626.

93. Hester, *Xenofeminism*, 4.

94. Hester, *Xenofeminism*, 13.

95. Gago, *Feminist International*, 778–779.

96. Marina Sitrin and Colectiva Sembrar (eds.), *Pandemic Solidarity: Mutual Aid during the COVID-19 Crisis* (London: Pluto Press, 2020); Catherine Rottenberg, Jo Littler, Andreas Chatzidakis, and Jamie Hakim, *The Care Manifesto: The Politics of Interdependence* (London: Pluto Press, 2020); Emma Dowling, *The Care Crisis: What Caused It and How Can We End It?* (London and New York: Verso, 2020).

97. Aaron Jaffe, "Social Reproduction Theory in and beyond the Pandemic," *Pluto Press* (blog), October 10, 2020, https://www.plutobooks.com/blog/social-reproduction-theory-in-and-beyond-the-pandemic/.

98. Berardi, *Futurability*.

99. Imani Perry, *Vexy Thing: On Gender and Liberation* (Durham: Duke University Press, 2018), 175.

100. Julia S. Jordan-Zachery and Duchess Harris (eds.), *Black Girl Magic Beyond the Hashtag: Twenty-First Century Acts of Self-Definition* (Tucson: University of Arizona Press, 2019).
101. Gago and Aguilar, "Women Rising in Defense of Life," 365.
102. Perry, *Vexy Thing*, 173.
103. Perry, *Vexy Thing*, 28.
104. Again, it's important not to romanticize all women's groups: the United Daughters of the Confederacy (UDC) sprang from women's hospital service groups and knitting circles.
105. Jo Freeman, W.I.T.C.H.—The Women's International Terrorist Conspiracy from Hell (n.d.), http://www.jofreeman.com/photos/witch.html.
106. Bratich, "The Digital Touch."
107. Jane Caputi, *Gossips, Gorgons and Crones: The Fates of the Earth* (Santa Fe: Bear & Company, 1993), 10.
108. Caputi, *Gossips, Gorgons and Crones*, xxii.
109. Gago, *Feminist International*, 818.
110. Gago, 819.
111. Hester, *Xenofeminism*, 142.
112. Perry, *Vexy Thing*, 175.
113. Perry, *Vexy Thing*, 176.
114. Gago, *Feminist International*, 818.
115. Hester, *Xenofeminism*, 5.
116. Perry, *Vexy Thing*, 28–29.
117. Lennard, *Being Numerous*, 56.
118. Wohlleben, "Memes without End." Italics added for emphasis.
119. Tarì, *There Is No Unhappy Revolution*, 5.
120. See Sophie Lewis, *Full Surrogacy Now: Feminism Against Family* (London and New York: Verso Books, 2019).
121. Hester, *Xenofeminism*, 30–31.
122. Hester, *Xenofeminism*, 31.
123. Burley, *Fascism Today*, 275.
124. Gago, *Feminist International*, 37; Hester, *Xenofeminism*, 46–47.
125. Lennard, *Being Numerous*, 66.
126. Guattari, *Chaosophy*, 166.
127. Meanwhile, those losses happen to women materially. Since such fear is materially grounded, abolition is directed at the conditions where that fear is in play, namely gender relations.
128. Foucault, *Society Must Be Defended*, 55.
129. For instance, if masculinity seeks to disappear into abstractions and to fulfill its catabolic subjective orientation, then society could provide honorable means to fulfill those social desires.
130. Tarì, *There Is No Unhappy Revolution*, 39.
131. Including the particularly odious Disney film *The Witches*, which sought to narratively recruit Black culture (even Black magic) into its war on women (by recoding the war as Black uprising).

Bibliography

Abrisketa, Olatz G., and Marian G. Abrisketa. "'It's Okay, Sister, Your Wolf-Pack Is Here': Sisterhood as Public Feminism in Spain." *Signs: Journal of Women in Culture and Society* 45, no. 4 (Summer 2020), https://doi.org/10.1086/707801.

Acker, Antoine. "How Fascism Went Digital: A Historian's Perspective on Bolsonaro's Victory in Brazil." In *Geschichte der Gegenwart*, November 7, 2018, https://geschichtedergegenwart. ch/how-fascism-went-digital-a-historians-perspective-on-bolsonaros-victory-in-brazil/.

Adam, Alison. "Cyberstalking and Internet Pornography: Gender and the Gaze." *Ethics and Information Technology* 4, no. 2 (2002): 133–142.

Alliez, Eric, and Maurizio Lazzarato. *Wars and Capital*, translated by Ames Hodges. South Pasadena: Semiotext(e), 2018.

Amorós, Celia. "Thinking Patriarchy." In *Feminist Philosophy in Latin America and Spain*, edited by María Luisa Femenías and Amy A. Oliver, 109–126. Amsterdam and New York: Editions Rodopi, 2007.

Anderson, Kristin J. *Modern Misogyny: Anti-Feminism in a Post-Feminist Era*. Oxford University Press, 2014.

Anderson, Reynaldo. "Afrofuturism 2.0 & The Black Speculative Arts Movement: Notes on a Manifesto." *Obsidian* 42, no. 1/2 (2016): 228–236.

Anderson, Reynaldo, and Tiffany E. Barber. "The Black Angel of History and the Age of Necrocapitalism." *Terremoto* 18, June 12, 2020, https://terremoto.mx/issue/issue-18-of-passageways-and-portals/.

Andersen, Robin. "That's Militainment! The Pentagon's Media-Friendly 'Reality' War." *Extra!*, May 1, 2003, https://fair.org/extra/thats-militainment/.

Armstrong, Aurelia. "Some Reflections on Deleuze's Spinoza: Composition and Agency." In *Deleuze and Philosophy: The Difference Engineer*, edited by Keith Ansell Pearson, 44–57. London and New York: Routledge, 1997.

Bailey, Moya, and Trudy. "On Misogynoir: Citation, Erasure, and Plagiarism." *Feminist Media Studies* 18, no. 4 (2018): 762–768.

Banerjee, Subhabrata Bobby. "Live and Let Die: Colonial Sovereignties and the Death Worlds of Necrocapitalism." *Borderlands* 5, no. 1 (2006).

Banerjee, Subhabrata Bobby. "Necrocapitalism." *Organization Studies* 29, no. 12 (2008): 1541–1563.

Banet-Weiser, Sarah. "'Ruined' Lives: Mediated White Male Victimhood." *European Journal of Cultural Studies* 24, no. 1 (2021): 60–80.

Banet-Weiser, Sarah. "*Radical Vulnerability: Feminism, Victimhood and Agency.*" In *Re-writing Women as Victims: From Theory to Practice*, edited by María José Gámez Fuentes, Sonia Núñez Puente, and Emma Gómez Nicolau, 167–181. New York and London: Routledge, 2019.

Banet-Weiser, Sarah. *Empowered: Popular Feminism and Popular Misogyny*. Durham: Duke University Press, 2018.

Banet-Weiser, Sarah, and Kate Miltner. "#MasculinitySoFragile: Culture, Structure, and Networked Misogyny." *Feminist Media Studies* 16, no. 1 (2015): 171–174.

Bataille, Georges, and Carl R. Lovitt. "The Psychological Structure of Fascism." *New German Critique* 16 (Winter 1979): 64–87.

Bates, Laura. *Everyday Sexism*. New York: Thomas Dunne Books/St. Martin's Griffin, 2016.

Beam, Louis. "Leaderless Resistance," *Inter-Klan Newsletter*, 1983. Republished in *The Seditionist*, no. 12 (February 1992).

Black Youth Project 100, https://www.byp100.org/.

Beauchamp, Zack. "Our Incel Problem." *Vox*, April 23, 2019, vox.com/the-highlight/2019/4/16/18287446/incel-definition-reddit.

Belew, Kathleen. *Bring the War Home: The White Power Movement and Paramilitary America*. Cambridge, MA: Harvard University Press, 2019.

Bell, Vicki. "Mimesis as Cultural Survival: Judith Butler and Anti-Semitism." *Theory, Culture & Society* 16, no. 2 (1999): 133–161.

Benjamin, Walter. *Illuminations: Essays and Reflections*. Translated by Harry Zohn. New York: Schocken Books, 2007.

Beran, Dale. "The Boogaloo Tipping Point: What happens when a meme becomes a terrorist movement?" *The Atlantic*, July 13, 2020, https://www.theatlantic.com/technology/archive/2020/07/american-boogaloo-meme-or-terrorist-movement/613843/.

Berardi, Franco "Bifo." *Futurability: The Age of Impotence and the Horizon of Possibility*. London and New York: Verso, 2017.

Berardi, Franco "Bifo." *Heroes: Mass Murder and Suicide*. London and New York: Verso, 2015.

Berardi, Franco "Bifo." "Reassessing Recomposition: 40 Years After the Publication of Anti-Oedipus." *Subjectivity* 5 (2012): 111–119.

Bergman, Hannah. "White Men's Fear of Women: Anti-Feminism and the Rise of the Alt-Right." *The Examined Life Lab*, March 31, 2018, https://mathias-nilges.com/student-projects-the-new-culture-wars/2018/4/1/white-mens-fear-of-women-anti-feminism-and-the-rise-of-the-alt-right.

Berlant, Lauren. "Slow Death (Sovereignty, Obesity, Lateral Agency)." *Critical Inquiry* 33, no. 4 (2007): 754–780.

Bogerts, Lisa, and Fielitz, Maik. ""Do You Want Meme War?": Understanding the Visual Memes of the German Far Right." In *Post-Digital Cultures of the Far Right: Online Actions and Offline Consequences in Europe and the US*, edited by Maik Fielitz and Nick Thurston, 147–153. Bielefeld, DE: transcript Verlag, 2019.

Borch, Christian, ed., *Imitation, Contagion, Suggestion: On Mimesis and Society*. Oxon and New York: Routledge, 2019.

Bordo, Susan. *The Flight to Objectivity: Essays on Cartesianism and Culture*. Albany: State University of New York Press, 1987.

Bosman, Julie, Kate Taylor, and Tim Arango. "A Common Trait among Mass Killers: Hatred toward Women." *The New York Times*, August 10, 2019, https://www.nytimes.com/2019/08/10/us/mass-shootings-misogyny-dayton.html.

Braidotti, Rosi. "Of Bugs and Women: Irigaray and Deleuze on the Becoming-Woman." In *Engaging with Irigaray: Feminist Philosophy and Modern European Thought*, edited by Carolyn Burke, Naomi Schor, and Margaret Whitford, 111–137. New York: Columbia University Press, 1994.

Branstetter, Gillian. "The Alt-Right is a Doomsday Cult." *Medium*, February 10, 2017, https://gillbranstetter.medium.com/the-alt-right-is-a-doomsday-cult-b40edd66062a.

Bratich, Jack. "Civil Society Must be Defended: Misinformation, Moral Panics, and Wars of Restoration." *Communication, Culture, and Critique* 13, no. 3 (2020): 311–332.

Bratich, Jack. "Digital Touch." *Ephemera* 10 (2010): 303–318.

Braune, Joan. "Erich Fromm and Thomas Merton: Biophilia, Necrophilia, and Messianism." *Fromm Forum* (English version), no. 15 (2011): 43–48.

Bray, Mark. *Antifa: The Anti-Fascist Handbook*. Brooklyn and London: Melville House, 2017.

Brock, Jr., André. *Distributed Blackness: African American Cybercultures*. New York: New York University Press, 2020.

Broderick, Ryan. "Christchurch: This Will Keep Happening." *BuzzFeed*, March 15, 2019, https://www.buzzfeednews.com/article/ryanhatesthis/murder-as-a-meme-white-male-violence-is-being-distributed.

Brown, Drew. "Toxic Masculinity Is at the Heart of This Darkness." *Vice*, April 25, 2018, https://www.vice.com/en/article/8xkjbx/toxic-masculinity-is-at-the-heart-of-this-darkness.

Brown, Wendy. *In the Ruins of Neoliberalism: The Rise of Antidemocratic Politics in the West*. New York: Columbia University Press, 2019.

Buck-Morss, Susan. "Aesthetics and Anaesthetics: Walter Benjamin's Artwork Essay Reconsidered." *October* 62 (1992): 3–41.

Burley, Shane. *Fascism Today: What It Is and How to End It*. Oakland: AK Press, 2017.

Burrell, Courtney Marie. "Otto Höfler's Männerbund Theory and Popular Representations of the North." *NORDEUROPAforum. Zeitschrift für Kulturstudien* [*Journal for the Study of Culture*] (2020): 228–266.

Butler, Judith. "Contingent Foundations: Feminism and the Question of 'Postmodernism.'" In *Feminists Theorize the Political*, edited by Judith Butler and Joan Scott, 3–21. New York: Routledge, 1992.

Butler, Judith. "Genius or Suicide." *London Review of Books* 41, no. 20 (2019), https://www.lrb.co.uk/the-paper/v41/n20/judith-butler/genius-or-suicide.

Butler, Judith. *Bodies that Matter: On the Discursive Limits of Sex*. Abingdon, Oxon and New York: Routledge, 2011.

Butler, Judith. "Anti-Gender Ideology and the New Fascism," paper presented at the New School for Social Research, New York City, February 21, 2019.

Butler, Judith, Zeynep Gambetti, and Leticia Sabsay, eds. *Vulnerability in Resistance*. Durham and London: Duke University Press, 2016.

Cammelli, Maddalena Gretel. "Fascism As a Style of Life: Community Life and Violence in a Neofascist Movement in Italy." *Focaal—Journal of Global and Historical Anthropology* 79 (2017): 89–101.

Caputi, Jane. *Gossips, Gorgons and Crones: The Fates of the Earth*. Santa Fe: Bear & Company, 1993.

Castronovo, Russ. *Necro Citizenship: Death, Eroticism, and the Public Sphere in the Nineteenth-Century United States*. Durham and London: Duke University Press, 2001.

Cavallero, Lucía, and Verónica Gago. "Feminism, the Pandemic, and What Comes Next." Translated by Liz Mason-Deese. *Critical Times: Interventions in Global Critical Theory*, https://ctjournal.org/2020/04/21/feminism-the-pandemic-and-what-comes-next/.

Césaire, Aimé. *Discourse on Colonialism.* Translated by Joan Pinkham. New York: Monthly Review Press, 2001.

Chappell, Bill. "'STOP GETTING TESTED' for Coronavirus, Ohio Politician Tells Constituents." *NPR*, July 9, 2020, https://www.npr.org/sections/coronavirus-live-updates/2020/07/09/889356233/stop-getting-tested-ohio-politician-tells-constituents.

Citarella, Joshua. "Irony Politics & GEN Z." *New Models*, April 2019, https://newmodels.io/proprietary/irony-politics-gen-z-2019-citarella.

Clark, Meredith. "DRAG THEM: A Brief Etymology of so-Called 'Cancel Culture.'" *Communication and the Public* 5, nos. 3–4 (September 2020): 88–92.

Cleary, Tom. "John Earnest: 5 Fast Facts You Need to Know." Heavy.com, Apr 29, 2019, https://heavy.com/news/2019/04/john-earnest/.

Cochran, Jason. "Those Confederate Statues Were Put There As Propaganda. Meet the Women Who Got Away With It." *Medium*, June 24, 2020, https://medium.com/@ReadJasonCochran/those-confederate-statues-were-put-there-as-propaganda-meet-the-women-who-got-away-with-it-c431d286ab37.

Collins, Patricia Hill. *Black Feminist Thought: Knowledge, Consciousness, and the Politics of Empowerment.* New York and London: Routledge, 2002.

Connolly, William E. *Aspirational Fascism: The Struggle for Multifaceted Democracy under Trumpism.* Minneapolis: University of Minnesota Press, 2017.

Coté, Mark. "What is a Media Dispositif? Compositions with Bifo." *Journal of Communication Inquiry* 35, no. 4 (2011): 378–386.

Crandall, Coryl, ed. *Swetnam the Woman-Hater: The Controversy and the Play.* West Lafayette: Perdue University Studies, 1969.

Crankshaw, Ned, Joseph E. Brent, and Maria Campbell Brent. "The Lost Cause and Reunion in the Confederate Cemeteries of the North." *Landscape Journal* 35, no. 1 (2016): 1–21.

CrimethInc. Ex-Workers Collective, "Why the Alt-Right are so Weak: And Why They're Becoming so Dangerous." *It's Going Down*, April 17, 2017, https://itsgoingdown.org/alt-right-weak-theyre-becoming-dangerous/.

Dalla Costa, Mariarosa, and Selma James. *The Power of Women and the Subversion of the Community.* Bristol: Falling Wall Press, 1975.

Daly, Mary. *Gyn/Ecology: The Metaethics of Radical Feminism.* Boston: Beacon Press, 2016.

Daly, Mary. The Mary Daly Reader, edited by Jennifer Rycenga and Linda Barufaldi. New York: New York University Press, 2017.

Daniels, Jessie. *Cyber Racism: White Supremacy Online and the New Attack on Civil Rights.* Lanham, Boulder, New York, Toronto, Plymouth, UK: Rowman & Littlefield Publishers, Inc., 2009.

Deleuze, Gilles. *Spinoza: Practical Philosophy.* Translated by Robert Hurley. San Francisco: City Lights, 1988.

Del Lucchese, Filippo. "Democracy, Multitudo and the Third Kind of Knowledge in the Works of Spinoza." *European Journal of Political Theory* 8, no. 3 (2009): 339–363.

De Seriis, Marco. *Improper Names: Collective Pseudonyms and Multiple Use Names.* Minneapolis: University of Minnesota Press, 2015.

DeVega, Chauncey. "Novelist and Screenwriter Aleksandar Hemon on the 'Magnitude of Catastrophe' Facing America." *Salon*, June 3, 2020, https://salon.com/2020/06/03/novelist-and-screenwriter-aleksandar-hemon-on-the-magnitude-of-catastrophe-facing-america.

Douglas, Susan J. *Enlightened Sexism: The Seductive Message That Feminism's Work Is Done* New York: Times Books/Henry Holt and Company, 2010.

Dowling, Emma. *The Care Crisis: What Caused It and How Can We End It?* London and New York: Verso, 2020.

Dragiewicz, Molly, Jean Burgess, Ariadna Matamoros-Fernández, Michael Salter, Nicolas P. Suzor, Delanie Woodlock, and Bridget Harris. "Technology facilitated coercive control: domestic violence and the competing roles of digital media platforms." *Feminist Media Studies* 18, no. 4 (2018): 609–625.

Driver, Alice. *More or Less Dead: Feminicide, Haunting, and the Ethics of Representation in Mexico*. Tucson: University of Arizona Press, 2015.

Dworkin, Andrea. *Woman Hating*. New York: Dutton, 1974.

Dyer-Witheford, Nick. *Cyber-Marx: Cycles and Circuits of Struggle in High-Technology Capitalism*. Urbana and Chicago: University of Illinois Press, 1999.

Eco, Umberto. "Ur-Fascism." *The New York Review of Books* 42, no. 11 (1995): 12–15.

Edwards, Stassa. "Dancing Through our Bad Year." *Jezebel*, April 22, 2020, https://jezebel.com/dancing-through-our-bad-year-1842274184.

Ehrenreich, Barbara. "Foreword." In *Male Fantasies: Women, Floods, Bodies, History*, edited by Klaus Theweleit, viiii–xxvi. Minneapolis: University of Minnesota Press, 1987.

Eliade, Mircea. *Rites and Symbols of Initiation: The Mysteries of Birth and Rebirth*. New York, Hagerstown, San Francisco, London: Harper & Row, 1958.

Eliade, Mircea. *Myths, Dreams and Mysteries*. Translated by Philip Mairet. New York: Harper & Row, 1967.

Evans, Brad, and Julian Reid. "Introduction: Fascism in all its Forms." In *Deleuze & Fascism: Security: War: Aesthetics*, edited by Brad Evans and Julian Reid, 1–12. London and New York: Routledge, 2013.

Evans, Robert. "Ignore The Poway Synagogue Shooter's Manifesto: Pay Attention To 8chan's /pol/ Board." *Bellingcat*, April 28, 2019, https://www.bellingcat.com/news/americas/2019/04/28/ignore-the-poway-synagogue-shooters-manifesto-pay-attention-to-8chans-pol-board/.

Evans, Robert. "Shitposting, Inspirational Terrorism, and the Christchurch Mosque Massacre." *Bellingcat*, March 15, 2019. https://www.bellingcat.com/news/rest-of-world/2019/03/15/shitposting-inspirational-terrorism-and-the-christchurch-mosque-massacre/

Evola, Julius. *Men Among the Ruins: Post-War Reflections of a Radical Traditionalist*. Translated by Guido Stucco. Rochester, VT: Inner Traditions, 2002.

Evola, Julius. *Ride the Tiger: A Survival Manual for the Aristocrats of the Soul*. Translated by Joscelyn Godwin and Constance Fontana. Rochester, VT: Inner Traditions, 2018.

Falasca-Zamponi, Simonetta. *Fascist Spectacle: The Aesthetics of Power in Mussolini's Italy*. Berkeley, Los Angeles, and Oxford, UK: University of California Press, 1997.

Federici, Silvia. *Caliban and the Witch*. Brooklyn: Autonomedia, 2004.

Federici, Silvia. "Occupy and the Struggle over Reproduction: An Interview with Silvia Federici." By Max Haiven. *Libcom.org*, November 27, 2011, https://libcom.org/library/feminism-finance-future-occupy-interview-silvia-federici.

Federici, Silvia. *Revolution at Point Zero*. Oakland: PM Press; Brooklyn: Common Notions and Autonomedia, 2012.

Federici, Silvia. *Witches, Witch-hunting, and Women*. Oakland: PM Press, 2018.

Fieldstadt, Elisha. "James Alex Fields, driver in deadly car attack at Charlottesville rally, sentenced to life in prison." *NBC News*, June 28, 2019, https://www.nbcnews.com/news/us-news/james-alex-fields-driver-deadly-car-attack-charlottesville-rally-sentenced-n1024436.

Fielitz, Maik, and Holger Marcks. "Digital Fascism: Challenges for the Open Society in Times of Social Media." *Berkeley Center for Right-Wing Studies Working Paper Series*, July 16, 2019, https://escholarship.org/uc/item/87w5c5gp.

Finchelstein, Federico. *A Brief History of Fascist Lies*. Oakland: University of California Press, 2020.

Florini, Sarah. *Beyond Hashtags: Racial Politics and Black Digital Networks*. New York: New York University Press, 2019.

Forchtner, Bernhard, and Christoffer Kølvraa. "Extreme Right Images of Radical Authenticity: Multimodal Aesthetics of History, Nature, and Gender Roles in Social Media." *European Journal of Cultural and Political Sociology* 4, no. 3 (2017): 252–281.

Fortunati, Leopoldina. "Social Reproduction, But Not As We Know It." *Viewpoint Magazine* 5, October 31, 2015, https://viewpointmag.com/2015/10/31/social-reproduction-but-not-as-we-know-it/.

Fortunati, Leopoldina. *The Arcane of Reproduction: Housework, Prostitution, Labor and Capital*. Translated by Hilary Creek. Brooklyn: Autonomedia, 1996.

Foucault, Michel. *"Society Must Be Defended." Lectures at the Collège de France, 1975–76*, edited by Mauro Bertani and Alessandro Fontana. Translated by David Macey. London: Picador, 2003.

Foucault, Michel. "Preface." In Gilles Deleuze and Félix Guattari, *Anti-Oedipus: Capitalism and Schizophrenia*, translated by Robert Hurley, Mark Seem, and Helen R. Lane, xixv. Minneapolis: University of Minnesota Press, 1977.

Franzinelli, Mimmo. "Squadrism." In *The Oxford Handbook of Fascism*, edited by R. J. B. Bosworth, 91–108. Oxford: Oxford University Press, 2009.

Freeman, Elizabeth. *Beside You in Time: Sense Methods and Queer Sociabilities in the American Nineteenth Century*. Durham and London: Duke University Press, 2019.

Freeman, Jo. W.I.T.C.H.—The Women's International Terrorist Conspiracy from Hell, http://www.jofreeman.com/photos/witch.html.

Fromm, Erich. *The Anatomy of Human Destructiveness*. New York: Holt, Rinehart and Winston, 1973.

Fromm, Erich. *War Within Man: A Psychological Enquiry into the Roots of Destructiveness*. Philadelphia: Peace Literature Service of the American Friends Service Committee, 1963, https://files.eric.ed.gov/fulltext/ED073981.pdf.

Gago, Verónica, and Raquel Gutiérrez Aguilar. "Women Rising in Defense of Life: Tracing the Revolutionary Flows of Latin American Women's Many Uprisings." *NACLA Report on the Americas* 50, no. 4 (2018): 364–368.

Gago, Verónica, Marta Malo, and Liz Mason-Deese. "Introduction: The New Feminist Internationale." *South Atlantic Quarterly* 119, no. 3 (2020): 620–628.

Gago, Verónica. *Feminist International: How to Change Everything.* Translated by Liz Mason-Deese. New York and London: Verso, 2020.

Gandesha, Samir, ed. *Spectres of Fascism: Historical, Theoretical and International Perspectives.* London: Pluto Press, 2020.

Gelderloos, Peter. *Worshiping Power.* Oakland: AK Press, 2017.

Genosko, Gary. "Black Holes of Politics: Resonances of Microfascism." *La Deleuziana* 5 (2017): 59–67.

Genosko, Gary. "Micro-Fascism in the Age of Trump." In *Spectres of Fascism: Historical, Theoretical and International Perspectives,* edited by Samir Gandesha, 164–176. London: Pluto Press, 2020.

Gibbs, Anna. "Panic! Affect Contagion, Mimesis and Suggestion in the Social Field." *Cultural Studies Review* 14, no. 2 (2008): 130–145.

Gibson-Graham, J.K. *A Postcapitalist Politics.* Minneapolis: University of Minnesota Press, 2006.

Gill, Rosalind. *Gender and the Media.* Cambridge, UK and Malden, MA: Polity, 2007.

Gill, Rosalind. "Sexism Reloaded, or, it's Time to Get Angry Again!" *Feminist Media Studies* 11, no. 1 (2011): 61–71.

Gilligan, Carol, and David A.J. Richards. *Darkness Now Visible: Patriarchy's Resurgence and Feminist Resistance.* Cambridge, UK and New York: Cambridge University Press, 2018.

Gilligan, Carol, and David A.J. Richards. *Deepening Darkness: Patriarchy, Resistance, and Democracy's Future.* Cambridge: Cambridge University Press, 2008.

Ging, Debbie, and Eugenia Siapera. "Introduction: Special Issue on Online Misogyny." *Feminist Media Studies* 18, no. 4 (2018): 515–524.

Goeschel, Christian. *Suicide in Nazi Germany.* Oxford: Oxford University Press, 2009.

Gramsci, Antonio. *Prison Notebooks, Volume II.* Edited and translated by Joseph A. Buttigieg. New York: Columbia University Press, 2011.

Griffin, Roger. "Interregnum or Endgame? The Radical Right in the 'Post-Fascist' Era." *Journal of Political Ideologies* 5, no. 2 (2000): 163–178.

Griffin, Roger. "From Slime Mould to Rhizome: An Introduction to the Groupuscular Right." *Patterns of Prejudice* 37, no. 1 (2003): 27–50.

Griffin, Roger. "Fascism's New Faces (and New Facelessness) in the 'Post-Fascist' Epoch." In *A Fascist Century: Essays by Roger Griffin,* edited by Matthew Feldman, 181–188. New York: Palgrave Macmillan, 2008.

Griffin, Roger. *A Fascist Century: Essays by Roger Griffin,* edited by Matthew Feldman. New York: Palgrave Macmillan, 2008.

Griffin, Roger. *The Nature of Fascism.* New York and London: Routledge, 1993.

Grottanelli, Cristiano. "War-Time Connections: Dumézil and Eliade, Eliade and Schmitt, Schmitt and Evola, Drieu La Rochelle and Dumézil." In *The Study of Religion under the Impact of Fascism,* edited by Horst Junginger, 303–314. Leiden and Boston: Brill, 2007.

Guattari, Félix. "Everybody Wants to Be a Fascist." In *Chaosophy,* edited by Sylvère Lotringer, translated by David L. Sweet, Jarred Becker, and Taylor Adkins, 154–175. New York: Semiotext(e), 2009.

Guattari, Félix. "Socially Significant Drugs." In *High Culture: Reflections on Addiction and Modernity*, edited by Anna Alexander and Mark S. Roberts, 199–208. Albany: State University of New York Press, 2003.

Guattari, Félix. "The Micro-Politics of Fascism." In *Molecular Revolution: Psychiatry and Politics*, trans. Rosemery Sheed, 217–232. Harmondsworth and New York: Peregrine Books, 1984.

Guattari, Félix, and Gilles Deleuze. *A Thousand Plateaus: Capitalism and Schizophrenia*, translated by Brian Massumi. Minneapolis: University of Minnesota Press, 1987.

Hackworth, Lucy. "Limitations of 'Just Gender.'" In *Mediating Misogyny: Gender, Technology, and Harassment*, edited by Jacqueline Ryan Vickery and Tracy Everbach, 51–70. Cham: Palgrave Macmillan, 2018.

Hardt, Michael, and Antonio Negri. *Assembly.* New York: Oxford University Press, 2017.

Harris, Joseph. "Love and Death in the Männerbund: An Essay with Special Reference to the Bjarkamál and The Battle of Maldon." In *"Speak Useful Words or Say Nothing": Old Norse Studies*, edited by Susan E. Deskis and Thomas D. Hill, 287–317. Ithaca: Cornell University Library, 2008.

Hart, Sam, Toby Shorin and Laura Lotti. "Squad Wealth." *Other Internet*, August 19, 2020, https://otherinter.net/squad-wealth/.

Hawley, George. *Making Sense of the Alt-Right.* New York: Columbia University Press, 2017.

Hay, James. *Popular Film Culture in Fascist Italy: The Passing of the Rex.* Bloomington: Indiana University Press, 1987.

Hayles, N. Katherine. "Survival as Mimesis: Microbiomimesis and the Production of Posthuman Bodies," keynote address for Posthuman Mimesis conference (HOM), Institute of Philosophy at KU Leuven, May 21, 2021, http://www.homomimeticus.eu/2021/07/05/survival-as-mimesis-katherine-hayles/.

Hedges, Chris. "America's Death March." *MintPress News*, August 10, 2020, https://www.mintpressnews.com/chris-hedges-hypernationalism-crisis-cults-signs-united-states-decline/270236/?fbclid=IwAR3o_z2WbYNGropx8KY5ooVKacWTnPn23u8CcWuPllfV-7x8h_-mh2FYsbM.

Herausgeber innenkollektiv [Editorial collective]. *Fantifa: Feministische Perspektiven Antifaschistischer Politiken.* Münster, DE: Edition Assemblage, 2013.

Hernandez, Joe. "A California Father Claims QAnon Conspiracy Led Him To Kill His 2 Children, FBI Says." *NPR*, August 13, 2021, https://www.npr.org/2021/08/13/1027133867/children-dead-father-claims-qanon-conspiracy-led-him-to-kill.

Hester, Helen. *Xenofeminism.* Cambridge, UK and Medford, MA: Polity Press, 2018.
Holland, Jack. *A Brief History of Misogyny: The World's Oldest Prejudice.* London: Little, Brown & Company, 2006.

Homo Mimeticus: Theory and Criticism (HOM). European Research Council-funded project, Department of Philosophy at KU Leuven, http://www.homomimeticus.eu/home/.

Huyssen, Andreas. "Behemoth Rises Again." *n+1*, July 29, 2019, https://nplusonemag.com/online-only/online-only/behemoth-rises-again/.

Indigenous Action, "Rethinking the Apocalypse: An Indigenous Anti-Futurist Manifesto." *Indigenous Action*, March 19, 2020, https://www.indigenousaction.org/rethinking-the-apocalypse-an-indigenous-anti-futurist-manifesto/.

Jackson, Sarah J., Moya Bailey, and Brooke Foucault Welles. *#HashtagActivism: Networks of Race and Gender Justice*. Cambridge: The MIT Press, 2020.

Jaffe, Aaron. "Social Production Theory in and beyond the Pandemic." *Pluto Press* (blog), October 10, 2020, https://www.plutobooks.com/blog/social-reproduction-theory-in-and-beyond-the-pandemic/.

Jane, Emma A. *Misogyny Online: A Short (and Brutish) History*. Los Angeles, London, New Delhi, Singapore, Washington, DC, and Melbourne: Sage Swifts, 2016.

Jarema, Kerri. "11 New Books With Kickass Girl Squads To Inspire You To Close Out 2018 With A Bang." *Bustle*, November 14, 2018, https://www.bustle.com/p/11-new-books-with-kickass-girl-squads-to-help-you-finish-out-the-year-strong-13115632.

Johannsen, Jacob. *Fantasy, Online Misogyny and the Manosphere: Male Bodies of Dis/Inhibition*. New York and London: Routledge, 2021.

Johnson, Andrew. "Ur-Fascism and Neo-Fascism." *The Journal of International Relations, Peace Studies, and Development* 5, no. 1 (2019): 1–33.

Jordan-Zachary, Julia S., and Duchess Harris, eds. *Black Girl Magic Beyond the Hashtag: Twenty-First-Century Acts of Self-Definition*. Tucson: University of Arizona Press, 2019.

Kay, Jilly Boyce. *Gender, Media and Voice: Communicative Injustice and Public Speech*. Chalm: Palgrave, 2020.

Khamis, Susie, Lawrence Ang, and Raymond Welling. "Self-Branding, 'Micro-Celebrity' and the Rise of Social Media Influencers." *Celebrity Studies* 8, no. 1 (2017): 191–208.

Klee, Miles. "4chan's 'Doomer' Memes Are A Strange Frontier In Online Extremism." *MEL Magazine*, July 14, 2020, https://melmagazine.com/en-us/story/4chan-doomer-gloomer-memes-music-playlists.

Klee, Miles. "We Stand Against 'No Simp September.'" *MEL Magazine*, March 15, 2021, https://melmagazine.com/en-us/story/no-simp-september.

Klinger, Cornelia. "The Concepts of the Sublime and the Beautiful in Kant and Lyotard." *Constellations* 2, no. 2 (1995): 207–223.

Koepnick, Lutz Peter. *Walter Benjamin and the Aesthetics of Power*. Lincoln: University of Nebraska Press, 1999.

Kølvraa, Christoffer, and Forchtner, Bernhard. "Cultural Imaginaries of the Extreme Right: An Introduction." *Patterns of Prejudice* 53, no. 3 (2019): 227–235.

Lavin, Talia. *Culture Warlords: My Journey into the Dark Web of White Supremacy*. New York: Hachette, 2020.

Lawtoo, Nidesh. *(New) Fascism: Contagion, Community, Myth*. East Lansing: Michigan State University Press, 2019.

Lazzarato, Maurizio. *Capital Hates Everyone: Fascism or Revolution*. Translated by Robert Hurley. South Pasadena: Semiotext(e), 2021.

Lee, Petronella. *Anti-Fascism Against Machismo: Gender, Politics, and the Struggle Against Fascism*. Hamilton: The Tower InPrint, 2019, https://north-shore.info/2019/10/03/anti-fascism-beyond-machismo/.

Lennard, Natasha. *Being Numerous: Essays on Non-Fascist Life*. London and New York: Verso, 2021.

Lewis, Rebecca. "Alternative Influence: Broadcasting the Reactionary Right on YouTube." *Data & Society*, September 18, 2018, https://datasociety.net/library/alternative-influence/.

Lewis, Sophie. *Full Surrogacy Now: Feminism against Family*. London and New York: Verso, 2019.

Linh Tu, Thuy, and Nikhil Pal Singh. "Morbid Capitalism and its Racial Symptoms," *n+1* 30 (Winter 2018), https://www.nplusonemag.com/issue-30/essays/morbid-capitalism/.

Lopez, Julyssa. "Donald Trump's History of Calling Women 'Dogs' Just Got Longer With New Omarosa Tweet." *Glamour*, August 14, 2018, https://www.glamour.com/story/donald-trump-history-of-calling-women-dogs-omarosa.

Lordon, Frédéric. *Willing Slaves of Capital: Spinoza and Marx on Desire*. London and New York: Verso, 2014.

Luna, Jack. "The Only Possible Way to Understand White Trump Voters." *Medium*, September 9, 2020, https://everythinghereistrue.medium.com/the-only-way-to-understand-white-trump-voters-6122ed88f4d2.

Lyons, Matthew N. "Jack Donovan on Men: A Masculine Tribalism for the Far Right." *Three Way Fight* (blog), November 23, 2015, http://three-wayfight.blogspot.com/2015/11/jack-donovan-on-men-masculine-tribalism.html.

Lyons, Matthew N. "CTRL-ALT-DELETE: The origins and ideology of the Alternative Right." *Political Research Associates*, January 20, 2017, https://www.politicalresearch.org/2017/01/20/ctrl-alt-delete-report-on-the-alternative-right.

Lyons, Matthew N. *Insurgent Supremacists: The U.S. Far Right's Challenge to State and Empire*. Oakland: PM Press, 2018.

Madani, Doha. "Dan Patrick on Coronavirus: 'More Important Things than Living.'" *NBC News*, April 21, 2020, https://www.nbcnews.com/news/us-news/texas-lt-gov-dan-patrick-reopening-economy-more-important-things-n1188911.

Maggs, Sam. *Girl Squads: 20 Female Friendships That Changed History*. Philadelphia: Quirk Books, 2018.

Manne, Kate. *Down Girl: The Logic of Misogyny*. New York: Oxford University Press, 2017.

Mantilla, Karla. *Gendertrolling: How Misogyny Went Viral*. Santa Barbara and Denver: Praeger, 2015.

Marcotte, Amanda. *Troll Nation: How the American Right Devolved into a Clubhouse of Haters*. New York: Skyhorse Publishing, 2018.

Marks, Laura U. "Which Came First, Fascism or Misogyny? Reading Klaus Theweleit's Male Fantasies." In *Spectres of Fascism: Historical, Theoretical and International Perspectives,* edited by Samir Gandesha, 109–119. London: Pluto Press, 2020.

Martel, James. "Histories of Violence: Why We Should All Read Walter Benjamin Today—Interview with James Martel." By Brad Evans. *Los Angeles Review of Books*, February 3, 2020, https://lareviewofbooks.org/article/histories-of-violence-why-we-should-all-read-walter-benjamin-today.

Maynard, Mary, and Jalna Hanmer, eds. *Women, Violence and Social Control*. Houndmills, Basingstoke, Hampshire, and London: Macmillan, 1987.

Mbembé, Achille and Libby Meintjes. "Necropolitics." *Public Culture* 15, no. 1 (2003): 11–40, muse.jhu.edu/article/39984.

McBrien, Justin. "Accumulating Extinction: Planetary Catastrophism in the Necrocene." In *Anthropocene or Capitalocene? Nature, History, and the Crisis of Capitalism*, edited by Jason W. Moore, 116–137. Oakland: PM Press, 2016.

McRobbie, Angela. *The Aftermath of Feminism: Gender, Culture and Social Change*. London, Thousand Oaks, New Delhi, Singapore: Sage, 2009.

Merrin, William. "President Troll: Trump, 4chan and Memetic Warfare." In *Trump's Media War*, edited by Catherine Happer, Andrew Hoskins, William Merrin, 201–226. Cham: Palgrave Macmillan, 2019.

M.I. Asma (J. Moufawad-Paul, Devin Zane Shaw, Mateo Andante, Johannah May Black, Alyson Escalante, D. W. Fairlane). *On Necrocapitalism: A Plague Journal*. Montreal: Kersplebedeb, 2021.

Michelsen, Nicholas. "Fascist Lines of the Tokkotai." In *Deleuze & Fascism: Security, War, Aesthetics*, edited by Brad Evans and Julian Reid, 148–172. London and New York: Routledge, 2013.

Mies, Maria. *Patriarchy and Accumulation on a World Scale*. New York: Zed Books, 1998.

Montag, Warren. "Necro-economics: Adam Smith and death in the life of the universal." *Radical Philosophy* 137, no. 7 (2005): 7–17.

Nagle, Angela. *Kill all Normies: Online Culture Wars from 4chan and Tumblr to Trump and the Alt-right*. Alresford, UK: John Hunt Publishing, 2017.

Neiwert, David. *Alt-America: The Rise of the Radical Right in the Age of Trump*. New York and London: Verso, 2017.

Neocleous, Mark. *The Monstrous and the Dead: Burke, Marx, Fascism*. Cardiff: University of Wales Press, 2005, 152.

Novak, Matt. "Why Are Trump Supporters Offering People 'Free Helicopter Rides' Online?" Gizmodo, October 12, 2018, https://gizmodo.com/why-are-trump-supporters-offering-people-free-helicopte-1829705238.

O'Donnell, Meghan. "Dangerous Undercurrent: Death, Sacrifice and Ruin in Third Reich Germany." *International Journal of Humanities and Social Sciences* 2, no. 9 (2012): 231–239.

O'Leary, Joseph S. "Steve Bannon's Ghostly Triumph." *B2o*, September 5, 2017, https://www.boundary2.org/2017/09/joseph-s-oleary-steve-bannons-ghostly-triumph/#comment-28958.

Pateman, Carole. "Feminist Critiques of the Public/Private Dichotomy." In *Public and Private in Social Life*, edited by S.I. Benn and G.F. Gaus, 281–303. London: Croom Helm, 1983.

Paxton, Robert O. *The Anatomy of Fascism*. New York: Vintage, 2007.

Pengelly, Martin. "Whitmer Won't Go 'Punch for Punch' with Republican who Called Her a Witch." *The Guardian*, April 11, 2021, https://www.theguardian.com/us-news/2021/apr/11/gretchen-whitmer-michigan-governor-witch-burn-stake.

Penny, Laurie. *Sexual Revolution: Modern Fascism and the Feminist Fightback*. New York: Bloomsbury Publishing, 2022.

Perry, Imani. *Vexy Thing: On Gender and Liberation*. Durham: Duke University Press, 2018.

Protevi, John. "'A Problem of Pure Matter': Deleuze and Guattari's Treatment of Fascist Nihilism in *A Thousand Plateaus*." In *Nihilism Now! Monsters of Energy*, edited by Keith Ansell Pearson and Diane Morgan, 167–188. Houndmills, Basingstoke, Hampshire and London: Macmillan, 2000.

Prupis, Nadia. "Bannon Heralds 'Deconstruction of Administrative State' and Trump's 'New Political Order.'" *Common Dreams*, February 23, 2017, https://www.commondreams.org/news/2017/02/23/bannon-heralds-deconstruction-administrative-state-and-trumps-new-political-order.

Puar, Jasbir K. *The Right to Maim: Debility, Capacity, Disability*. Durham and London: Duke University Press, 2017.

Quart, Alyssa. "The Age of Hipster Sexism." *The Cut*, October 30, 2012, https://www.thecut.com/2012/10/age-of-hipster-sexism.html.

Rainey, Lawrence. "Introduction: F. T. Marinetti and the Development of Futurism." In *Futurism: An Anthology*, edited by Lawrence Rainey, Christine Poggi, Laura Wittman, 1–39. New Haven: Yale University Press, 2009.

RedPill Living, https://www.redpillliving.com/we-believe/.

Renton, David. *The New Authoritarians: Convergence on the Right*. Chicago: Haymarket Books, 2019.

Roediger, David. *The Wages of Whiteness: Race and the Making of the American Working Class*. London and New York: Verso, 1991.

Romano, Aja. "How the alt-right's sexism lures men into white supremacy." *Vox*, April 26, 2018, https://www.vox.com/culture/2016/12/14/13576192/alt-right-sexism-recruitment.

Roose, Kevin. "A Mass Murder of, and for, the Internet." *The New York Times*, March 15, 2019, https://www.nytimes.com/2019/03/15/technology/facebook-youtube-christchurch-shooting.html.

Ross, Alexander Reid. *Against the Fascist Creep*. Chico: AK Press, 2017.

Rottenberg, Catherine. *The Rise of Neoliberal Feminism*. Oxford: Oxford University Press, 2018.

Rottenberg, Catherine, Jo Littler, Andreas Chatzidakis, and Jamie Hakim. *The Care Manifesto: The Politics of Interdependence*. London and New York: Verso, 2020.

Rubin, Gayle. "The Traffic in Women: Notes on the 'Political Economy' of Sex." In *Toward an Anthropology of Women*, edited by Rayna R. Reiter, 157–210. New York: Monthly Review Press, 1975.

Russell, Diana E. H. "The Origin and Importance of the Term Femicide," Filmed December 1, 2011, 22:02, https://www.youtube.com/watch?v=fk9VNHYMOrE.

Savigny, Heather. *Cultural Sexism: The Politics of Feminist Rage in the #Me Too Era*. Bristol: Bristol University Press, 2020.

Schaefer, Kayleen. *Text Me When You Get Home*. New York: Dutton, 2018.

Schreckinger, Ben. "World War Meme: How a group of anonymous keyboard commandos conquered the Internet for Donald Trump—and plans to deliver Europe to the far right." *Politico*, March/April 2017, https://www.politico.com/magazine/story/2017/03/memes-4chan-trump-supporters-trolls-internet-214856/.

She Safe, We Safe, https://www.shesafewesafe.org.

Shifman, Limor, and Dafna Lemish. "Between Feminism and Fun(ny)mism." *Information, Communication & Society* 13, no. 6 (2010): 870–891.

Shukaitis, Stevphen. *Imaginal Machines: Autonomy & Self-Organization in the Revolutions of Everyday Life*. London, New York, Port Watson: Minor Compositions, 2009.

Sibertin-Blanc, Guillaume. *State and Politics: Deleuze and Guattari on Marx*. Translated by Ames Hodges. South Pasadena: Semiotext(e), 2016.

Siegel, Jacob. "Teens Bring 4chan Politics to Boston." *The Daily Beast*, May 15, 2017, https://www.thedailybeast.com/teens-bbring-4chan-politics-to-boston.

Singh, Rianka, and Sarah Banet-Weiser. "Sky High: Platforms and the Feminist Politics of Visibility." In *Re-Understanding Media Feminist Extensions of Marshall McLuhan*, edited by Sarah Sharma and Rianka Singh. Durham: Duke University Press, 2022 [pre-press proof].

Sitrin, Marina, and Colectiva Sembrar, eds. *Pandemic Solidarity: Mutual Aid during the COVID-19 Crisis*. London: Pluto Press, 2020.

Solnit, Rebecca. "Not Caring is a Political Art Form." *Literary Hub*, June 22, 2018, https://lithub.com/rebecca-solnit-not-caring-is-a-political-art-form/.

Sontag, Susan. "Fascinating Fascism." *The New York Review of Books*, February 6, 1975. https://www.nybooks.com/articles/1975/02/06/fascinating-fascism/

Spotts, Frederic. *Hitler and the Power of Aesthetics*. New York: The Overlook Press, 2003.

Stahl, Roger. *Militainment, Inc.: War, Media, and Popular Culture*. New York and Abingdon, Oxon: Routledge, 2009.

Stanley, Jason. *How Fascism Works: The Politics of Us and Them*. New York: Random House, 2020.

Steele, Catherine Knight. *Digital Black Feminism*. New York: New York University Press, 2021.

Stern, Alexandra Minna. *Proud Boys and the White Ethnostate: How the Alt-Right is Warping the American Imagination*. Boston: Beacon Press, 2019.

Sunshine, Spencer. "Three Pillars of the Alt-Right: White Nationalism, Antisemitism, and Misogyny." *Political Research Associates*, December 4, 2017, https://www.politicalresearch.org/2017/12/04/three-pillars-of-the-alt-right-white-nationalism-antisemitism-and-misogyny.

Swetnam, Joseph. *The Arraignment of Lewd, Idle, Froward, and Unconstant Women: Or, The Vanity Of Them; Chuse You Wheter. With A Commendation of The Wise, Vertuous, and Honest Women. Pleasant for Married-Men, Profitable for Youngmen, and Hurtfull To None*. London: B. Deacon, 1707.

Sternhell, Zeev, with Mario Sznader and Maia Ashéri. *The Birth of Fascist Ideology: From Cultural Rebellion to Political Revolution*. Translated by David Maisel. Princeton and Chichester, UK: Princeton University Press, 1994.

Taguieff, Pierre-André. "Discussion or Inquisition: The Case of Alain de Benoist." *Telos* 98–99 (Winter 1993–Spring 1994): 99–125.

Tarì, Marcello. *There Is No Unhappy Revolution*. Brooklyn: Common Notions, 2021.

Taussig, Michael. *Mimesis and Alterity: A Particular History of the Sense*s. New York and London: Routledge, 1993.

Taussig, Michael. *The Magic of the State*. New York and London: Routledge, 1997.

Theweleit, Klaus. *Male Fantasies, Volume 1: Women, Floods, Bodies, History*. Minneapolis: University of Minnesota Press, 1987.

Theweleit, Klaus. *Male Fantasies, Volume 2: Psychoanalyzing the White Terror*. Minneapolis: University of Minnesota Press, 1991.

Thorburn, Elise. "Networked Social Reproduction: Crises in the Integrated Circuit." *tripleC: Communication, Capitalism & Critique. Open Access Journal for a Global Sustainable Information Society* 14, no. 2 (2016): 380–396.

Thornton, Cassie. *The Hologram: Feminist, Peer-to-Peer Health for a Post-Pandemic Future*. London: Pluto Press, 2020.

Thorpe, Charles. *Necroculture*. New York: Palgrave Macmillan, 2016.

Threadcraft, Shatema. "North American Necropolitics and Gender: On #BlackLivesMatter and Black Femicide." *South Atlantic Quarterly* 116, no. 3 (2017): 553–579.

TIME staff. "Here's Donald Trump's Presidential Announcement Speech." *TIME*, June 16, 2015, https://time.com/3923128/donald-trump-announcement-speech/.

Torba, Andrew. "The Silent Christian Secession." Gab.com, February 1, 2021, https://news.gab.com/2021/02/01/the-silent-christian-secession/.

Torino, Paul, and Adrian Wohlleben. "Memes with Force – Lessons from The Yellow Vests." *Mute*, February 26, 2019, https://www.metamute.org/editorial/articles/memes-force---lessons-yellow-vests.

Toscano, Alberto. "The Long Shadow of Racial Fascism." *Boston Review*, October 28, 2020, https://bostonreview.net/race-politics/alberto-toscano-long-shadow-racial-fascism.

Traverso, Enzo. *The New Faces of Fascism: Populism and the Far Right*. New York and London: Verso, 2019.

Trudy. "Explanation of Misogynoir." *Gradient Lair*, April 28, 2014, https://www.gradientlair.com/post/84107309247/define-misogynoir-anti-black-misogyny-moya-bailey-coined.

Trudy. "Misogyny, In General vs. Anti-Black Misogyny (Misogynoir), Specifically." *Gradient Lair*, September 11, 2013, https://www.gradientlair.com/post/60973580823/general-misogyny-versus-misogynoir.

Tuchman, Gaye. "The Symbolic Annihilation of Women by the Mass Media." In *Hearth and Home: Images of Women in the Media*, edited by Gaye Tuchman, Arlene Kaplan Daniels, and James Benét, 3–38. New York: Oxford University Press, 1978.

Turner, Graeme. Ordinary People and the Media: The Demotic Turn. London: Sage, 2010.

Udupa, Sahana. "Extreme Speech| Nationalism in the Digital Age: Fun as a Metapractice of Extreme Speech." *International Journal of Communication* 13 (2019): 3143–3163.

Vickery, Jacqueline Ryan, and Tracy Everbach. "The Persistence of Misogyny: From the Streets to Our Screens, to the White House." In *Gender, Technology, and Harassment*, 1–27. Cham: Palgrave Macmillan, 2018.

Wendling, Mike. *Alt-Right: From 4chan to the White House*. London: Pluto Press, 2018.

Wildman, Sarah. "Trump's Speech in Poland Sounded like an Alt-Right Manifesto." Vox.com, July 6, 2017, https://www.vox.com/world/2017/7/6/15927590/trump-alt-right-poland-defend-west-civilization-g20.

Williams, Raymond. *Marxism and Literature*. Oxford and New York: Oxford University Press, 1977.

Williamson, Judith. "Sexism with an alibi." *The Guardian*, May 31, 2003, https://www.theguardian.com/media/2003/may/31/advertising.comment.

Wilson, Jason. "What do incels, fascists and terrorists have in common? Violent misogyny." *The Guardian,* May 4, 2018, https://www.theguardian.com/commentisfree/2018/may/04/what-do-incels-fascists-and-terrorists-have-in-common-violent-misogyny.

Winch, Alison. "Brand Intimacy, Female Friendship and Digital Surveillance Networks." *new formations: a journal of culture/theory/politics* 84 (2015): 228–245.

Winter, Aaron. "Online Hate: From the Far-Right to the 'Alt-Right,' and from the Margins to the Mainstream." In *Online Othering: Exploring Violence and Discrimination on the Web,* edited by Karen Lumsden and Emily Harmer, 39–64. Cham: Palgrave Macmillan, 2019.

Wohlleben, Adrian. "Memes Without End." *Ill Will,* May 16, 2021, https://illwill.com/memes-without-end.

Woolf, Virginia. *A Room of One's Own and Three Guineas.* Oxford: Oxford University Press, 2008.

Worsdale, Hope. "Anti-Fascism Is a Feminist Issue." *Red Pepper,* December 7, 2018, https://www.redpepper.org.uk/anti-fascism-is-feminist-issue/.

Wright, Jennifer. "Why Donald Trump Keeps Calling Women 'Bloody.'" *Bazaar,* June 29, 2017, https://www.harpersbazaar.com/culture/features/a10241058/mika-brzezinski-donald-trump-tweet/.

Wright, Melissa W. "Necropolitics, Narcopolitics, and Femicide: Gendered Violence on the Mexico-US Border." *Signs: Journal of Women in Culture and Society* 36, no. 3 (2011): 707–731.

Wright, Steve. *Storming Heaven: Class Composition and Struggle in Italian Autonomist Marxism.* London: Pluto Press, 2002.

Wulf, Christoph, and Gunter Gebauer. *Mimesis: Culture, Art, Society.* Translated by Don Reneau. Berkeley: University of California Press, 1995.

Wynter, Sylvia, and McKittrick, Katherine. "Unparalleled Catastrophe for Our Species? Or, to Give Humanness a Different Future: Conversations." In *Sylvia Wynter: On Being Human as Praxis,* edited by Katherine McKittrick, 9–89. Durham and London: Duke University Press, 2015.

Zechner, Manuela. "A politics of network-families? Precarity, crisis and care." In *The Nanopolitics Handbook,* edited by Paolo Plotegher, Manuela Zechner, and Bue Rübner Hansen, 183–198. Wivenhoe, New York, and Port Watson: Minor Compositions, 2013.

Zemmour, Éric. *Le Suicide Français.* Paris: Éditions Albin Michel, 2014.

Ziarek, Ewa Plonowska. "Mimesis in Black and White: Feminist Aesthetics, Negativity and Semblance." In *The New Aestheticism,* edited by John J. Joughin and Simon Malpas, 51–67. Manchester and New York: Manchester University Press, 2003.

Zuckerberg, Donna. *Not All Dead White Men: Classics and Misogyny in the Digital Age.* Cambridge, MA and London: Harvard University Press, 2018.

Index

About the Author

Jack Z. Bratich is professor of journalism and media studies at Rutgers University. He has written dozens of articles, book chapters, and essays about the intersection of popular culture and political culture. His work applies autonomist social theory to such topics as social movements, social media, and the cultural politics of secrecy.

Bratich has edited special journal issues on Occupy Wall Street and on the tenth anniversary of *Empire* by Michael Hardt and Antonio Negri. He is author of *Conspiracy Panics: Political Rationality and Popular Culture* (2008) and coeditor, along with Jeremy Packer and Cameron McCarthy, of *Foucault, Cultural Studies, and Governmentality* (2003). He has been a zine librarian at ABC No Rio in New York City and now sits as a member of its advisory board.

About Common Notions

Common Notions is a publishing house and programming platform that advances new formulations of liberation and living autonomy. Our books provide timely reflections, clear critiques, and inspiring strategies that amplify movements for social justice.

By any media necessary, we seek to nourish the imagination and generalize common notions about the creation of other worlds beyond state and capital. Our publications trace a constellation of critical and visionary meditations on the organization of freedom. Inspired by various traditions of autonomism and liberation—in the United States and internationally, historically and emerging from contemporary movements—our publications provide resources for a collective reading of struggles past, present, and to come.

Common Notions regularly collaborates with editorial houses, political collectives, militant authors, and visionary designers around the world. Our political and aesthetic interventions are dreamt and realized in collaboration with Antumbra Designs.

commonnotions.org / info@commonnotions.org

Become a Monthly Sustainer

These are decisive times, ripe with challenges and possibility, heartache and beautiful inspiration. More than ever, we are in need of timely reflections, clear critiques, and inspiring strategies that can help movements for social justice grow and transform society. Help us amplify those necessary words, deeds, and dreams that our liberation movements and our worlds so need. Movements are sustained by people like you, whose fugitive words, deeds, and dreams bend against the world of domination and exploitation.

For collective imagination, dedicated practices of love and study, and organized acts of freedom.

By any media necessary. With your love and support.

Monthly sustainers start at $12 and $25.

Join us at commonnotions.org/sustain.

More From Common Notions

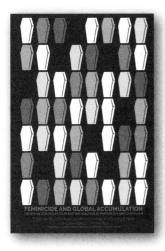

Feminicide and Global Accumulation: Frontline Struggles to Resist the Violence of Patriarchy and Capitalism

Edited by Silvia Federici, Susana Draper, and Liz Mason-Deese

With Otras Negras ... y ¡Feministas!

Afterword by Sheila Gruner, Epilogue by Betty Ruth Lozano Lerma

978-1-942173-44-1
$20
240 pages

Feminicide and Global Accumulation brings us to the frontlines of an international movement of Black, Indigenous, popular, and mestiza women's organizations fighting against violence—interpersonal, state sanctioned, and economic—that is both endemic to the global economy and the contemporary devalued status of racialized women, trans, and gender non-conforming communities in the Global South.

These struggles against racism, capitalism, and patriarchy show how crucially linked the land, water, and other resource extraction projects that crisscross the planet are to devaluing labor and nature and how central Black and Indigenous women and trans leadership is to its resistance.

The book is based on the first ever International Forum on Feminicide among ethnicized and racialized groups—which brought together activists and researchers from Colombia, Guatemala, Italy, Brazil, Iran, Guinea Bissau, Bolivia, Canada, the U.S., Ecuador, Spain, Mexico, among other countries in the world to represent different social movements and share concrete stories, memories, experiences and knowledge of their struggles against racism, capitalism and patriarchy.

Feminicide and Global Accumulation reflects, in a collective fabric, the communitarian and enraged struggles of women, trans, and gender non-conforming communities who commit themselves to the transformation of their communities by directly challenging the murder and assassination of women and violence in all its forms.

More From Common Notions

For Antifascist Futures:
Against the Violence of Imperial Crisis

Edited by Alyosha Goldstein and Simón
Ventura Trujillo

978-1-942173-56-4
$24
304 pages

We must, as *For Antifascist Futures* urges, take antifascism as a major imperative of movements for social change. But we must not limit our analysis or historical understanding of the rise of the right-wing authoritarianism in our times by rooting it in mid-twentieth century Europe. Instead we turn to a collection of powerful BIPOC voices who offer a range of anticolonial, Indigenous, and Black Radical traditions to think with.

For Antifascist Futures takes seriously what is new in this moment of politics, exploring what the analytic of fascism offers for understanding the twenty-first century authoritarian convergence by centering the material and speculative labor of antifascist and antiracist social movement coalitions. By focusing on the long history of Black and Brown antifascist resistance that has been overlooked in both recent conversations about racial justice as well as antifascist resistance, the essays, interviews, and documents included here make clear how racialized and colonized peoples have been at the forefront of theorizing and dismantling fascism, white supremacy, and other modes of authoritarian rule.

By linking a deep engagement, both scholarly and practical, of racial justice movements with an antifascist frame, and a global analysis of capitalism the contributors have assembled a powerful toolbox for our struggles. The editors, widely recognized ethnic and American studies scholars, offer a groundbreaking collection with contributions from Johanna Fernández, Manu Karuka, Charisse Burden-Stelly, Zoé Samudzi, and Macarena Gomez-Barris among others.